ArtScroll® Series

Rabbi Nosson Scherman / Rabbi Gedaliah Zlotowitz

General Editors

Rabbi Meir Zlotowitz ז״ל, *Founder*

HaMahn

Its Enduring Message of Parnassah and Bitachon

DOV WELLER

INCLUDES TEFILLOS AND SEGULOS FOR PARNASSAH

צנצנת לאה שרה

פָּרָשַׁת הַמָּן

Parashas

Published by

ArtScroll®

Mesorah Publications, ltd

FIRST EDITION
First Impression … January 2025

Published and Distributed by
MESORAH PUBLICATIONS, LTD.
313 Regina Avenue / Rahway, N.J 07065

Distributed in Europe by
LEHMANNS
Unit E, Viking Business Park
Rolling Mill Road
Jarow, Tyne & Wear, NE32 3DP
England

Distributed in Australia and New Zealand by **GOLDS WORLDS OF JUDAICA**
3-13 William Street
Balaclava, Melbourne 3183
Victoria, Australia

Distributed in Israel by
SIFRIATI / A. GITLER — BOOKS
POB 2351
Bnei Brak 51122

Distributed in South Africa by
KOLLEL BOOKSHOP
Northfield Centre, 17 Northfield Avenue
Glenhazel 2192, Johannesburg, South Africa

ARTSCROLL® SERIES
PARASHAS HAMAHN

The author can be reached at wellerdov@gmail.com

ISBN 10: 1-4226-4290-9 / ISBN 13: 978-1-4226-4290-0
ITEM CODE: PHAMH

Typography by CompuScribe at ArtScroll Studios, Ltd.
Bound by Sefercraft, Quality Bookbinders, Ltd., Rahway N.J. 07065

Lovingly and respectfully, we dedicate this volume in memory of our unforgettable and inspirational mother, mother-in-law, and grandmother,

Laura Weissman ע״ה

לאה שרה בת מרדכי ע״ה

נלב״ע כ״ז טבת תש״פ

Her life was a living example of *emunah*, generosity, and unwavering *bitachon* in Hashem.

Throughout her life, she displayed a profound belief in Hashem, always turning to Him with complete trust for everything she needed. No matter the circumstance, she knew that her sustenance, her well-being, and her strength came directly from the Creator. Like the manna in the Desert, she believed that Hashem would provide for her and for those around her, no matter the situation. She had the rare and powerful ability to ask Hashem for what she needed, with a heart full of humility and a *neshamah* open to His will.

Her generosity knew no bounds. She gave not only of her resources, but of her spirit. Whether it was with a kind word, a helping hand, or a financial contribution, she gave with an open heart, without hesitation or expectation. She understood the true essence of *tzedakah*, recognizing that the blessings in her life were meant to be shared with others. Just as the manna was given freely and abundantly to the Children of Israel, so too did she give wholeheartedly to all who came to her in need.

May this volume serve as a small token of gratitude for all she has taught us and countless others. Her life was a beacon of *emunah*, *chesed*, and generosity, and it is our hope that this work will inspire others to emulate her faith and her giving spirit.

ת.נ.צ.ב.ה.

קהלת כולל בני הישיבות

הרב משה יוסף שיינערמאן שליט״א

מרא דאתרא

מוצש״ק פ׳ ויחי תשפ״ה

כתוב בפרשת כי תבוא (כט-ה) ״לחם לא אכלתם ויין ושכר לא שתיתם למען תדעו כי אני ה׳ אלוקיהם״ וכתב ה׳תרגום יונתן׳ ״לחמא דאיבורא לא אכלתון וחמר ומירת במדרשיכון מטול דתתעסקין בה״. והעיר מו״ר הגרמ״ד זצ״ל (שיעורי עה״ת שם) ״וצ״ב מה המעלה המיוחדת בזה שאכלו מן ולא לחם, ומהו החסרון באכילת לחם וכו׳. [ופי ה׳תרגום יונתן׳] מבואר דהמעלה של אכילת המן היתה שלא היו צריכים להתעסק בו, וממילא היו פנויים ללימוד התורה בלא שום טרדות דגן ויין, דאפילו כשיש שפע צריך עכ״פ להתעסק עמו מעט. אבל כשהיה להם את המן לא היה להם שום טרדה, והיו פנויים לגמרי ללימוד התורה.

הזכות לכתוב מאמרים על פרשיות ׳המן׳ כמו שכתב ידידי הרב ר׳ דוב שליט״א ייתכן רק על ידי התעסקות בתורה ללא הפסקות וחציצות עוה״ז, וכדוגמת אוכלי המן. כדאי לן כבוד ידידי את כל החיבור שלך רק כדי שיצא מזה חיזוק ללימוד התורה כי זה חלקנו מכל עמלנו. ובפרט בזמנינו שהרבה מבני אחינו חושבים שיציאה מבית המדרש לצורך פרנסה הוא הנהגה דלכתחילה, והרי הם מחליפים חיי נצח בשביל נזיד עדשים.

חן חן לך שאתה עמל ומתמיד בתורה הקדושה, ולוואי שילמדו ממך שצריך כל אחד לדרוש מעצמו לעשות למען כבוד שמים למעלה מכוחותיו, כי זה הוא מה שעשה כבוד ידידי – ולא פחות! אשריך שזכית להביא פרי עמלך לדפוס, דבר ששייך רק על ידי הרבה סייעתא דשמיא.

והנני לברך את יד״נ הנעלה שימשיך בעבודתו הק׳ ולהוציא לאור הרבה ספרים לאור עולם לזכות הרבים מתוך מנוחת הנפש והרחבת הדעת ובריות גופא ונהורא מעליא ונחת ושמחה ממשפחתו

הכו״ח לכבוד התורה ולומדי׳ ומרביצי׳

משה יוסף שיינערמאן

Simcha Bunim Cohen
Rav K'hal Ateres Yeshaya
Lakewood, New Jersey

שמחה בונם קאהן
רב קהל עטרת ישעי'
לעקוואד, ניו דזערסי

יום ג' פרשת שמות תשפ"ב

לכבוד הרב החשוב מאד מרביץ תורה ברבים ר' דוד שליט"א

נהנתי מאד מספרך על פרשת המן שהוא מלא וגדוש בביאורים נפלאים ודקדוקים נפלא ונושאי הלכה שכנסתה לאחד חיבור חשוב כזה. ורצוני שרבים יתעוררו מספרך ללימוד ושאר עניני יראת שמים

הכותב בשמחה גדולה
שמחה בונם הכהן קאהן

37 FIFTH STREET | LAKEWOOD, NJ 08701 | 732-370-8239

Table of Contents

Acknowledgments

Going to work and supporting our families is *chesed*; it is holy work. Chazal (*Avodah Zarah* 3b) tell us that Hashem spends a third of the day supporting and providing for His creations, and He maintains sole control over the key to *parnassah* (*Taanis* 2a). Our central purpose in life is to follow in the ways of Hashem. Through supporting and providing for our families we are actively walking in His ways. How vital it is to remember this.

I would like to thank Hashem for the tremendous opportunity, with His *siyata d'Shmaya*, to enable readers to come closer and follow in His ways as we earn our *parnassah*.

This *sefer* is divided into three parts. The first part provides the reader with insights into Parashas HaMahn. It contains inspirational *divrei Torah*, practical ideas centered around *emunah* and *parnassah*, and relatable stories focused on energizing us toward growth. The second section is a list of *segulos* and practical advice from Torah-based sources on *parnassah* and attaining financial stability. The third section is a compilation of *tefillos* for financial success.

Our relationship with work and money is an enormous test, whose outcome defines the very nature of our lives and those of our families. The allure of what money can bring is blinding; in the words of the Chasam Sofer, it is the main *nisayon* that we are presented with here in this world (*Derashos Zayin Adar*). *Parnassah* forces us to deal with the challenges of *emunah*, honesty, work-life balance, prioritizing, and ensuring we are focused on spiritual growth and Torah learning while meeting the growing financial needs of supporting a Jewish family. It is so easy to get distracted, disconnected, overwhelmed, stressed, and blinded by money, our careers, and the pressures of work in general. Through absorbing the messages of Parashas HaMahn, may we merit to be uplifted, inspired, calm, and connected to Hashem throughout it all. May Hashem grant us success in all matters of *parnassah* and shower us with *parnassah, berachah*, contentment with our lot, and *siyata d'Shmaya* in all our endeavors.

May the words of Torah and inspiration gleaned from this *sefer* serve as a *zechus l'ilui nishmas* our Aunt Debbie Wachsman, חוה דבורה בת אברהם יצחק הכהן ע״ה. Debbie was an extraordinary person and *mechaneches* who inspired and uplifted generations. Her smile and positivity were magnetic. Like her name Devorah, a bee, she spread sweetness to all those around her, and like Chava, she gave life and purpose to so many through her teachings, sincere care, and positive influence.

This *sefer* is also written as a *zechus l'ilui nishmas* our Uncle Tuli Mayer, יעקב נפתלי בן יוסף צבי ע״ה. Uncle Tuli was an exceptional man, who lived with Hashem every moment of his life. He could be working in Manhattan, yet he was with Hashem. He could be involved in business, yet he was with Hashem. He had an iron compass of Torah values. Learning and mitzvos were a priority. He was a man of principles, had a deep love for his family, and had a sensitive heart that helped and healed hundreds in a quiet and unassuming way. Uncle Tuli embodied the dual *middos* of Yissachar and Zevulun. He raised the banner of Yissachar, as he was always learning and dedicated to Torah and mitzvos. He personified Zevulun through supporting Torah and understanding that the *berachos* one has been bestowed with should be used for a higher order.

I thank **Yonatan and Malki** for dedicating this *sefer* in memory of Yonatan's mother Leah Sarah ע״ה. May the special merit of spreading Torah be a *zechus* for her *neshamah*. Hashem should shower you and your family with much *nachas, berachah*, and success.

ఆ

To my parents, **Dr. Judah and Harriet Weller**, thank you for your continuous love, support, and encouragement. We have learned from you how to rise over challenges, be relentless in the pursuit of our goals, and use our talents to inspire and help others. Abba, your leadership at P'tach for more than forty years helping champion the cause of Jewish children is a source of deep pride for your family. May Hashem grant you and Mommy *arichus yamim,* both qualitatively and quantitatively, in good health, and much *nachas* from your family. To my in-laws, **Dr. Eli and Feige Mayer**, thank you for your constant love, support, and continuous vote of confidence. We appreciate all that you do for us and may Hashem grant you much *nachas*, good health, and happiness. To my brother, **Rabbi Avi Weller**, thank you for your encouragement, for expertly reviewing the manuscript, and for being a wonderful positive example for our family. Thank you to **Mr. Yehuda (Marc) Vorchheimer** of Integrated Financial Consulting. Your valuable insights and real-life example of what it means to be a successful God-fearing Jew in the workplace have greatly enhanced this *sefer* and our lives.

To **Rabbi Gedaliah Zlotowitz**, thank you for seeing the potential for this *sefer* and encouraging it every step of the way. Thanks also to **Mrs. Miriam Zakon** for expertly coordinating and shepherding the project all the while providing keen insights along the way, and **Mrs. Esther Rabi** for a thorough and professional editing job.

A special thank you to **R' Eli Kroen** for the magnificent cover design; to **R' Mendy Herzberg** for supervising the publication process; and to **Mrs. Judi Dick, Mrs. Esther Feierstein, Mrs. Estie Dicker,** and **R' Yisroel Perkowski** for their proficient editing, paginating, and proofreading.

To the **Weller children**, thank you for allowing Totty the time to work on this project. We are so proud of every one of you. This *sefer* is our *sefer*. To **Rochel**, thank you for your encouragement, inspiration, support, editing, and insights that guided this *sefer* from its start to its ultimate fruition. May we merit to see much *nachas* from our children and continue to have the *zechus* of spreading Torah.

Dov Weller
Teves 5785 (January 2025)
Monsey, NY

The author dedicates this work in memory of:

אברהם יצחק בן יחזקאל הכהן ע״ה
כ״ט ניסן תשל״ג
ואשתו
חנה מלכה בת משה ע״ה
כ״ו תשרי תש״מ

דוב בער בן אברהם יואל ע״ה
י״ד אייר תשמ״ה
ואשתו
פיגא רחל בת משה ע״ה
א׳ תשרי תשפ״ב

מנחם מענדל בן אלתר שמואל אהרן ע״ה
י׳ חשון תשע״ז

יוסף צבי בן שמעון ע״ה
י״ג אדר תשע״ג
ואשתו
פריידא בת יעקב ע״ה
כ״ג תשרי תשע״ח

יעקב נפתלי בן יוסף צבי ע״ה
ז׳ אדר א׳ תשפ״ד

חוה דבורה בת אברהם יצחק הכהן ע״ה
כ״ג שבט תשפ״ד

שמואל משה זאב בן יהודה צבי ע״ה
כ״ו שבט תשפ״ד

ת. נ. צ. ב. ה.

Introduction

◆ Parashas HaMahn: Its Segulah and Source

From the time Adam and Chavah ate from the *Eitz HaDaas*, the Tree of Knowledge, and were exiled from Gan Eden, man was cursed with having to earn his living. Yet, there was a time when this curse was suspended. When Hashem redeemed the Jewish nation from Egypt, He led them into the Wilderness. It was there, in that barren expanse, far from civilization or any source of nourishment, that Hashem supported His nation of millions for forty years with the miraculous *mahn*.

Reading the Parashas HaMahn (*Shemos* 16:4–36) transports us to the time when Hashem provided sustenance miraculously, and the Jewish nation was totally dependent on Hashem (see *Ohr HaChaim, Bamidbar* 21:8). This increases our *emunah* that today as well Hashem takes care of all our needs — and this *emunah* prompts Hashem's blessings.

Rav Shamshon Raphael Hirsch explains that the Torah's recounting of Parashas HaMahn is not a mere historical description; it is the blueprint, the very guidebook, of how a Jew views money, finances, *hishtadlus*, and *bitachon*. The forty years of the *mahn* shine a perpetual light on Hashem's role in all aspects of our survival and sustenance. "Not by bread alone does man live; rather, by everything that emanates from the mouth of God does man live" (*Devarim* 8:3).

Sefer HaManhig quotes the Talmud Yerushalmi that says, "One who recites Parashas HaMahn each day is promised that he will have a place in the World to Come and his financial needs will not be lacking" (*Hilchos Shabbos* §44). *Tashbetz Katan* (§256), a student of the Maharam MiRottenberg, quotes the Yerushalmi and adds, "And I am a guarantor!" *Rabbeinu Bachya* (*Shemos* 16:16) also writes about the *segulah* of reciting Parashas HaMahn each day. He says, "There is a tradition from the Rabbis that whoever recites Parashas HaMahn each day is promised that he will never experience a lack of sustenance."

We need to stop right here and reread what was just communicated: The Rishonim promised that one's *parnassah* will be secured through reciting *and internalizing* the message of Parashas HaMahn — that it is Hashem Who provides for each of His children! *Sefer Yafah L'Lev* explains that there are 486 words in Parashas HaMahn, which is the same as the numerical value of פִּתּוֹ — one's bread. One who recites Parashas HaMahn each day will ensure that his bread — his sustenance — will always be available.

The young daughter of a relative of ours attended Morah Chanie's playgroup. Morah Chanie is a loving and caring teacher who cares deeply for each of her students. Her husband is a talmid chacham learning in kollel and the money she earned helped to support the family. They lived simply and struggled at times to pay for even the basics.

When the time came to marry off her children, the pressure was overwhelming. Morah Chanie called to say that one of her children was engaged. She was quite embarrassed to ask, but she wanted to know if I could help raise funds. With much siyata d'Shmaya we raised a considerable sum for her child's wedding.

When I heard, a few months ago, that another of Morah Chanie's children was engaged, I knew that she faced huge financial obligations yet again. I called Morah

Chanie to wish her mazel tov and to let her know that I was dedicated to helping raise money for this noble cause and that I had already collected a decent sum. Morah Chanie started to cry and said, "You will not believe it. When our child got engaged, I was so happy, but at the same time felt the enormous financial pressure of how we were going to afford even the basics. I then remembered the segulah of Parashas HaMahn, which I began to recite, and placed my bitachon in Hashem. And here you are. I did not even pick up the phone to call you. You were the one to call me to offer your help! It is like mahn!"

◆§ *Parashas HaMahn and Emunah*

Why is reciting Parashas HaMahn such a powerful *segulah* for *parnassah*?

The *Shulchan Aruch* says that it's good to say Parashas HaMahn every day (*Orach Chaim* 1:5). The *Beis Yosef* explains that the reason is "so that one should believe that all his sustenance comes directly from Hashem with Divine Providence."

The *Mishnah Berurah* (1:13) explains that in order to tap into the *segulah* of Parashas HaMahn, it must be recited with concentration. This way one internalizes its lesson and comes to the firm belief that Hashem provides *parnassah* through *hashgachah pratis,* as it says, regarding gathering the *mahn*, "Whoever gathered much did not have more, and whoever gathered little did not have less" (*Shemos* 16:18). As we recite Parashas HaMahn, we need to truly believe that every dollar reaches its recipient through Hashem's direction and providential guidance. The *segulah* of Parashas HaMahn is not in its mere recitation — it is not some magical incantation. Rather, its power and effectiveness lie in its strengthening our *emunah* in Hashem and in His direct role in our financial well-being. A conduit of *berachah* is then opened, which allows for the flow of *parnassah* (see *Yismach Yisrael, Beshalach* 4).

The Bas Ayin explains that the word מָן (*mahn*) is related to the word אֱמוּנָה (*emunah*). When the *mahn* fell, the Jews said מָן הוּא (*mahn hu*), the letters of which, when rearranged, form the word אֱמוּנָה (*emunah*). It was at this time that they strengthened their absolute belief in Hashem and came to the realization that there is none other than Hashem — *ein od milvado*. Emunah is the key to *berachah*. When one strengthens his *emunah* through the recitation of Parashas HaMahn, he taps into this special channel of *berachah*.

The distribution of the miraculous *mahn* was not just a phenomenon that took place in the Wilderness thousands of years earlier. Hashem told Moshe to store a small amount of *mahn* and keep it for generations to come as a reminder that Hashem continuously provides for us. Look back at your own life to see how you experienced receiving *mahn* from Hashem. It may have been in the form of your first job, or money that came in from an unexpected source just when you needed it, or in any of a myriad of Divine Providence's other methods. The *Noam Elimelech* (*Beshalach*) notes an allusion to this in the words Hashem used to tell Moshe that He was going to provide support: "*Hineni mamtir lachem lechem* — "Behold, I will cause bread to rain down on you." The word *hineni* is in the present tense, meaning that Hashem continues to provide miraculous support from His loving and caring hand in all generations.

Rav Pinchas of Koritz (*Mishmeres Shalom* 14:2) encouraged those requiring assistance with *parnassah* to recite Parashas HaMahn and the Thirteen Principles of Faith each morning. Rav Yosef Chaim Sonnenfeld and many other *gedolim* also urged those having *parnassah*-related challenges to recite Parashas HaMahn with concentration.

> *A rebbi recounted that his financial situation was bleak. Both he and his wife had lost their jobs within a few weeks of each other and they could not put bread on the table for their family. "One day after Shacharis," the rebbi recounted, "I poured out my heart to a rav. He walked with me to the bookshelf and pulled out a Mishnah Berurah. There he showed me the words, black on white, that say that one should recite Parashas HaMahn each day, to strengthen his*

emunah that his parnassah is from Hashem. Then the rav asked, 'What greater segulah do you need than this?'

"I decided at that very moment to begin reciting Parashas HaMahn with concentration and to truly ingrain in my heart the knowledge that my parnassah comes from Hashem and only Hashem. That very morning, I was offered a teaching position with better hours and better pay than my previous job. Moreover, my wife was hired shortly thereafter at a great company. This is a story I experienced personally and I am determined to publicize it" (Aleinu L'Shabei'ach, Eikev, p. 267).

◆§ *Foundational Lessons*

There is a fascinating halachah that states that if a congregation doesn't know which *parashah* is to be read that Shabbos, Parashas HaMahn should be read (*Sefer HaIttim* 184, in the name of Rav Saadiah Gaon). Why, of all possible Torah portions, was Parashas HaMahn designated as *the parashah* to be read in such a situation?

The Rambam's Thirteen Principles of Faith are at the core of what it means to be an observant Jew. The *Alshich* (*Shemos* 16:4–7) explains how each of the Rambam's Thirteen Principles can be gleaned from Parashas HaMahn. Perhaps it is for this reason that Parashas HaMahn is read when the week's *parashah* is unknown. Parashas HaMahn contains the DNA of Judaism and is therefore relevant every week.

Moreover, Shabbos is the day when our minds and thoughts are unshackled by the bonds of work and the bustle of the workday. We can assess our spiritual state and try to calibrate ourselves to live a Torah life. The message of Parashas HaMahn and the need to truly trust in Hashem for our livelihood is always relevant; it is always the *parashah* of the week.

Many *sefarim* explain that the prohibition of going out to gather *mahn* on Shabbos was in essence the first time the Jewish nation was commanded to observe the Shabbos and understand the gift that is Shabbos (*Devarim Rabbah* 3:1; *Gur*

Aryeh [see *Tiferes Yosef, Beshalach*]; *Sfas Emes, Beshalach* 643). As such, on any given Shabbos on which the correct Torah portion is unknown, it is appropriate to read Parashas HaMahn, which describes the first Shabbos the Jewish Nation was commanded to actively observe.

✂ *Reciting Parashas HaMahn Each Day*

The Vilna Gaon explains the source for reciting Parashas HaMahn each day. He points to the Gemara in which Rabbi Shimon ben Yochai was asked why Hashem chose to provide the *mahn* on a day-to-day basis, as opposed to just once a year (*Yoma* 76a). Rabbi Shimon answered with a parable of a king who had one son, whom he supported. If the king sent his son a full year's support at once, his son would come to greet him only once a year. Instead, he only gave him adequate support for each day. This way, his son came to greet him daily. Similarly, Hashem desires a connection with each one of us. He wants us to daven to Him each day and show a continuous reliance on Him. Hence the custom to recite Parashas HaMahn each day. It is for this reason, explains the *Chasam Sofer* (*Toras Moshe, Eikev*), that in the *berachah* of *Borei Nefashos,* we thank Hashem for "creating man and his deficiencies (*chesronan*)." Hashem does not give us all our needs, but ensures that we are "lacking things"; we have weaknesses, anxieties, worries, and deficiencies so that we will call out to Hashem for support on a regular basis.

Within Parashas HaMahn, Moshe and Aharon asked the Jewish nation, "Why are you complaining to us? Who are we?" Despite their exalted positions, they demonstrated the humility that itself is a *segulah* for wealth (Rav Chaim Palagi, *Ruach Chaim*).

The *Me'il Tzedakah* writes that when one recites Parashas HaMahn, recounting how Hashem provided His nation with sustenance in a miraculous way, his *ahavas Hashem* is aroused and he is spurred to further dedicate himself to Torah and mitzvos. This dedication is a *segulah* for *parnassah.*

☙ When to Recite Parashas HaMahn

The *Shulchan Aruch* implies that Parashas HaMahn should be recited at the start of davening (see *Seder HaYom*). The *Zohar* states that one should daven for *parnassah* only after Shacharis and as such, Parashas HaMahn should be recited after davening (see *Mekor Chaim* 1:5). Parashas HaMahn should not be recited during the chazzan's repetition of *Shemoneh Esrei*. Some say that one should recite Parashas HaMahn when doing *shenayim mikra v'echad Targum* (*Noheig Katzon Yosef* quoting Rabbeinu Tam; *Me'am Loez*; *Shevet Mussar*, Ch. 40). Parashas HaMahn can be recited on Shabbos as well as Yom Tov (*Mishnah Berurah* 1:13 — one should omit the *tefillos* recited before and after the *parashah*).

☙ Parashas HaMahn on the Tuesday of Parashas Beshalach?

Sefer Yalkut Menachem (published in 1991, p. 286) quotes Rav Shlomo Yehuda Weinberger in the name of Rav Avraham Shalom of Stropkov who attributed a *minhag* to Rav Menachem Mendel of Rimanov (1745–1815) that the Tuesday of *Parashas Beshalach* is a special time to recite Parashas HaMahn (*shenayim mikra v'echad Targum*).

Perhaps Tuesday is an especially auspicious day for this because it was on Tuesday, the third day of Creation, that Hashem formed the dry land and the earth produced plants and trees, the mainstay of human consumption.

This *segulah* is not found in any of Rav Menachem Mendel's writings nor in those of his students. This is quite a glaring omission because for twenty-two years, Rav Menachem Mendel spoke about Parashas HaMahn each Shabbos, and many of his writings on the topic are readily available in print. Moreover, the *segulah* is to recite Parashas HaMahn *each day*, not just one day a year (see *Otzar Tu B'Shevat*, p. 262, for a lengthy discussion on this). Rav Shlomo Yehuda Weinberger, the source for this *minhag*, wrote in his notebook that it was on a Tuesday of *Parashas Beshalach* that Rav Avraham

Shalom of Stropkov told him that Rav Menachem Mendel of Rimanov said that one should recite Parashas HaMahn *each day*. Perhaps someone misheard and thought that the Rebbe of Stropkov had said that the Tuesday of *Parashas Beshalach* is a special day to recite Parashas HaMahn.

Rav Chaim Kanievsky and Rav Aharon Leib Steinman both stated that this *segulah* was unsourced. A *segulah* for *parnassah* that the students of Rav Menachem Mendel of Rimanov mentioned in the name of their Rebbe is to be happy and trust in Hashem (*Be'eros Mayim,* Vol. 2, *Hashmatos*). This is alluded to in the words וְהָיִיתָ אַךְ שָׂמֵחַ (*v'hayi**sa** a**ch** samei'**ach***), whose end letters form the acrostic *Chasach,* the name of the angel that's responsible for *parnassah.*

◆§ *Parashas HaMahn: A Daily Reminder to Live a Broad Life*

There are some who think that there are two distinct worlds: the world of full-time Torah learning — kollel, spiritual growth, and pure dedication to the ways of Hashem — and the world of working, career, and money, where spiritual growth is on the back burner. This is a fallacy. They are not two disparate worlds.

One of Rav Yitzchok Hutner's students was leaving kollel to earn a livelihood, and he felt that he was abandoning his previous life. Rav Hutner wrote to him, "Thinking that having a secular career means living a 'double life' is a mistake. One who has a home where he lives and then has another room at a hotel, where he lives as a guest, is living a 'double life.' But one who has a two-room apartment is living a *broad life*, not a double life. I recall that I once visited Dr. Moshe Wallach's hospital (Shaarei Tzedek hospital in Yerushalayim) and I saw how he approached a patient who was about to undergo surgery. He asked the patient for his name and the name of his mother so he could daven for him. Is Dr. Wallach living a 'double life' when he recites *Tehillim* for a patient?" (*Igros* 94).

Rav Hutner is telling us that pursuing a career is not an

antithesis to Torah. Rather, doing so enables a person to live a *broader* and more *expansive* life, as he can infuse what it means to be a Yid into his business pursuits.

In a letter to someone leaving the yeshivah to enter the workforce, Rav Wolbe writes, "Whereas in yeshivah you *learn* the *Chovos HaLevavos's Shaar HaBitachon*, when you go out to work you have the opportunity to *live* the *Shaar HaBitachon*" (*Letters*, Vol. 2, p. 397). Every day that we go to work, we can broaden and put into practice so much of what we learned in prior years. We can transform the earthly into something holy. *Emunah* is belief in Hashem; *bitachon* is the practical application of this belief in our daily life.

The *Meor Einayim* (*Likkutim*) writes that a person should not think that the only time he connects with Hashem is while he is learning or davening, and that he has turned away from Hashem when he is working or eating. No! The Torah commands us to "Know Him in all your ways" (*Mishlei* 3:6). Every moment of the day, in every event and in every situation, a person can connect himself to Hashem. This is what Dovid HaMelech said: "*Es'haleich lifnei Hashem b'artzos hachaim* — I will walk before Hashem in the land of the living" (*Tehillim* 116:9). The word "בְּאַרְצוֹת" (*b'artzos*) can also mean בְּאַרְצִיּוּת (*b'artziyus)* — worldliness. It is as if Dovid were saying, "Even when בְּאַרְצִיּוּת — when I am involved in matters of This World, such as earning a living, doing errands, eating, sleeping, and the like — I am walking in front of You, Hashem."

When one goes to work to support his family, send his children to yeshivos, and give *tzedakah*, the work is itself a mitzvah and *avodah* of Hashem (*Pri Tzaddik, Mishpatim*). Such a mindset transforms a mundane day of work into a day of spiritual accomplishment. Hashem views such a day of work as if it were a *terumah* donation to the Beis HaMikdash (*Zera Kodesh, Terumah*). On average, a person spends more than one-third of his life working (90,000 hours). That is a significant allotment of time. But these hours can be transformed into something spiritual when one spends them with Hashem at his side. "Know Him in all your ways" (*Mishlei* 3:6). This is a small *parashah* that encapsulates all the main ideas of the Torah (*Berachos* 63a).

The *Midrash Chazis* tells us something puzzling: Yosef HaTzaddik merited to be freed from jail and became the second-in-command in Egypt because he served his master Potiphar to the best of his abilities. The Sfas Emes explains that Yosef understood that the position Hashem placed him in at that moment was what was best for him. He accepted his situation and served Potiphar and his family wholeheartedly. With full *emunah* in Hashem, Yosef knew this was what Hashem wanted from him, although he found himself in this situation because he'd been sold by his own brothers, and was now a slave in morally depraved Egypt. He accepted it with love and *emunah*. Because of this he was catapulted to a position of authority and prestige.

One who is in the working world is often called a בַּעַל הַבַּיִת (*baal habayis*). The numerical value of בַּעַל הַבַּיִת is 519, the same numerical value as that of "הַשְׁלֵךְ עַל ה׳ יְהָבְךָ — throw your burden on Hashem" (*Tehillim* 55:23). The very essence of a *baal habayis* should be someone who goes to work knowing that Hashem is there for him every step of the way. He goes to work with relaxed shoulders, assured that he can throw onto Hashem the weight, stress, and pressures that he faces (*Imrei Yosef, Emor*).

Parashas HaMahn is the text that enables us to tap into this, to remind ourselves that Hashem is providing for us every step of the way. It is so easy to forget, to become confused and lost. The daily Parashas HaMahn is there to remind us; it is a guidepost for our minds and hearts and inspires constant awareness of Hashem's presence in our lives.

פרשת המן

Parashas HaMahn

ד **וַיֹּאמֶר** יהוה אֶל מֹשֶׁה, הִנְנִי מַמְטִיר לָכֶם לֶחֶם מִן הַשָּׁמָיִם,

וַיֹּאמֶר ה׳ אֶל מֹשֶׁה הִנְנִי מַמְטִיר לָכֶם לֶחֶם מִן הַשָּׁמָיִם — ***Hashem said to Moshe, "Behold, I will cause bread to rain down on you from heaven"*** (*Shemos* 16:4).

◈ *The Miracles of the Mahn*

The *mahn* was an exceptionally unique and dynamic miracle that the Bnei Yisrael experienced during their forty-year sojourn in the Wilderness.

Ibn Ezra writes that the miracle of the *mahn* was extraordinary in its longevity. Most miracles last just a brief amount of time, but the miracle of the *mahn* continued for a full forty years!

Yalkut Me'am Loez enumerates twenty-five different miracles that were involved in the descent of the *mahn*! These miracles demonstrated Hashem's deep love for the Jewish nation, showing them how He cares and provides for them under any and all circumstances. The *mahn* was untouched by human hands; it was a gift purely from Hashem's hands, *min haShamayim* — directly from Heaven.

Recanati (*Shemos* 16:4) tells us that the word פַּרְנָסָה (*parnassah)* has the same numerical value as the word הַשָּׁמַיִם *(haShamayim)* — 395 — to drive home the message that *parnassah* comes directly from Hashem.

Below is a partial list of the miracles that took place during the descent of the *mahn*:

- ✧ The *mahn* fell in direct proportion to the number of people in each household. Having a large family did not detract from the family's *parnassah* in any shape or form.
- ✧ The place in which the *mahn* fell was determined by one's observance of Torah and mitzvos. The *mahn* fell

right at the doorsteps of the righteous. It fell outside the encampment for the *beinoni* (average person). The daily portion of *mahn* for the *rasha* fell far away, necessitating him to travel quite a distance to gather his sustenance (*Yoma* 75a).

- ✧ The *mahn* for the *tzaddik* fell like bread that could be eaten immediately, without any preparation. The *beinoni* had to bake it, and the *rasha* needed to grind and then bake his portion of the *mahn* (*Yoma* 75a).
- ✧ The Gemara (*Yoma* 76a) tells us that the height of the *mahn* that fell each day was sixty *amos*! It towered so high that all the kingdoms to the east could see it, which resulted in a magnificent *kiddush Hashem.*
- ✧ The Midrash (*Yalkut Beshalach* 258) tells us that each day, the quantity of *mahn* that fell was sufficient to sustain each Jew for 2,000 years — meaning, the *mahn* fell in huge proportions, but when the time came to pick it they were each only able to take the amount necessary for their family.
- ✧ When each person gathered their *mahn*, it transformed to a standard size of a tenth of an *eifah.*
- ✧ Spices fell along with the *mahn* to enhance the experience.
- ✧ Perfume and jewelry fell with the *mahn* so that the women could adorn themselves (*Yoma* 75a).
- ✧ The *mahn* brightened the complexion, softened the skin, and gave the body a pleasant scent (*Ben Yehoyada*).
- ✧ The *mahn* had an exceptionally delicious fragrance. The *mahn* that fell in honor of Shabbos had an extra-special smell and composition (*Mechilta, Beshalach*).

- ✧ Jewelry and Shabbos clothing also fell with the Erev Shabbos *mahn* (*Tosafos HaShalem*).
- ✧ Precious stones and pearls fell along with the *mahn*. These stones were later used for the construction of the Mishkan and the Kohen Gadol's vestments (*Yoma* 75a).
- ✧ The *mahn* tasted like nearly any food one wanted. The *Yalkut* writes that the *mahn* had 546 different flavors, which equates to the numerical value of *matok*, sweet. If one did not have any thought in mind, then the flavor depended on one's age: For the elderly it tasted like bread, for middle-aged people it tasted like oil, and for the younger children it tasted like honey.
- ✧ Rav Yosef Engel writes that the *mahn* could also take the form of a liquid and taste like wine. Hence, on Shabbos, they were able to recite Kiddush on the *mahn* (*Gilyonei HaShas, Berachos* 48b).
- ✧ The *mahn* was referred to as *lechem abirim*, angel's bread. It was spiritual in nature, perfectly pure, and as such, when it was consumed, it permeated the 248 limbs of the human body and resulted in no physical digestive waste (*Yoma* 75b).

  Rav Menachem Mendel of Rimanov explains that because the *mahn* was a spiritual food it was digested in the trachea, not in the esophagus! (*Menachem Tzion, Vayeitzei*). The *Ramban* (*Devarim* 8:4) writes that the clothing the Jews wore in the Wilderness did not wear out. Sweat often wears out clothing. As the *mahn* was of utmost purity it did not cause the body to perspire and as such the clothing remained in good condition. Rav Aryeh Tzvi Frommer, the Kozhoglover Rav, writes that on Yom Kippur, when we are prohibited to eat, we are sustained by the *mahn* (*Sefer Eretz Tzvi*). That is why the Talmud discusses the *mahn* in *Yoma*. On Yom Kippur we are compared to angels and just as the angels are sustained by the *lechem abirim*, the *mahn*, we too, on this day when we do not partake of any physical food, are given strength by the *mahn*.

- ✧ The *mahn* gave *daas,* wisdom, to those who consumed it. With this *daas* they were able to delve into the Torah, as Chazal (*Mechilta* 16:4) tell us, "The Torah was only given to the generation that consumed the *mahn*" (*Baal HaTurim*). Moreover, through eating the *mahn*, which was a spiritual food, one was protected from having any forbidden thoughts and his level of holiness was uplifted (*Me'am Loez; Sifsei Kohen*).

☙ *Primary Lessons of the Mahn, From the Malbim*

The Malbim succinctly summarizes the many practical and inspirational lessons we can learn from the *mahn*:

- ✧ **"I will cause bread to rain down on you"** (16:4) — Hashem Himself provides the *mahn*, and not an intermediary. The key to *parnassah* is solely in the hands of Hashem (*Taanis* 2a). It is never our boss, clients, or relatives to whom we need to turn for *parnassah,* but to Hashem.
- ✧ **"Bread from heaven"** (16:4) — The *mahn* came from heaven. It was the food of angels, a spiritual food. The primary purpose of *parnassah* is to enable spiritual nutrition; it is to satisfy a person's *neshamah,* so that he has time and energy to learn and perform mitzvos.
- ✧ **"The people will go out and gather each day's portion"** (16:4) — The *mahn* was gathered daily, providing each person and his family exactly what they needed for that day. Do not worry about tomorrow. Worrying about the future is a lack of trust. Place your trust in Hashem. Just as you trust that He will keep you alive today, trust that He will give you sustenance tomorrow as well.
- ✧ **"On the sixth day... there will be double"** (16:5) — One does not lose anything from keeping Shabbos and honoring Shabbos, or from providing resources for a mitzvah. We see this firsthand from the double portion

of *mahn* that fell on Erev Shabbos. Additionally, we see that the following six days of the work week are blessed by our honoring Shabbos. The *Zohar* says that all *berachah* comes from Shabbos.

✧ **"It happened on the sixth day that they gathered... what you wish to bake, bake; and what you wish to cook, cook"** (16:22,23) — Shabbos requires proper preparation, both physically and emotionally. Anything holy (Yom Tov, a *simchah*, davening...) needs proper preparation. One must prepare if one wants to experience the full breadth and depth of *kedushah*.

✧ **Moshe said to Aharon, "Take a single earthenware jar and place in it an *omerful* of *mahn*, and set it down before Hashem as a keepsake for your generations"** (16:33) — The *mahn* was not just a miracle that took place in the Wilderness. It is available today to those who dedicate themselves to a life of observance of Torah and mitzvos.

וַיֹּאמֶר ה׳ אֶל מֹשֶׁה הִנְנִי מַמְטִיר לָכֶם לֶחֶם מִן הַשָּׁמָיִם —
Hashem said to Moshe, "Behold, I will cause bread to rain down on you from heaven" (16:4).

Today's Mahn

The word "*Hineni,* Behold," is in the present tense. The Noam Elimelech writes that the miraculous *mahn* exists today just as it did during the forty years the Jewish nation journeyed the barren Wilderness. The same channel of *berachah* that brought the *mahn* then, exists today in the guise of nature. Hashem is prepared to provide sustenance to everyone, each day. The prosperity is there, waiting to be released. *Bitachon* in Hashem, internalizing in both thought and action that one's financial state is directly dependent on Hashem's flow of goodness, is the key to opening the floodgates of *berachah*. But when a person is lacking in *bitachon* and thinks that it is his actions, his education, his hustle, his intelligence, his connections, and his energy that are responsible for his *parnassah,* he creates a barrier.

Chovos HaLevavos tells us that *bitachon* is the key to *parnassah*. Reliance on Hashem not only frees us from the shackles of worry, it is the conduit that connects us directly to the *mahn*, which was given to us directly from Hashem. *Sefer Rav Ye'ivi* writes succinctly, "*Parnassah* is the result of *bitachon*. The more *bitachon* the more *parnassah*, as the verse states, 'Hashem desires those who fear Him, those who yearn for His kindness'" (*Tehillim* 147:11).

In the Chofetz Chaim's lifetime, most Jews suffered from grueling poverty and financial challenges. Even in our present time of prosperity, many suffer financial hardships due to the steep costs of mortgages, tuition, taxes, and daily needs. Yet the Chofetz Chaim provided us with a solution to the problem. In his writings to his fellow Jews, he says, "When the Jewish people strengthen their *bitachon* they will most certainly bring *berachah* into their homes, as the verse (*Yirmiyah* 17:7) says, 'Blessed is the man who trusts in Hashem.' Now, when financial hardship is the lot of so many, there is nothing to do but trust in Hashem, and for this, He will send *berachah* from his Holy Abode" (*Nefutzos Yisrael,* Ch. 8; *Zechor L'Miriam,* Ch. 20).

Chovos HaLevavos (*Shaar HaBitachon*) tells us that when a Jew places his *bitachon* in Hashem, Hashem can and will provide for him. There is no situation too bleak or circumstance too impossible for Hashem to provide us with our needs. The following story shows us how the flow of *mahn* exists today, and if Hashem wants someone to receive *parnassah* he will, even in the most unusual and unlikely means.

> *A young man in Eretz Yisrael became a sofer so he could provide parnassah for his family. This fellow was not gifted with artistic talent by any stretch of the imagination. Despite his perseverance, he could not write all the letters in the same size and style.*

His first completed project was a Megillas Esther. He tried to sell the megillah but everyone who looked at it immediately rejected it. The father of this sofer was pained that his son was having such a hard time. He decided to ask a well-known safrus merchant if he could try to sell his son's megillah. This would give him the confidence he needed to continue, as well as much-needed funds.

A few weeks before Purim, the safrus merchant traveled to America to sell tefillin, mezuzos, and megillos. One evening he was invited to the home of a wealthy man who was interested in purchasing a megillah. The merchant showed the wealthy man the most beautiful megillos, but none were of interest to him. Megillah after megillah was rejected. The merchant had one left; it was the megillah written by the sofer whose handwriting was so messy that he did not even want to show it to the man. But the megillah caught the wealthy man's eye and he said, "Wait, I see you have one more megillah. Please let me see it."

The merchant responded, "If you didn't like the others I showed you, you most definitely won't like this one." Yet the wealthy man wanted to see it. The merchant unrolled it in front of him and the wealthy man's eyes lit up. "Yes! This is the exact one I was looking for!" He paid the merchant $2,500 and was proud of his new megillah.

"Pardon me for asking, but I am a bit puzzled," the merchant said. "I showed you the most gorgeous megillos with the most beautiful, nearly-perfect writing, yet you did not want them. The megillah you took is anything but perfect. Its script is uneven, some words are bold and some are thin, some are elongated and some are abbreviated. It is far from excellent. Please enlighten me."

The wealthy man replied, "The megillos you showed me at first are beautiful; in fact, too beautiful. They look like they were computer-printed. I wanted a megillah that was clearly written by a human hand. This one fit the bill exactly!"

◆ Mahn in the Merit of Moshe

The Gemara tells us that *mahn* fell because of Moshe Rabbeinu (*Taanis* 9a). It was for this reason that one of Moshe's names was Yered (which means descent), as it was in his *zechus* that the *mahn fell* (*Megillah* 13a).

When we look at Moshe's life, we see that it was by no means easy. At the tender age of three months, he was torn from his mother and family, placed in a basket in the river, and brought to the house of Pharaoh, the nemesis of the Jewish nation. For the next twenty years he was raised in the palace of the evil and conniving ruler whose primary goal was eradicating the Jewish people. He was brought up in an environment of idolatry and moral depravity such as the world had never seen. Then, with his life on the line, Moshe was forced to flee to Midian. It was only at the age of eighty that Moshe became the leader of Klal Yisrael. Despite his hardships, or more likely because of his hardships, Moshe became the Jewish nation's leader and a prophet like no other.

The Gemara (*Menachos* 29a) tells us that there were three things that Moshe struggled to understand, and Hashem had to show Moshe firsthand what He intended. The three things were: the form of the *Menorah* for the Mishkan, the species of insects (*sheratzim*) that are non-kosher, and the appearance of the moon when Rosh Chodesh is to be sanctified. The name מֹשֶׁה is the acrostic formed by the initial letters of the words מְנוֹרָה, שְׁרָצִים, הַחֹדֶשׁ — ***M**enorah*, ***sh**eratzim* (insects), **h**achodesh. This alludes to the message that we are defined, elevated, and praised by our struggles! Our challenges and battles are the ultimate definition of our identity. It is our essence. Moshe shows us that we can never give up. When things are difficult, when we do not understand, when we struggle to see the light, the solution is to turn toward Hashem. We can overcome the challenges that come our way when we internalize the reality that we have a loving Father Who is tenderly holding our hand at every step. Millions of men, women, and children followed Hashem into the barren Wilderness, trusting that He would care for them. Despite the uncertainty, the overwhelming hardship of not knowing where their next meal was coming from, the Jews armed themselves with *bitachon* in Hashem and were nourished by the Heavenly *mahn*.

☙ Forty Days of Mahn in the Merit of Yehoshua

The Gemara (*Yoma* 76a) relates that there was a period in which the *mahn* fell on behalf of Yehoshua. The *Meshech Chochmah* (*Shemos* 16:10) explains that the *mahn* fell primarily on account of Moshe Rabbeinu's deeds. Moshe died on the seventh of Adar, which should have been the last day that Bnei Yisrael partook of the *mahn*. But the *mahn* that they had was still edible for another forty days, until the sixteenth of Nissan (see *Kiddushin* 38a). The extra forty days of *mahn* were granted due to Yehoshua's deeds; he waited forty days at the foot of Har Sinai for Moshe, his rebbi, to return. We see from here that there is unbelievable reward for those who serve, assist, honor, and support *talmidei chachamim*. The entire nation — millions of people — were given an extra forty days of *mahn* because of Yehoshua's dedication and respect for Moshe, his rebbi.

> *While on a walk with his son one evening, Reb Moshe Reichman was interrupted by a tzedakah assistant who informed him that a rosh yeshivah had phoned and left a message. Reb Moshe changed his route and headed to his mother's home to return the call. The gabbai protested that the call had not been urgent; it could wait till after his walk. Reb Moshe told his son, "Yechezkel, remember that one doesn't keep a talmid chacham waiting." Reb Moshe's financial support of Torah was only matched by his kavod haTorah (Building for Eternity, p. 244).*
>
> *"My father had two poses," reflects one of Reb Moshe's daughters. "There was Paul Reichman — tall, confident,*

> *and erect, clearly the dominant figure in any business meeting. Then there was Moshe Reichman in the presence of a talmid chacham — stooped, deferential, and ready to listen" (ibid., p. 261).*

Yehoshua was chosen to be Moshe Rabbeinu's successor, the leader of Klal Yisrael who would bring them into Eretz Yisrael. Why was Yehoshua selected for this lofty position? The Midrash states that Yehoshua served Moshe with utmost devotion, even arranging the benches and floor mats in the study hall (*Bamidbar Rabbah* 21:14). It was Yehoshua's attention to detail, his care for the *beis midrash's* cleanliness and orderliness, that proved to be one of the defining reasons for his success. [*Tosafos HaRosh* (*Sanhedrin* 20a) writes that the angel of wealth resides in homes and locations which are clean and well-organized.] We all too often overlook and undervalue the small things in life. The small *chesed* opportunities that come our way — returning the *sefarim* to their proper place in shul, thanking the chazzan, or picking up a tissue from the floor — are truly important. We see from Yehoshua that the small things, the details, really matter and define the greatness and depth of who we are.

הִנְנִי מַמְטִיר לָכֶם לֶחֶם מִן הַשָּׁמָיִם וְיָצָא הָעָם וְלָקְטוּ דְּבַר יוֹם בְּיוֹמוֹ —
Behold, I will cause bread to rain down on you from heaven, and the people will go out and gather each day's portion in its day (16:4).

◆§ *Tefillah: The Key to Parnassah*

D'var can mean either a thing or a word. What does the word *d'var* mean here? It seems to be out of place. The Torah could have written, "each day they went out and gathered *mahn*"!

In the barren and arid Wilderness, the Jewish nation

understood there was nothing, literally nothing, they could do to sustain themselves. What should they do? There was one possible *hishtadlus*, and that was to daven. Each day they could pour out their hearts with *dibburim* — words of *tefillah* to Hashem to provide for them and their family's needs. This was their *hishtadlus* (*Maor VaShemesh*; *Sefer Aron HaEidus*).

The numerical value of the words מִן הַשָּׁמַיִם (*min haShamayim*), from the Heavens, is the same value as the numerical value of the word תְּהִלִּים (*Tehillim*) — 485. Through the words of *tefillah*, through connecting to Hashem and understanding that only He provides for us, we can activate the key to *parnassah* that He holds. Hashem could have easily provided enough *mahn* to last for an extended period of time. Yet, He chose to send only enough for each day so that every day His children, Bnei Yisrael, would reach out to Him in *tefillah*.

The *mahn* remained fresh until the fourth hour of the day. Then the sun began to melt the *mahn*, and it began to spoil. Rav Pinchas of Koritz explains that the *mahn* melted and spoiled specifically at this time because it is until this time that one can daven Shacharis (*Imrei Pinchas, Beshalach*). Mahn and *parnassah* were provided specifically at this time because it is a time of *tefillah*.

As a loving Father, Hashem wants nothing more than to provide for us. But He wants us to connect with Him. From the time of Creation, *tefillah* has been the means to connect, and to open the flow of *berachah* (*Rashi*, *Bereishis* 2:5). The *shefa,* the abundance that Hashem wants to provide for us, is waiting, and *tefillah* is the key to that *shefa.* A cognate of the word "*tefillah*" is *pesil,* a wick (*Rashi*, *Bereishis* 30:8; *Be'er Mayim Chaim, Bereishis*). A wick is a bridge, the connection between oil and fire. It enables us to enjoy light and warmth. When we daven, we are connecting ourselves directly to Hashem. Every time we daven to Hashem, whether through formal *tefillah* or through impromptu conversations throughout the day, we are strengthening our bond with Him. The *Zohar* writes that one who davens to Hashem each day for *parnassah* is considered a child who can claim *berachos* from Hashem, His Father in Heaven.

Rav Wolbe (*Alei Shur,* Vol. 2, p. 348) writes that This World is like a clock. The average analog clock can have up to three hundred moving parts — the gears and wheels that turn the clock's hands. All these parts are moved by one single powered gear. The same is true in This World. It is *tefillah* that powers everything. A person thinks that this happened because of this and that happened because of that; they need to understand what Dovid HaMelech said in *Tehillim,* "*Va'ani tefillah* — I am prayer" (109:4), and all that happens to me and around me is due to *tefillah.* My very essence, like that of Dovid HaMelech, is *tefillah.*

At times, the burden of providing for our families can feel overwhelming. It weighs us down, causing anxiety, stress, and, at times, anger and confusion. It is a great responsibility to provide for a Jewish family. There is tuition, camp, cleaning help, groceries, Shabbos, Yom Tov, the mortgage, taxes, clothing, charity, supporting the married children, bills, *simchos,* and so much more. When we need help for *parnassah* it is so easy to look around and blame our boss, the client, the market, the political atmosphere, ourselves, our family, and everyone around us. But we need to remember that there is one gear that powers it all. That is *tefillah.* We need to remember to Whom to turn in a time of need. Hashem wants nothing more than for us to reach out to Him and to share with Him our fears and needs.

Rav Shimshon Pincus once said, "If I accomplished anything significant in my life or managed to overcome challenges, it is all because of one thing that I trained myself to do continuously: to speak to Hashem throughout the day as a person speaks to his friend. I poured my heart out to Hashem and told Him everything that was bothering me, upsetting me, making me happy... everything, good and bad."

In a letter addressed to a young man struggling for direction, Rav Shimshon writes:

It appears you are trying as hard as you can... and you have done all that you can. Now you are at the point where you need help from the outside, and therefore, I will give you the name and the address of someone who can help you to overcome your challenges and rise to the goals you have set for yourself.

He is called Hashem. He is very powerful, He created everything, and I know that He loves you, personally, dearly. He waits with longing for you to turn toward Him. It is not difficult to find Him or His address. He is everywhere, and even at the very moment you are reading this letter you can turn toward Him... Go directly to the One Who can truly help you, and grab onto Him and do not let go.... (Nefesh Shimshon, Letters, p. 43).

Rav Pincus relates an extremely powerful story that provides us with guidance and inspiration to tune into the awesome power of *tefillah* and relying on Hashem:

The ICU was in desperate need of a doctor to cover the upcoming night shift. They managed to locate a doctor who was still doing his residency. Although inexperienced, he had the necessary qualifications. The ICU was unusually full that night, and the young doctor was nervous about singlehandedly taking responsibility for each of these critically ill patients. The hospital administrator tried to allay his fears. He told him that hopefully the night would pass quietly. "But," he said, "if you need something, if you are overwhelmed with crises, pick up the emergency line and we will make sure that a doctor from another department will come to assist you within moments."

The night began quietly. The patients' vital signs were all stable. Then the peace was broken; a patient needed emergency assistance. The doctor ran over and began doing what was necessary. While he was busy with that, another patient's alarm began to ring. The doctor stabilized the patient he was with and ran to the next patient. Then three other patients needed emergency attention. The young doctor ran valiantly from patient to patient but, as night began to turn to dawn, there was a tragedy. He didn't get to one of his patients in time, and the patient passed away.

Sometime later, the young doctor was summoned to court. He was being sued for negligence. He defended himself by saying, "I made heroic efforts to treat every single patient in the ICU that night! Why am I being sued and punished for my heroic efforts?"

The judge responded, "You were instructed to pick up the phone and call for help if you needed it. No one asked you to handle the situation alone, without help. You were given a simple instruction: Call for help in case of need. Since you did not call out in a time of need, you are being sued for negligence."

This is exactly what Hashem tells each of us. "No one asked you to shoulder all the burden of providing for your family. Call out to Me, daven to Me, reach out to Me at any time, in any language, and I will be there to assist." This is tefillah. We need to understand and internalize that we need Hashem and we cannot manage on our own, that we have a Father Who is capable of anything. Let us make the call, make the connection, and shift the weight from our shoulders to Hashem, Who is waiting for us to reach out to Him.

◆§ *Tefillah:* Our Lifeboat in the Stormy Sea

The Torah details the story of Noach, the *Teivah*, and the *Mabul* at great length. Baal HaTanya explains that figuratively, the stormy, turbulent seas of the *Mabul* are an allusion to the stormy and often challenging world of going to work, earning a livelihood, and staying spiritually afloat in the outside world. The stormy sea, which represents *gashmiyus*, threatens to capsize the *teivah*, which represents the *neshamah*. Stormy turmoil threatens to sink, frighten, overwhelm, confuse, and distract from the *neshamah's* mission (*Ohr Torah, Noach*).

At times we may feel that a gale of challenges and pain is swirling around us, especially as it relates to our financial obligations and pressures. What are we to do in such a situation? What is a Yid to do when his struggles are mounting and he feels it is difficult to remain afloat in the sea of life? The Baal Shem Tov (*Al HaTorah,* p. 108) provides us with an extraordinary insight: The Torah tells us, "Noach, with his sons, his wife, and his sons' wives with him, went into the *Teivah* because of the waters of the Flood" (*Bereishis* 7:7). *Teivah* can be translated not only as "ark" but also as "word." The Torah is insinuating that when one is facing a personal flood that threatens to submerge him in the struggles of life, the solution is to come into the *teivah* — the **words** of *tefillah.* They will protect you from the fury of the storms that are raging. *Tefillah* is the lifeboat in the stormy sea of life, it is the life jacket Hashem provides for each one of us. Our job is to grab on and hold tight. When we are stressed, anxious, nervous, confused, challenged — it's time to reach out to Hashem. Whether we are having a hard time with a client, an employee, looking for a job, trying to close a deal, or wondering how we are going to make it until the end of the month, always remember that *tefillah* is our first response.

How powerful is *tefillah* and our desire to connect to Hashem? The Baal Shem Tov spoke about a simple Jew who is working all day to support his family. The work is so all-encompassing that he gets caught up and forgets to even think about Hashem. Then, just before sundown, he remembers that he has not davened Minchah yet. A sigh escapes his lips as he thinks about how he'd been too busy to spend even a moment thinking about Hashem. He runs to a quiet corner and davens Minchah. The sigh that emanated from the deep recesses of his *neshamah* had a profound effect, piercing the highest Heavens (see *Magen Avraham, Balak, Dibbur* 3).

The *Kuzari* (3:5) asks why a Yid davens three times a day. He compares davening to food. Breakfast gives a person the energy to begin his day. Lunch provides him with the strength for a productive afternoon, and dinner ensures that he has the stamina to get through the night. It is the same with *tefillah*. Our three daily *tefillos* energize us, provide us with strength, and give us the stamina and *siyata d'Shmaya* for all that we do.

וְלָקְטוּ דְּבַר יוֹם בְּיוֹמוֹ —
And gather each day's portion in its day (16:4).

❧ *We Are a Product of Our Daily Habits*

The Maharal (*Nesivos Olam, Nesiv Ahavas Rei'a,* Ch. 1, quoting *Ein Yaakov*) quotes a fantastic Midrash:

There was a discussion among the Tannaim about which verse defines what it means to be a Yid. What is *the* verse that encapsulates the definition of a Jew and contains within it a microcosm of the entire Torah? Most of us, if not all, would say it's *Shema Yisrael, Hashem Elokeinu, Hashem Echad.* It is this verse that expresses our allegiance to Hashem and declares Hashem's omniscience. It is this verse that Jews throughout history cry out as they prepare to give up their lives *al kiddush Hashem.* This is the opinion of Ben Zoma.

Ben Nanas says that "*V'ahavta l'rei'acha kamocha* — Love your friend as yourself" (*Vayikra* 19:18) is *the* verse that contains the entirety of the Torah. It is this verse that teaches the centrality of interpersonal relationships in Judaism and the importance that the Torah places on loving and respecting a fellow Jew.

The third opinion is that of Shimon ben Pazi, who says that the verse that serves as the Jews' banner, their slogan, the verse that contains within it the Torah's DNA and what it means to be a Yid, is "You shall offer one sheep in the morning and the second sheep you shall offer in the afternoon" (*Shemos* 29:39). This verse informs us of our obligation to bring morning and afternoon offerings daily.

How do we rule? We rule like Shimon ben Pazi. "You shall offer one sheep in the morning and the second sheep you shall offer in the afternoon" is *the* verse that encapsulates the Torah's essence.

What is the meaning of this cryptic Midrash?

Parashas HaTamid describes the offering that was brought on the *Mizbei'ach* each day, day in and day out, regardless of circumstances. The *tamid* teaches us the importance of consistency in daily life. It informs us that what we do in the morning and what we do in the afternoon *every day* is who we really are! We are direct products of our daily habits and schedules. Yes, we need to go to work. But what we do before we go to work in the morning, what we do after work in the evenings, on Friday night, Shabbos afternoon, Motzaei Shabbos, Sunday, and legal holidays — that is what defines our identity. Snow, rain, sunshine, cold, grumpy, happy, not interested, not feeling it... The most important part of our *avodas Hashem* is consistency. Building solid, healthy, balanced habits that combine Torah study, family time, and work is vital for a productive and successful life. The *tamid* is what builds you; it is what transforms you over time.

People I know personally who work full time have finished *Shas*, written *sefarim*, and completed *masechtos* and *sefarim* by consistently committing to carving out time to learn. What they chose to do daily and over time is what enabled them to accomplish. It did not happen overnight; it did not take a month or a year. But a habitual commitment to Torah and learning leads to remarkable growth and accomplishments.

When the Romans besieged Jerusalem, they were unable to penetrate the holy city's walls. Eventually they discovered why. They had been sending two sheep over the wall every day in exchange for money. This allowed Bnei Yisrael to continue to offer the *korban tamid*. Then they learned that this was the secret to the impenetrability of the walls: The *korban tamid*, the daily offering, is what kept the city walls intact. That day, instead of a sheep, the Romans sent a pig. When it was halfway up the wall, it dug its hooves into the wall and Eretz Yisrael trembled (*Bava Kamma* 82b). Such is the power of consistency and the *tamid*.

Greatness is in consistency; it is in the *tamid*. It is not hard to recite *Bircas HaChamah* — an opportunity that happens once every twenty-eight years — with feeling. The real indicator of spiritual success is the ability to recite *Asher Yatzar* with feeling. True greatness is to come home from work exhausted but still go to *seder*. To get up in the morning when it's dark and cold, your car is freezing, and the world is sleeping; but you are showing up, you are there to learn and grow, day in and day out.

In his bestselling book, *Atomic Habits*, James Clear writes, "If you want to predict where you will end up in life, all you have to do is follow the curve of tiny gains or tiny losses (hence the name "atomic habits") and see how your daily choices will compound ten or twenty years down the line. A slight change in your daily habits can guide your life to a very different destination. Making a choice that is one percent better or one percent worse seems insignificant at the moment, but over the span of moments that make up a lifetime, these choices determine the difference between who you are and who you could be. Success is the product of daily habits" (p. 18).

The impact of a small change is hard to gauge in the short term, which is why many people become disillusioned and abandon their goals when the results they crave are not immediately forthcoming. It is vital to mentally commit to your goals and stay focused on the long term. With time and consistency, small changes compound and lead to profound change and growth. If a pilot, taking off from Los Angeles International Airport on his way to New York, changes his direction by a mere eighty-five inches south, he will land in Washington, D.C.! As the plane is taking off, the discrepancy of a little more than seven feet is almost unnoticeable. But when magnified over five hours of traveling time and 2,800 miles, that seven-foot divergence becomes a major difference.

The same is true with our small changes and commitments. Over time, they will compound and lead to true, impactful change and growth. A small change to your schedule, a consistent learning *seder* in the morning and in the afternoon, magnified over time, will change your life and give you and your family more purpose and more *simchah*. Your day-to-day choices are what shape you. Daily habits are what mold and create your identity. As the slogan has it, "It's not about the *daf*, it's about the *yomi*!" This is true for any learning *seder* or program, whether it be a page a day of a *sefer*, a Mishnah a day, *amud yomi, daf yomi, Dirshu, Oraysa, Zichru, V'haarev Na,* or *Hachzek*. Keep the commitment going no matter how small it is. Even a small *seder* at work has a huge impact. I know working people who have five-minute *sedarim* during lunch, or before Minchah, and they have completed many *sefarim* and *limudim* this way. Make the commitment to start. It will exponentially transform you.

Rav Alexander Moshe Lapidus (*Sefer Divrei Emes,* p. 158) writes something so remarkable. The Talmud tells us, "There are those who acquire their portion in the Next World in one hour" (or in one moment; *Avodah Zarah* 17a). Rav Alexander Moshe explains that this applies to one who spends most of his day working to support his family, so that he has only a short period of time each day in which to study Torah. If he is consistent about studying Torah in that time, he acquires a place in the Next World as if he studied Torah the entire day!

The power of your commitment is more than just what you accomplish on any given day. It is a gravitational push that creates vital forward momentum. A study by Lorene Whitehead (*American Journal of Physics*, 1983) demonstrated how a domino can knock over another domino that is one and a half times its size. A miniature size domino 0.2 inches tall and 0.04 inches thick (it almost looks like a piece of rice) can knock over another domino that is 1.5 times its size. If you follow the math, this little domino one-fifth of an inch tall can, within thirteen dominos, each 1.5 times its predecessor's size, cause a domino that is more than three feet tall, weighing one hundred pounds, to fall. If you lined up twenty-nine such dominos, the gravitational energy generated from the first little domino, magnified by all the successive ones, could knock over a domino as high as the Empire State Building! We learn from here that starting, pushing, moving, and making a minuscule change, can, in time, create an energy that leads to bigger and more profound accomplishments.

Greatness is building your day in a way that every day you add something small, something tangible, to the edifice that will become *you*. When you are not in yeshivah or in growth-oriented surroundings, the challenge is even greater. It is up to you to power your own engine. That is accomplished by standing firm in your commitments. It is just you and Hashem.

Decorated Navy SEAL and author Jocko Willink writes about greatness, "My glory does not happen in front of a crowd. It does not happen in a stadium or on a stage. There are no medals handed out. It happens in the darkness of early morning. Where I try. And I try and I try again, with everything I have, to be the best that I can possibly be. And claim one victory that is earned every single day. A victory of determination and will and discipline. A victory achieved because I will not stop." Take the time today to chart out your day. See how you can take better advantage of your time. What you accomplish in a few minutes here and a few minutes there is transformative when magnified over time.

> *I was fortunate to have Dr. Nachman Schorr as an optometrist for many years. I watched him, for many years, learn first seder every single day in Yeshiva of Far Rockaway. Only after a morning of serious learning did he open his practice. Dr. Schorr was a stalwart participant in daf yomi, completing Shas in depth many times. He lived and breathed the daily daf, reviewing it many times. He gained supreme clarity of sugyos and took the monthly Dirshu tests.*
>
> *I remember one story as if it happened yesterday. It was Purim. I went to my rebbi, Rav Moshe Brown, who was hosting a kabbalas kahal for the Yeshiva of Far Rockaway bachurim and for his shul, which was where Dr. Schorr davened (and participated in Rav Brown's morning daf yomi shiur). We were sitting around Rav Brown's table singing and being merry when Dr. Schorr*

walked in. Rav Brown, slightly inebriated, stood up and screamed to Dr. Schorr, "Nachman, Nachman. Tell them. Tell everyone here today. Tell the bachurim. Tell them how many blatt Gemara you were tested on in last week's Dirshu test. Tell them, Nachman. They need to know!"

Dr. Schorr, a modest person, but inebriated, said, "Rebbi, it was six hundred blatt! That was the last Dirshu test I took — on six hundred blatt!"

Rav Brown took Dr. Schorr by the hand and began dancing with him. The great Rav Brown and the great Dr. Schorr. Dr. Schorr organized his life and set his priorities straight. He was consistent, mornings and evenings. He became a paradigm of a working person who continued to grow and become one with the Torah, and an inspiration to so many.

I was learning in Eretz Yisrael when the 12th Siyum HaShas took place in the summer of 2012. During this time, I had been davening next to Professor Zecharya Dershowitz, who was in his late eighties, and had been a professor at Bar Ilan for many years. One morning after davening, we were discussing the upcoming siyum. Knowing Professor Dershowitz learned the daf yomi each day, I asked him if this would be his first time completing the cycle and how he would be celebrating. The professor smiled at me and said, "You know, this will be my ninth Siyum HaShas, the ninth cycle I am completing of the daf yomi." He knew Shas because at the young age of twenty, he made the decision that the daf would become part of his day. Nearly seventy years later, that daily commitment of forty-five minutes had formed a man who knew Shas and knew it well.

so that I can test them, whether they will walk according to My teaching or not.

Rav Avraham Danzig, author of the landmark sefarim Chayei Adam and Chochmas Adam, was a renowned talmid chacham whose sefarim and halachic rulings have played a role in daily Jewish life for generations. Rav Avraham was also a businessman. In the introduction to Chochmas Adam he writes, "I know that people will whisper and wonder about me, the man who was a businessman who traveled to Leipzig (the marketplace) for more than fifteen years. So, when did I learn? Know my brothers, that I did not travel to gain wealth. Hashem will testify that I traveled to support my family, my ten sons. My fellow businessmen will testify that even when I was traveling, I always had a Gemara, a Chumash, and a Mishnayos with me. And even on market days I learned at least one and a half pages of Gemara and Mishnayos. I am not telling you this to inflate my ego but to encourage other people who are working and traveling, so that they realize they can and need to learn each day. Maybe from me, my children and grandchildren will learn and I will get some credit for that."

וְלָקְטוּ דְּבַר יוֹם בְּיוֹמוֹ לְמַעַן אֲנַסֶּנּוּ הֲיֵלֵךְ בְּתוֹרָתִי אִם לֹא —
And gather each day's portion in its day, so that I can test them, whether they will walk according to My teaching or not (16:4).

◆§ *Bitachon: Our Connection to Hashem*

The Gemara (*Yoma* 76a) explains that Hashem sent the Jewish nation a daily portion of *mahn*, exactly what they needed for that day (except on Erev Shabbos, when a double portion fell). He did not send them a large amount of *mahn* that would last for an extended period of time. There are several reasons for this:

Firstly, receiving the *mahn* daily ensured that Bnei Yisrael had only the freshest and most tasty food.

Secondly, gathering the *mahn* daily meant that it was relatively easy to gather and carry home; they did not have to transport and store large amounts of food.

Thirdly, the *mahn* fell daily so that the Jews would turn their eyes to Hashem in prayer every day, confident in the knowledge that He would provide for them. Hashem wanted Bnei Yisrael to look to Him, to understand that they needed to connect with Him daily for their every need. Going to sleep with nothing in the fridge forced the nation to strengthen their trust in Hashem and their reliance on Him. This *bitachon* was the foundation stone of the education of all future generations; the daily portion of *mahn* showed that Hashem is the Source of *parnassah*. It is easy to speak about *bitachon* when things are going well at work or when the stock market is flourishing. The true test is when there are struggles, when the bills are mounting, the markets are down, and things are tight. Our *avodah* is to glean inspiration and direction from Parashas HaMahn. The *segulah* of reciting Parashas HaMahn daily is to affirm the knowledge that it is Hashem — and only Hashem — Who controls our *parnassah*.

Rav Moshe Chaim Luzzatto explains an amazing and powerful fact about trust in Hashem. Dovid HaMelech tells us, "*Kavei el Hashem* — Rely on Hashem" (*Tehillim* 27:14). The root of the word קַוֵּה (*kavei*), rely, is קַו (*kav*), a line. When we are "*kavei el Hashem*," when we rely on Hashem, we create a direct *kav*, line, to Heaven, connecting us to Hashem's *Kisei HaKavod*! (*Otzros Ramchal*, p. 246). This is the power of relying on Hashem and only on Hashem! Do you want a direct line to Hashem's Throne of Glory? You can have it by strengthening your *bitachon* in Hashem. "Hashem is good to those who trust in Him; to the soul that seeks Him" (*Eichah* 3:25).

The Midrash expounds on the verse "I have greatly relied on Hashem" (*Tehillim* 40:2), telling us that the Jewish people will enjoy the ultimate redemption because they "greatly relied on Hashem" (*Shachar Tov*).

The Kedushas Levi explains that the root of the word *bitachon* is *tach,* adhere. *Bitachon* creates a "sticking agent," attaching us to Hashem and firmly attaching Him to us. The more *bitachon* we have in Hashem the stronger the bond and the more resolutely Hashem is connected to us (*Arugos HaBosem, Parashas Beshalach*).

After the snake convinced Chavah to eat from the *Eitz HaDaas,* Hashem cursed him, decreeing that he lose his legs and crawl on the ground, and eat the dust of the earth. Rav Moshe Minder asks, "Why is that a curse? Dust is readily available in every place. The snake now has permanent and continuous access to food. Apparently, that's a blessing!" He explains that the biggest curse is Hashem saying, "Here, take it all. You will have what you need forever; I do not want a relationship with you, I do not want to connect with you." When we are struggling with *parnassah,* or any matter, it is Hashem telling us, "My child, I want to be close to you, I want you to connect with Me. Call out to Me. Extend a hand. Look upward. Rely on Me. Transfer to Me all the weight of anxiety, stress, and worry that you are feeling. I will bear it for you."

◆§ *Strengthening Our Bitachon Each Day: Sefer Chovos HaLevavos, Shaar HaBitachon*

Sefer Chovos HaLevavos, and particularly the *Shaar HaBitachon,* has been a life raft for many generations in the stormy and turbulent sea of our history. Many *gedolim* of all sectors studied this *sefer,* on their own and with their students. The Shelah, Chida, the great Kabbalist Rav Shalom Sharabi (Rashash), the Yismach Moshe, Chasam Sofer, and so many others all made time each day to learn from and teach *Chovos HaLevavos.* Rav Chaim Soloveitchik, the Brisker Rav, once passed by his son, the young Rav Yitzchok Zev, when he was avidly studying *Chovos HaLevavos.* He said to him, "Learn and learn from this *sefer.* The *Chovos HaLevavos* is the *Shulchan Aruch* of what it means to be a Yid!"

Learning *Shaar HaBitachon* is itself a *segulah* for *parnassah.*

Strengthening one's *bitachon* opens the gates of *berachah* (Apter Rebbe). The Vilna Gaon is quoted as saying that studying *Shaar HaBitachon* is a *segulah* for *hatzlachah* in all areas (*Zichron Yaakov Yosef*). Make this *sefer* a part of your daily life. Let the teachings of this *sefer* change your thoughts and actions. The more you tap into *bitachon*, the better you are prepared to handle whatever life brings with serenity and the knowledge that Hashem is always with you.

> *Rav Yitzchok Zev Soloveitchik, the Brisker Rav, received a block of buildings in Warsaw as a dowry. It was valuable real estate, worth a fortune. But shortly thereafter, he lost the property. "Are you worried about the future?" someone asked. He replied, "People think that a wealthy person is someone who has properties in Warsaw. A wealthy person is someone who has Shaar HaBitachon ingrained in his heart" (Uvdos V'hanhagos L'Beis Brisk, Vol.1, p. 73).*

וַיֹּאמֶר ה׳ אֶל מֹשֶׁה הִנְנִי מַמְטִיר לָכֶם לֶחֶם מִן הַשָּׁמָיִם... לְמַעַן אֲנַסֶּנּוּ — *Hashem said to Moshe, "Behold I will cause bread to rain down on you from heaven... so that I can test them"* (16:4).

Growth Through Struggles

The Gemara (*Bava Metzia* 86b) tells us that Bnei Yisrael received the miraculous *mahn* directly from Hashem and not through an intermediary in the merit of a specific deed of Avraham Avinu.

What did he do? On the third day after his *bris milah*, the most painful of the recuperation days, Hashem made the sun blaze. This was so that no one would venture outdoors and, without any guests to serve, Avraham could remain in his tent to rest and recover. However, Avraham was disturbed at not being able to fulfill the mitzvah of welcoming guests. So Hashem sent three angels, dressed as Arabs. Despite all the excuses — his age, the pain, the heat — Avraham arose with alacrity to welcome and feed his guests.

Whatever foods Avraham himself prepared for his guests, like the bread and cakes, Hashem Himself provided for Bnei Yisrael in the Wilderness; therefore, Hashem's children received *mahn* directly from Heaven. The items that Avraham sent an emissary to prepare were provided for Bnei Yisrael via an emissary. So the water, which Avraham sent an emissary to retrieve, was provided by Hashem through an emissary — the well. [Moreover, the *mahn* fell for the first time when Bnei Yisrael were in the city of Alush, the name of which prompts us to recall Avraham telling Sarah, "***Lushi*** *va'asi ugos* — knead and make cakes," reminding Bnei Yisrael that they were receiving *mahn* as a form of *middah k'neged middah* for Avraham and Sarah having provided cake for the guests (*Yerushalmi Beitzah* 2:1; see also *Nachal Kedumim*, who explains that the word "מָן" (*mahn*) is an acrostic of "מַעֲשֵׂה נִסִּים" (*maaseh nissim*) — a miraculous action. Although generally one should not benefit from miracles, Bnei Yisrael were permitted to benefit from the *mahn* since it was remuneration for Avraham's acts of *chesed*.)]

Rav Yosef Tzvi Salant (*Be'er Yosef*, p. 41) asks, why was **this** *chesed* of Avraham's the one that determined how Hashem would sustain Avraham's progeny in the Wilderness years later? Avraham performed thousands of other acts of *chesed*; Avraham is the pillar of *chesed*! Why did Hashem pinpoint this incident? His answer is so powerful. He asks, "When was it hardest for Avraham to do *chesed*? When was it challenging, uncomfortable, even painful to do *chesed*? It was at this time, the third day after his circumcision — it was hot, he was elderly, they appeared to be Arabs — and yet, Avraham rose above it all." He passed the ultimate test. We laser in on this story of Avraham's *chesed* because it was hard, it was a battle for him. Muscles are built by overcoming resistance. The same is true for *ruchniyus* and character development. Growth, development, and reward come when we are challenged but we overcome. That is why this incident is the one that set the stage for how his children were to be sustained in the Wilderness years later.

In a letter to a student undergoing a difficult time, Rav Hutner (*Igros U'Kesavim* §128) wrote, "Know, my beloved, that the root of your soul is not the peaceful times of the *yetzer tov*, but rather the battles of the *yetzer tov* [in its continual battle with the *yetzer hara*]. You will certainly fall again and lose battles, but I am confident that despite lost battles, you will arise victorious in war, adorned with a crown of triumph. The path to glory is not a straight one; it winds like a serpent on the road. Shlomo HaMelech writes, 'The righteous one will fall seven times, and he will arise' (*Mishlei* 24:16). There are those who erroneously construe the verse to mean that the righteous one rises despite having fallen seven times. This is incorrect. Rather, the true understanding of the verse is that one is *transformed into a tzaddik because he has fallen seven times*." We are not born great. We become great through failing and through rising up and overcoming our challenges. We are a resilient people who have become the great nation we are because we have faced challenges and overcome them.

Often, we are trained to gauge our success on a barometer of pure results. It is overwhelmingly difficult not to judge ourselves based on outcomes when society places unprecedented stress on money, breadth of social circles, looks, and tangible possessions. One either has or lacks these. It is a results-oriented world. Yet, when it comes to our relationship with Hashem, it is not an all-or-nothing paradigm. Our efforts, our challenges, our struggles, even our falls and mistakes are beloved by Hashem. "Hashem wants our hearts" (*Sanhedrin* 106b) and uses our hearts and efforts as indicators of our success. Know that when we are tested, when we have a *nisayon* in any aspect of life, it is not easy, but it is a God-given opportunity for growth and *berachah*. We were given the miraculous *mahn* because Avraham successfully passed his test. And getting the *mahn* was a test for us, to see if we would continue to keep the Torah, as the verse says, "I will cause bread to rain down on you... so that I can test them, whether they will walk according to My teaching or not." We all experience trials throughout our day, and specifically at work. Tests in honesty, tests in avoiding looking at forbidden sights, tests in maintaining a healthy work-life balance, tests in setting priorities, tests in *bitachon*... We can learn from Avraham that embracing these challenges and working to overcome them results in the *berachah* of *mahn* and *parnassah*.

Navy Admiral William McRaven, commander of the Joint Special Operations Command and Special Operations Command Europe and a former Navy SEAL, delivered these comments to eight thousand graduates at the University of Texas at Austin in 2014:

> *Every day during SEAL training you were challenged with multiple physical tests — long runs, long swims, obstacle courses, hours of calisthenics — something designed to test your mettle. Every event had standards — times you had to meet. If you failed to meet those standards your name was posted on a list, and at the end of the day, those on the list were invited to a "circus." A circus was two hours of additional calisthenics designed to wear you down, to break your spirit, to force you to quit.*
>
> *No one wanted a circus.*
>
> *A circus meant that for that day, you did not measure up. A circus meant more fatigue — and more fatigue meant that the following day would be more difficult — and more circuses were likely. But at some time during SEAL training, everyone — everyone — made the circus list.*
>
> *But an interesting thing happened to those who were constantly on the list. Over time those students — who did two hours of extra calisthenics — got stronger and stronger. The pain of the circuses built inner strength, built physical resiliency.*
>
> *Life is filled with circuses. You will fail. You will likely fail often. It will be painful. It will be discouraging. At*

times it will test you to your very core. But if you want to change the world, don't be afraid of the circuses.

Rav Ezriel Tauber was a visionary leader, kiruv innovator, speaker, talmid chacham, and businessman. On one trip, his connecting flight was delayed and the airline put him up in a hotel. It was an extremely long and tiresome day for Rav Ezriel, and by the time he arrived at his hotel room it was close to one in the morning. He sat down in an armchair, took out his Gemara, and began to learn daf yomi, something he did every day, religiously. But his eyes could not stay open; he was exhausted. After a few more attempts to continue learning, he berated himself and said, "I don't come close to my father, just one generation past, who spent hours learning at night and never let sleep get in the way of his daily learning obligations." Rav Ezriel paused, looked at the TV in front of him, and said with an air of triumph, "Yes, maybe my learning is not up to my father's level. But my father never had the test of being in a hotel room alone with a TV!" The tests of life are what make us a stronger, more resilient, and more elevated people.

וְלָקְטוּ דְּבַר יוֹם בְּיוֹמוֹ לְמַעַן אֲנַסֶּנּוּ הֲיֵלֵךְ בְּתוֹרָתִי אִם לֹא —
And gather each day's portion in its day,
so that I can test them, whether they will walk
according to My teaching or not (16:4).

Learning Each Day

Hashem told Klal Yisrael that in the merit of learning Torah each day, they would receive the Heavenly *mahn*. Chazal (*Shemos Rabbah* 25:9) learn this from the verse, "Praiseworthy is a person who listens to Me, to be constantly at My doors every day" (*Mishlei* 8:34). "Moreover," Hashem says, "I will bless you each day," as the verse says, "Blessed is Hashem; every day He loads our salvation on us" (*Tehillim* 68:20).

Hashem gives us the *berachah* of *parnassah* when we commit to study Torah daily. When a soldier is serving in the army and protecting his country, the king provides his food and daily needs. When one commits to Torah study, he is enlisting as a soldier in the army of Hashem, and is therefore supported directly by Hashem! (*Ha'amek Davar, Bereishis* 26:5).

Daily Torah study becomes our anchor in the stormy sea of life. It gives us purpose and meaning, and elevates us. Rav Meir Shapiro, the innovator of the *daf yomi*, highlighted this with the Gemara (*Yevamos* 121a) that recounts a sea voyage that Rabban Gamliel once took. When he saw another boat capsize, he was pained by the loss of Rabbi Akiva, who was on that boat. Yet, upon landing, Rabban Gamliel met Rabbi Akiva, who came and sat next to him. Rabban Gamliel asked him how he had survived. Rabbi Akiva explained, "A *daf* (a board) of a ship came to me, and I let all the waves that came my way wash over my head." Rav Meir explained that this *daf* is the *daf* of Gemara that saved Rabbi Akiva. Daily Torah study saves each of us from the waves of life that seek to capsize us. "[The Torah] is a tree of life to those who grasp it" (*Mishlei* 3:18). It is like a wooden board that a drowning person can grab onto in the stormy sea (*Ruach Chaim* 6:1).

Let us be sure to study Torah each day. The Torah is what saves us, anchors us, transforms us, and blesses us.

In *HaSiyum*, which was published in honor of the 13th Global Siyum HaShas of Daf Yomi, Rav Noach Isaac Oelbaum wrote:

> *When someone dedicates himself to a daily regimen of limud haTorah, the Torah's influence elevates him and changes his entire behavior. It transforms him into a Torahdige person in every aspect of his life. I have been privileged to witness the transformation that occurs when the Gemara penetrates a Jewish heart. Beyond the tremendous accomplishment of the learning itself, we have found profound benefit from a great spiritual lift. People's middos improve, their shalom bayis is greater,*

their speech is refined, their bein adam lachaveiro is on a different level, and their days are filled with Torah and kedushah. As a rav of a kehillah for close to forty-five years, I have seen repeatedly how baalei batim have become bnei Torah after they married. For whatever reason, some were not very successful in yeshivah, but after they married and settled down, and became attendees of our daf yomi shiurim, they became outstanding bnei Torah. This is the magic of limud haTorah.

I recall one man who was heavily involved in sports. It was an important part of his life; he had no interest in shul activities or in learning. One time, our daf yomi shiur was completing a masechta and we needed a tenth man to say Kaddish. This man came and amazingly, he so enjoyed hearing the shiur on the last blatt of the masechta that he showed up the next day for the first blatt of the next masechta. Although it was a difficult masechta, he took to it with determination and kept coming to the shiur. Today, he's on his fifth cycle of daf yomi and deeply involved in tzorchei tzibbur, the community's needs.

Elisha Loewenstern, father of six, was killed defending Israel on the seventh night of Chanukah, 2023. His wife, Hadas, recounted that Elisha was passionate about Torah study. The last photo of Elisha was taken a few hours before he was killed. It is a picture of him and his team in a bombed-out building in Gaza, resting after spending days cooped up in the tank. Elisha is sitting there in his uniform learning from a paperback Rambam.

When his mother saw the picture, she started crying. "I told Elisha that he needs to take off his shoes the minute he leaves the tank. Having those big, heavy military boots on in the extremely oppressive tank for days was unhealthy. Yet, look at this picture. Elisha is still wearing his boots. The first thing Elisha did after leaving the tank was to pick up a sefer. His soul was parched. He did not even take off his shoes, but went straight to the Rambam, to his precious Torah."

Hadas added, "Elisha loved to learn. On Shabbos, during the evenings after work, and whenever he had time, he always prioritized his learning and davening. ***Elisha did not just die a hero. He lived as a hero.****"*

☙ *Trying Our Hardest*

At times, it is a struggle to incorporate Torah study into the daily schedule, especially for those working long hours. Even those who make the time to study may feel as though the material is not being absorbed, as their minds are swimming in a hundred directions, or simply turned off. Despite trying, at times it just does not go. The Chazon Ish addresses this. He said, "Hashem loves our *chizuk* of even one moment." When we make the effort to be better people, this in and of itself is highly valued in Heaven and has a lot of influence there (*Maaseh Ish*, Vol. 4, p. 59).

Avnei Nezer writes that the word "רָצוֹן" (*ratzon*), desire, has the same letters as "צִנוֹר" (*tzinor*), pipe. When one demonstrates a desire to do what is right, it creates a pipeline of *berachah* and success.

An Israeli taxi driver said that he was once fortunate enough to drive the renowned Rav Yaakov Yisrael Kanievsky, the Steipler Gaon. The Steipler spoke with the driver and asked if he had a set time to learn Torah each day. The taxi driver responded that yes, every night he went to a shiur, but he was so exhausted he always fell asleep and only woke up when the shiur was over. The driver expressed his disappointment and frustration about his inability to remain awake during the shiur. The Steipler smiled and said encouragingly, "Here in This World it appears that you are not accomplishing much. But I can promise you that in Heaven you are a great general because you are doing the best you can. Continue to attend the shiur. Even if you fall asleep, in Heaven, they consider you a great tzaddik!" The Steipler's message is so simple but so vital: As long as we try our best, whether we can see quantifiable results or not, we are considered great generals in Heaven. Rav Gifter said that the minimum Hashem expects from us is the maximum of our ability.

Rav Nosson Tzvi Finkel, the rosh yeshivah of Mir Yerushalayim, suffered from Parkinson's. The disease disabled the rosh yeshivah's body, but not his spirit. He worked tirelessly to create the magical place that is Yeshivas Mir. There were many times that Rav Nosson Tzvi overcame great pain and difficulty to go and give a shiur, getting as far as opening the Gemara, but then no words came out. He was unable to speak. At one particular shiur in which this happened, the yeshivah students held their breaths, hoping that their rosh yeshivah would be able to deliver the shiur. But not even one sound emerged; the words just would not come out. Rav Nosson Tzvi asked for a pen and paper and wrote, "Nisisi, selichah — I tried, I apologize" (B'chol Nafshecha, p. 418).

Hashem wants every one of us to come to Him with our own paper stating that in whatever endeavor we struggled, or whatever goal we set for ourselves, we can proclaim, like Rav Nosson Tzvi, "*Nisisi* — I tried." This is what is incumbent upon us. Take the first step. Try, and with Hashem's help you will be successful. When one takes a step to live with greater purity, Hashem will help him (*Yoma* 38b). Take that first step today.

לְמַעַן אֲנַסֶּנּוּ הֲיֵלֵךְ בְּתוֹרָתִי אִם לֹא —
So that I can test them, whether they will walk according to My teaching or not (16:4).

Emunah: The Key to Improving Interpersonal Relationships

The *mahn* fell even before the Jews accepted the Torah. There was a reason for this. We know that a prerequisite to receiving the Torah is *derech eretz*, character refinement and respectable *middos*, as it says, "*Derech eretz kadmah laTorah*" (see *Vayikra Rabbah* 9:3). To be a receptacle that can accept the Torah, Jews need to be upstanding, righteous people who get along with one another on a personal, communal, and national level. The Torah places an extraordinary emphasis on interpersonal relationships; Rabbi Akiva stated: "'*V'ahavta l'rei'acha kamocha,' zeh klal gadol baTorah* — 'Love your neighbor as yourself,' this is a great principle in the Torah!" (*Sifra, Kedoshim* 4). Yet, as we know, interpersonal relationships with family, friends, coworkers, and neighbors pose a daunting test, especially when it comes to money.

How can one improve his interpersonal skills and love for his fellow Jew? The *sefarim* tell us that the prerequisite for good *middos* is *emunah* and *bitachon* in Hashem (see *Sefer HaChinuch* §241 and *Sefer HaYashar L'Rabbeinu Tam*). *Emunah* and *bitachon* allow us to see that everyone's actions are directed by Hashem. One cannot become upset with others when one has this knowledge. One does not lose one's temper, nor slander, nor seek revenge. When we internalize that Hashem is in control of every detail of our lives, and that we will get every dollar that is supposed to come to us, and will not get a single dollar that is not meant for us; when we realize that no one can touch what is mine, then we can avoid *lashon hara*, hatred, anger, jealousy, disagreements, and more. Hence, the *mahn* — the purpose of which was to teach us to recognize Hashem as the director of everything — changes our outlook on our fellow Jew, and our interactions. (Of course, this doesn't mean that someone who wronged us will not have to answer for it, but that *cheshbon*, that accounting, is in Hashem's hands.) The daily gathering of *mahn* taught us to rely on and trust in Hashem. *Bitachon* leads to an improvement of interpersonal relationships and upstanding *derech eretz*. Only one with good *middos* and *derech eretz* can earn the privilege of receiving the Torah (*Yalkut Menachem*, p. 158).

The *Bas Ayin* (*Parashas Bo*) writes that the mitzvah of loving one's neighbor as oneself is a wondrous *segulah* for one's *tefillos* to be accepted! The Arizal writes that before one begins davening one should resolve to observe the mitzvah of loving each Jew like himself. This will allow his *tefillah* to join together with those of the entire nation, rising to the greatest heights and bearing fruit (*Magen Avraham* 46).

Rav Shimshon Pincus explains that our relationship with Hashem and with our fellow man are not two distinct parts of *avodas Hashem*; they are intrinsically and intimately connected. If we have an issue with another Yid, we have an issue with Hashem's precious child, and that affects our relationship with Hashem!

Rav Shimshon even takes it a step further. *Tefillah* is *emunah* in Hashem. Getting along with our fellow Jew is *emunah* as well. When we have *emunah* in Hashem, we know that there is no reason to be angry at another Yid, who is a mere emissary of Hashem. There is no need for jealousy, either, as everything is apportioned with Divine precision. Unfortunately, we see that when it comes to matters of money, disagreements soon become heated. Business partners, families, and communities have been ripped asunder by disputes about money. The *mahn* teaches us that all money is directed by Hashem to exactly where it should go. I will have what I am supposed to have and no one in the world can touch that.

With this awareness, let us work to de-escalate money-related disagreements. There is nothing more beloved and desired by Hashem than for us to have peace between ourselves. There is no greater *segulah* for *berachah* in our lives than peace.

◆§ *Lag BaOmer: Never Giving Up*

Rashi (*Beshalach* 16:1, based on *Shabbos* 87b) tells us that the *mahn* fell for the first time on the sixteenth of Iyar. A second opinion is that the *mahn* fell for the first time on the fifteenth of Iyar. The Chasam Sofer, basing his opinion on a

Midrash, cites a third (minority) opinion that the first day the *mahn* fell was on the eighteenth of Iyar. This is one reason we rejoice on Lag BaOmer, the eighteenth day of Iyar.

Lag BaOmer is a day of joy and celebration. The night begins with festive dancing, singing, *divrei Torah,* and happiness. By day, overgrown beards are trimmed and haircuts are taken as the thirty-three-day mourning period that falls during *sefirah* is lifted. Weddings and other *semachos* commence, and music is heard in homes, cars, stores, and schools.

What is the reason for the joy of Lag BaOmer? The most well-known answer is that this is the day on which the 24,000 students of Rabbi Akiva ceased to perish. So the mourning period is over and we can rejoice.

The *Pri Chadash* (493:2) asks the obvious question: How can we celebrate the fact that the students of Rabbi Akiva ceased to die when so many were lost? He answers: The *simchah* on Lag BaOmer is that Rabbi Akiva rebuilt Torah through five new students.

Picture the scene: Rabbi Akiva begins to learn Torah at the age of forty, an exceptional accomplishment. He eventually becomes the eminent Tanna and the leader of a Torah empire, the rosh yeshivah of 24,000 students. But in a flash, they are all gone. Every single one died. Each student a child, each student a diamond, an investment, a bright star... all gone. One could imagine that the leader of 24,000 deceased students might feel life is not worth living, choose an early retirement, or somehow just fade into oblivion. Not Rabbi Akiva. Rabbi Akiva did not wallow in sorrow, he did not quit, and he did not become disgruntled. Rabbi Akiva was a warrior, a warrior who never gave up, who never stopped battling, and after losing so much, he started again. This was the same Rabbi Akiva who started learning Torah at the age of forty! This is the *simchah* of Lag BaOmer.

We learn from here that no matter what age we are or what has happened in the past, we can forge on, we can start again, we can grow and accomplish. The Klausenberger

Rebbe lost his wife, eleven children, and his entire *kehillah* in the Holocaust. Following in the footsteps of Rabbi Akiva, he rose from the ashes to rebuild a flourishing and successful international *chassidus* with yeshivos, kollelim, and hospitals of *chesed*. The Ponevezher Rav lost his wife, many children, a yeshivah, and a *kehillah*. Yet he came to Eretz Yisrael, forged ahead, and built a Torah empire that is still going strong today.

Rav Tzadok HaKohen (*Divrei Sofrim* 16) writes that our nation is built on the premise that a Jew never loses hope. Sarah, Rivkah, and Rachel were physically unable to bear children, but they did. They gave birth to the Jewish nation. Never give up, never settle.

I have the privilege of knowing a special Jew who made a fortune, but then lost it all and then some. During this time, his neshamah began to awaken, and he began to connect to Hashem. Despite enormous financial and legal losses and negative publicity, he started to learn Torah and live a life of mitzvos. He did not give up; he did not throw in the towel. He made a conscious decision to forge on, to move ahead, to become different, better, more elevated. This is Rabbi Akiva's message. This is the message of the eighteenth day of Iyar.

I recently met a working man in his sixties who told me that after the tragedy in Eretz Yisrael that happened on Simchas Torah, October 7, 2023, he wanted to do something on behalf of the hostages and soldiers. He decided to begin reviewing the parashah each week. How impressive! A man who, for fifty-plus years of his life, has not performed this mitzvah, makes the commitment to begin anyway. It is never too late to start. It is never too late to change.

◆§ *Nisyonos — Life Itself*

The battles we face with the *yetzer hara* are opportunities for growth and development. It is not easy. The tests are great and often constant. The *yetzer hara* is relentless, looking for every and any opportunity to trip us up and bring us down. Earning a living presents a plethora of challenges and tests. Know that a test is a Heaven-sent opportunity for us to graduate to the next step, to build our spiritual muscles, and earn stupendous *berachah*. Hashem does not expect perfection. We will not win every battle. But in today's time of spiritual darkness, the light created from battling and working as hard as you can is immense.

Before his demise, Moshe reminds the Jewish nation that they provoked God time after time, and that he sacrificed so much to battle for their forgiveness, survival, and ultimate success: "When I ascended the mountain to receive the Tablets of Stone, the Tablets of the Covenant that Hashem sealed with you, I remained on the mountain for forty days and forty nights: I did not eat bread and I did not drink water" (*Devarim* 9:9). Moshe seems to be telling the Jewish nation that he sacrificed so much by not eating or drinking for these forty days. But during these forty days he was in direct communication with the Shechinah itself, basking in Hashem's presence, and earning a closeness to God that no other human has ever experienced! Why the concern about food and drink?

Tiferes Shlomo explains something unbelievable. Our job here in This World is to battle our *yetzer hara*. The essence of life is when our body (*yetzer hara*) is pitted against our *nefesh* (*yetzer tov*) and we battle to do the will of Hashem. This continuous, lifelong, unceasing battle is life itself; the reason we are here in This World is to wage war against the *yetzer hara* and fight as best as we can to perform the mitzvos. Moshe Rabbeinu was telling the Jewish nation: I sacrificed forty days of life for you! While I was in heaven accepting the Luchos and beseeching Hashem to have mercy on you, I did not need to eat or drink, I did not have a *yetzer hara*, I had no battle, no fight with my *yetzer hara*. In essence I sacrificed forty days of life for you! (*Rosh Hashanah; Nitzavim*).

After Yaakov's struggle with the angel, he is given a new

name. The angel tells him (*Bereishis* 32:29), “No longer will it be said that your name is Yaakov, but Yisrael, for you have struggled (*sarisa*)with the Divine and with man, and you have overcome (*vatuchal*). Rav Leibel Eiger points out that the word used to say “you have overcome” is *vatuchal.* If so, why wasn’t Yaakov’s name changed to Michael to commemorate his victory? The name Yisrael comes from the word *sarisa,* you struggled; it just recalls the fight. He answers that Hashem is showing us that it is not only the victory that’s precious, but the efforts we make when waging war. It is the fight, the struggle, that Hashem values. Therefore, each of us is called a Yisrael! (*Imrei Emes*).

☙ *The Test of Setting Priorities*

The Torah tells us that *mahn* was given to test the Jewish nation, to see if they would follow Hashem’s instruction not to leave over *mahn* from one day to the next, as well as obey the prohibition of going out on Shabbos to look for *mahn* (*Rashi*). Similarly, the *Chovos HaLevavos* explains that one reason Hashem decreed that man should work is to test him, to see if he will earn his living with honesty and integrity, and safeguard the relevant halachos. It is no wonder that the first question man is asked when arriving at the Heavenly Court is, “Did you conduct business with integrity?” (*Shabbos* 31a). Knowing ahead of time that going to work will undoubtedly present us with tests enables us to be on the lookout for challenges and prepare accordingly.

Chazal tell us that one had the ability to taste almost anything he desired when eating *mahn.* What was the reason for this miracle? Rav Yonasan Eibeschutz tells us something so important: that a clear ordering of priorities is a requirement for success in leading a meaningful and elevated life. Without that, the allure of excess, of tasting everything that This World has to offer, is so blinding that it distracts us from what we truly want (*Taamei HaMinhagim,* p. 145).

People can spend decades totally unaware of why they go

to work. Earning a living, amassing more and more, and feeling the constant pressure to taste the delicacies of This World becomes an end in itself; it becomes the sole purpose of life, it becomes one's identity.

When the *mahn* was gathered in the Wilderness, it was a test. Would time and energy be spent to experience a culinary delight and increase personal pleasure, or to study Torah? The same applies to us today. Will time be spent with family, or pursuing another fleeting pleasure? How many months and years of learning and time spent with our family are sacrificed to the allure of what we think will bring us more happiness? This is the question each of us needs to answer every day. What are our priorities, what are our goals?

The test today is so strong, stronger than it has ever been. Every advertisement tells us to think about money, food, clothing, homes, cars, vacations, and worldly experiences; these pull our attention, mind space, and resources away from what is eternal and important. Dovid Hamelech davened to Hashem, הַצִּילֵנִי מִדָּמִים אֱלֹהִים (*Tehillim* 51:16). The Baal Shem Tov homiletically explained that Dovid beseeched Hashem, "Save me so that money (דָּמִים) does not become like a god (אֱלֹהִים), that it not define who I am. Let it not blind me and coerce me to live in a way that I know is not good for me or my family."

The Maharal writes (*Nesiv HaOsher* 2) that the word for money, *kesef,* shares a root with the word *kisufin,* desires and yearning. There is nothing more universally chased, desired, longed for, and motivating than money. But *kesef* also shares a root with the word *kisufa,* the Aramaic word for embarrassment. The pursuit of money and the drive for its accumulation may bring one to disregard one's *neshamah* and one's mission in This World, and there is nothing more embarrassing than that.

At a *pidyon haben,* the Kohen lifts the five silver coins and asks the new father, "What do you want more, the five silver coins or your child?" It is a rhetorical question, as the father is required to give the Kohen the five coins and take his child. But the truth is that the father and mother answer the Kohen's question each day of their lives: "What do you want more, what is most important to you? Is it the five silver coins — money, your standard of living, the grinding pursuit of the material — or the *neshamah* of your precious child?"

It is intriguing to note that in the Jewish calendar the new day begins at sundown. Perhaps this tells us that the new day truly commences when we arrive home from work. When you are with your family, and free to study Torah, a new day dawns and your priorities become clear.

Rav Moshe Weinberger, the rav of Aish Kodesh, recounts a day when he was distraught.

> *I went to the nearest payphone to call my father, who had a dry-cleaning business on Third Avenue in Manhattan. My mother, who worked in the store as well, picked up the phone and I asked, "Mommy, can I speak to Daddy, please?"*
>
> *My mother said, "Can you call back later? It's very busy right now at the store."*
>
> *"Ma, I just need to speak to Daddy for a minute."*
>
> *Daddy came to the phone and asked, "Moshe, is everything okay?"*
>
> *I told him what happened, and he said to hold on a minute. A minute or two passed and it was quiet. He then got back on the phone and we spoke for the next forty-five minutes, while he helped me work through the issue.*
>
> *That night when I came home, my mother greeted me and said, "You know, when you called Daddy at three o'clock, it was very busy at the store. Do you know what Daddy did?"*
>
> *"No, what did Daddy do?" I asked.*
>
> *"Daddy asked all the customers to leave, then he closed the store and went to the back to speak with you."*
>
> *I went to apologize to my father. I did not realize how busy the store was, or that he would close the store just so he could speak to me.*

Daddy said to me, "Apologize? You are the whole reason I go to work; I live for you. I am here for you."

May Hashem grant each of us the insight and the courage to overcome the enormous test of getting our priorities straight. Let today be the day we make a commitment to pay more attention to what is truly important and meaningful — Torah study, *chesed,* mitzvos, and our precious families.

☙ *The Test of Staying Focused*

The *mahn* presented the Jews with a test. Would they adhere to the halachos given along with the *mahn* (such as not leaving over from one day to the next)? Would they use their time for Torah study? Would they use this blessing to get their priorities straight?

We, too, are faced with similar tests. *Mesillas Yesharim* (Chapter 1) writes that this is *olam hanisyonos* — a world of tests. Every individual has his own set of tests. Wealth presents one set of tests and financial instability another. Working, unemployment, retirement, semi-retirement, learning in kollel, and every job presents its own set of *nisyonos.* Each day presents specific tests as well. The tests at work on a Monday are not the same as the tests of a Shabbos afternoon or Sunday morning.

The word for bread and sustenance is לֶחֶם, from the word מִלְחָמָה — battle. We are in the *olam hanisyonos* to battle; we grow from these battles, as each victory, no matter how small, brings us closer to Hashem. It is the test of *neshamah* vs. *guf* — which will we prioritize?

We need to be aware of one of the primary weapons the *yetzer hara* yields, especially as it relates to working and money. That weapon is *bilbul,* confusion and constant toiling. When Hashem expelled Adam from Gan Eden, the *pasuk* (*Bereishis* 3:24) says, "וַיְגָרֶשׁ אֶת הָאָדָם." *Targum Yonasan* translates it as "וּטְרַד יָת אָדָם, and Adam was made to be busy." The *yetzer hara* seeks to overburden us, to confuse us, to overwhelm us, to seduce us with the allure of what money can bring, so that years pass, and we lose sight of the true purpose of our existence.

After Avraham successfully defeated the armies of the four kings, the king of Sodom, who was saved, told Avraham, "Give me the souls and take the possessions for yourself" (*Bereishis* 14:21). Chasam Sofer explains that the king of Sodom is an allegory for the *yetzer hara*. The *yetzer hara* has his eyes on our souls and whispers in our ears on a daily basis, "Give me your soul; that is what I want. Money, wealth, and the pleasures of This World are here for you to take."

In Egypt, Pharaoh ordered the forced labor of the Jews to be relentless, not giving them a moment of respite. This was to prevent them from having the time to think, even for an instant, about themselves, their lives, and possible ways to end their acute suffering. This, explains the *Mesillas Yesharim*, is the same strategy that the *yetzer hara* uses today. It seeks to blind us, using our obsession with consumerism. The false appeal of "what more will bring" prevents us from thinking, and questioning the purpose of our existence. *Why am I here in This World? What are my ultimate goals and responsibilities? What is my relationship with Hashem? How are my eternal investments looking? What am I doing here to make myself and those around me better and more elevated people?* These are the penetrating questions we should be thinking about, but the *yetzer hara* does all it can to keep us from asking them — and from acting on the answers.

> *A rabbi from Eretz Yisrael traveled to Germany and was hosted by a local congregant. After conversing with his host, a simple Jew, the conversation somehow shifted to mezuzos, whereupon the rabbi offered to check his host's mezuzos. The host mentioned that he had purchased the mezuzos from a well-known Meah Shearim sofer years earlier, but he had not had them checked since then and would appreciate the rav examining them. The rabbi removed each of the mezuzah cases from its doorpost and opened each case only to discover, to his utter*

disbelief, that each mezuzah case was empty! The rabbi was astounded and asked his host what was going on. The host replied, "Rabbi, I know how to hang mezuzos, so I threw out the instructions that came inside the case." This man had thought that the whole essence of mitzvas mezuzah was the case, and that the scrolls inside were merely instructions on how to hang them!

No one will deny the importance of a mezuzah case. It serves as the purpose of encasing and beautifying the mezuzah. But one who gives significance to the case over the scroll is clearly and dangerously misguided. Hashem gave each of us a body and a *neshamah*. The body houses and covers the *neshamah*, a vital role. Our mission is to ensure that the *neshamah* that Hashem gave us is on the right trajectory to fulfill its mission. In an era in which we are busier than ever, life swirls by at a dizzying speed; the need to step back and introspect becomes even more necessary. Of course, we need to go to work, pay the bills, and care for our families, but we must never forget the primacy of our *neshamos*. It is time to check the mezuzos within us, our *neshamos*, to ensure that they are kosher, holy, and protected. The *mahn* teaches us that our *parnassah* is in the hands of Hashem, that He is always providing for us. This should give us the serenity to rally our minds and hearts around what is important. Let us therefore daven to Hashem that He should grant us clarity, serenity, strength of character, fortitude, and the ability to always remain focused on our *neshamos*.

Despite his wealth, the noteworthy baal chesed, Shlomie Gross, worked hard to ensure that money did not control his life or his decision making. When they decided to move, as their home had some glaring deficiencies, Shlomie was adamant that they buy an existing house that was in move-in condition. Building from scratch, he felt, was making a statement that materialism was a major factor in his life, which was not the case. He also did not want his time to be taken up with the details of major construction. "I should build a house and be busy with it day and night?" he asked. He was also concerned that it might arouse jealousy. "I don't want the whole world walking by and seeing that Shlomie Gross is building himself a house." To the Grosses, "low key" was the approach in any public venue (Shlomie!, pp. 75–76).

☙ *The Test of Taking Advantage of Our Time*

Rabbeinu Bachya explains that the test of the *mahn* was a test in time management. Now that the Jewish nation did not have to spend the entire day working to support themselves, they could capitalize on their newfound time, dedicating it to Torah study and other pursuits with higher meaning. This was a test then, and is perhaps one of society's greatest tests today. How do we manage our time? Because how we manage our day determines who we are and who we will become. We have so much *berachah* that life is easier and simpler than ever. We can accomplish in minutes what used to take days and hours — washing the dishes and laundering our clothes, traveling, buying food, and pretty much anything you need. This should mean that we have more time. What we do with that time is a test and a responsibility. How much time we spend working, and what we do with our time before we go to work and when we get home from work, during lunchbreak, Friday nights, Shabbosos, Sundays, and legal holidays, indicates the value we put on life and on our *neshamos*.

It is no secret that today's phones present a serious challenge to our level of *kedushah*. But what perhaps gets overlooked is the amount of time spent on the phones. The average adult spends four and a half hours a day on their phone. Over fifty years, that adds up to 82,000 hours, or more than nine precious years of life! Some of it is important — phone calls, emails, business, and chores. But four and a half (or more) hours of it? How much of that is a mindless habit of scrolling sites and a zombie-like ritual of checking emails, news, and updates?

The Gemara (*Chagigah* 4a) explains that a *shoteh,* a person who by halachah is considered mentally incompetent, is defined as someone who breaks what he is given. For example, a person who is given a beautiful piece of china and throws it to the ground is not normal and qualifies as a *shoteh*. Hashem gives each person seconds, minutes, hours, days, weeks, and years. Each moment has the potential to be used for eternal reward. But what do we do with this time? Do we throw it to the ground, spending days, weeks, and years in the pursuit of trivialities, and wasting time?

At the end of Neilah, we beg Hashem to forgive us for stealing. Rav Yechezkel Abramsky explains that we are asking Hashem for forgiveness for improperly using the time He has given us, our greatest gift — life itself.

Sefer HaChaim (10:1) writes, "Man worries about lost money, but does not worry about lost time. Money will not help him; his days will not return to him."

I was present in a meeting with the CEO of a large company and his team. The introductory part of the meeting is for each participant to recount a professional and personal accomplishment of the past three months. When it was the CEO's turn, he recounted that his personal achievement was having bought a second phone that has no internet browser, no texting, no WhatsApp, and no email — it's just a phone. This is the phone that comes home with him at night. His other phone stays in the car, so that he can focus on and be present for his family and his learning. He values the gift of time that Hashem has given him and understands the pitfall of the misuse of time.

After speaking to a financial advisor and discussing a few points, there was some information he requested I obtain. I asked if I should phone him that evening with the information or if it would be better to touch base in the morning. He said, "For about twenty years, I have been proactively working on creating a healthy life-work balance. One decision I made was not to give clients my cell phone number. If I did, I would have to answer calls even after normal business hours. How can I concentrate on my family and Torah study if my clients all have my phone number? Let us speak in the morning."

A family member told me that she minimized her phone time thanks to a feature that Apple rolled out, reporting on your average daily time spent on the phone. This young mother was shocked to see that it was upward of four hours a day. Yes, some of the time was for work and for important calls, but not four hours a day. Since then, once she gets home from work, she puts her phone in a closet and does not take it out until the children are asleep. It was not easy; it was a challenge. She was defining her priorities. Choosing her children over WhatsApp, her husband over mindless scrolling. Life well spent over life frittered away.

When we show Hashem that we carefully make the most of the time He gives us, He has a reason to grant us more life. Let today be the day in which we take a few moments to see where, in our daily lives, we can prioritize the real over the transient, the important and the meaningful over the fleeting and the hollow. Yes, we all need to relax and take a breather, but let us ensure we are making the best use of the most precious gift we have — time.

The Lubavitcher Rebbe said, "The key to successful time management is to see and understand the value of every moment."

☙ *The Test of Being Calculated*

When it comes to business and money, we all want to see growth, return on our investment, and consistent progress. This can only happen through strategic planning and execution, exacting tracking, and personal accountability.

It is the same with progressing toward who we want to become and what we want to accomplish as Torah Jews. How am I living now? Do I have a plan to become more elevated and closer to Hashem? Am I developing a path in life that leads me to where I want to go? What is going to be my legacy? How am I creating good in This World, real meaningful good? The Torah tells us, "Regarding this, the *moshlim* (rulers) would say, 'Come to Cheshbon! Let it be built and established as the city of Sichon'" (*Bamidbar* 21:27). The Gemara (*Bava Basra* 78b) tells us that *moshlim* refers to those who rule over their *yetzer hara*. They are telling us, "Let us make a *cheshbon,* an accounting. Let us weigh the loss of not fulfilling a mitzvah and contrast it to the reward of fulfilling it." If you do, the verse promises, you will be "built [in This World] and established [in the World to Come]."

The Torah is telling us that we need to have a *cheshbon*, a calculation of our spiritual growth and inventory. Where are we heading, what is our trajectory, what is succeeding and what is not. How can I enhance what is succeeding and repair what is not? How can I see growth year after year in my learning, davening, *chesed*, and relationships? An uncalculated life is a life not lived. The Piaseczna Rebbe, Rav Klonymus Kalman Shapiro, writes that each year on one's birthday one should look at himself and say, "Today I am Reuven, and this is who I am. What do I want to look like in a year? What do I need to do during this year to shed the parts of me that I want to reject and to add dimensions of growth and depth?" This way, come next year, Reuven will not be the same Reuven he was the previous year. He will be a new Reuven, a Reuven who has worked on himself, improved his character, and deepened his commitment to Torah and mitzvos.

> *An investment advisor recounted that one of his longtime clients has a special birthday custom. For the past ten years, on each of his birthdays, he resolved to learn an additional ten minutes per day. It may not seem like much, but over twelve years it adds up to an additional*

two hours per day, in addition to his regular study schedule. This is a real-life example of someone who took small but calculated steps to see, year after year, growth in his Torah study and avodas Hashem.

☙ *The Test of Being Ehrlich*

During the Cuban Missile Crisis of October 1962, many feared the onset of World War III. Tensions between the United States and Russia were at an all-time high, and many believed a nuclear attack was imminent. At the time, the esteemed *mashgiach* of Lakewood, Rav Nosson Wachtfogel, recounted an unbelievable tradition dating back directly to the Maharil Diskin, Rav Yehoshua Leib Diskin, Rav of Brisk and Yerushalayim. He'd said, "In the last war before Mashiach's arrival all the *ehrliche Yidden* will be protected. Who are '*ehrliche Yidden*'? Those who are not bound by the culture around them. One need not be one of the thirty-six hidden *tzaddikim*. The path to becoming worthy of protection is to be separated from the values, trends, and ideals that are not in line with what Hashem wants from His children. One who can answer the clarion call of '*mi laShem eilai* — whoever is dedicated to Hashem come to me!' with strength, conviction, and resolve will be brought under Hashem's protective wing, unharmed by the *chevlei Mashiach,* birth pangs of Mashiach" (*Leket Reshimos, Chanukah,* p. 41).

Chazal tell us that it was because of three things that the Jews were redeemed from Egypt: They did not change their language, their names, or their clothing. Even though they had slipped to an extremely low level of spirituality, by holding onto their standards in these three areas, they retained their identities and could eventually be redeemed. The *Maor VaShemesh* explains that not changing their language meant that they did not use profanity. They spoke in an elevated, clean, and refined manner (*Rimzei Pesach*).

The *rasha,* the wicked son in the Haggadah, says, **מָה הָעֲבֹדָה הַזֹּאת לָכֶם** — "What is this service **to you**?" What is the seemingly extra word לָכֶם (to you) teaching us? לָכֶם is an acrostic for לָשׁוֹן, כִּנּוּי, מַלְבּוּשׁ — language, name, clothing. The *rasha* does not understand why we are so careful about the way we speak, the names we go by, and the way we dress. But we understand these three areas are the pillars of our identity. They reflect our essence — who we are, and how we are different.

A Yid came to tell the Chofetz Chaim that he was going to Eretz Yisrael to avoid being drafted into the army. The Chofetz Chaim asked if he could deliver a letter to his cheder rebbi, Rav Yaakov, who was living in Yerushalayim.

A few months later, the man went to Rav Yaakov's home to deliver the letter. Rav Yaakov, already advanced in years, took the letter from his talmid, the Chofetz Chaim, who by now had gained worldwide fame for his leadership and sefarim. It read, "As the Rebbi is closer to the holy sites, and one's tefillos are more effective there [in Eretz Yisrael, and especially in Yerushalayim], I am asking you to daven that I be an ehrliche Yid."

At the funeral of a relative who had truly been a God-fearing Jew and also a successful businessman, his younger brother recounted that as young men, they used to take the train together to Manhattan, where they were both attending classes. Upon alighting from the train — without saying anything, without any fanfare or announcements — the older brother would remove his glasses and take his younger brother's hand in his, so that his eyes would remain holy. Wherever he traveled, he dressed like a Yid. He was physically in the business world, but he behaved like a striving and growing Yid, ever so close to Hashem.

The Test of Not Losing Our Identity

There are vital questions each and every person needs to ask himself: "Who am I? What am I? Where am I? How do I define myself? What is my purpose here in This World? What is my legacy?" When Adam committed the world's first sin by eating from the *Eitz HaDaas*, he and Chavah hid. Hashem called out to Adam: "*Ayekah* — Where are you?" What have you done? This is the question that Hashem asks each of us every day: "*Ayekah*? Where are you, My child? I gave you a pure and holy *neshamah* that emanated from My Throne of Glory. Inside of you is a *chelek Elokah mimaal,* a portion of Godliness. I gave you a mission in This World that you and only you can accomplish. How well are you managing this mission? What have you done with your life, this beautiful and fleeting opportunity I gave you?"

It is these questions we have to answer. The question is how. The challenge they present is particularly difficult for those who are out in the working world.

Many have the custom, at the end of *Shemoneh Esrei*, to recite a verse that starts with the first letter of their name and ends with the last letter of their name (see *Kitzur HaShelah*; *Kaf HaChaim* 122:11). When one is brought to the Heavenly Court for judgment after 120 years, the fear will be so great that one may not even remember his own name. It may help to recite a verse that contains a reference to one's name.

Some forget their name even prior to being brought to the Heavenly Court. They forget their essence, the Godliness that resides within them; they forget their mission here in This World, and neglect to identify their latent potential. They forget their true purpose, what meaning and joy look like, as they drown in the pressures of work, career, making ends meet, and keeping up with perceived societal pressures. They forsake what is unique about them, and instead try to gain for themselves what others have — the possessions of others, the dreams of others.

When the ship Yonah the prophet was on was about to capsize, drowning everyone on it, the sailors asked Yonah, "What is your job, and where did you come from?" Yonah responded, "I am an *Ivri* and I fear Hashem, the God of the Heavens"

(*Yonah* 1:8,9). Do you know who I am? Do you know what my essence is? My definition? My identity? My calling? My lifelong mission? I am a Yid. A Yid who fears Hashem. But not just a Yid because I was born to a Jewish mother. I am an *Ivri*. I am a grandchild of Avraham who was called an *Ivri,* signifying that "the whole world was on one side and he (Avraham) was on the other side" (*Bereishis Rabbah* 42:8).

While the entire world was serving idolatry, Avraham had the fortitude to challenge societal norms, to be independent and not bound by peer pressures. To be different. "This is who I am," said Yonah. "I am different." I work not merely to exist in This World, but for a higher purpose — to serve and fear Hashem. That is who I am and that is how I am defined. When I go to work, I remember this in the way I think, in my relationship with money, in the way I dress, in the way I speak, in the way I run my business. I am an *Ivri*. The world may idolize money and possessions. They may all speak one way, act one way, think one way, and be pulled in one direction. That is fine. But I strive to be different. I strive to live an elevated existence. I try my best to never forget my *neshamah*, who I am and what my purpose is in This World. I understand that money is transient, success is ephemeral, life is fleeting, and ultimately no one is remembered in This World or the Next for their money, only for who they were as a person: their charity, Torah study, family, and values. That is what matters in life, that is the true currency of a Jew.

Klal Yisrael is compared to a rose maintaining its beauty while surrounded by thorns (*Shir HaShirim* 2:2). The Sfas Emes tells us that Klal Yisrael is eternally praised for being the singular rose in a bed of thorns. The thorns represent This World and everything that is the antithesis of what it means to be a Jew. The Jew lives in This World, not in a cave far removed from all the world's challenges and lures. The ultimate praise of the Jew is his ability to blossom beautifully *specifically* in a setting of thorns. The Jew can live in This World, exposed to the thorns of life, and yet blossom, grow, and retain inner beauty.

ה וְהָיָה בַּיּוֹם הַשִּׁשִּׁי, וְהֵכִינוּ אֵת אֲשֶׁר
יָבִיאוּ, וְהָיָה מִשְׁנֶה עַל אֲשֶׁר יִלְקְטוּ
יוֹם יוֹם. ו וַיֹּאמֶר מֹשֶׁה וְאַהֲרֹן אֶל כָּל
בְּנֵי יִשְׂרָאֵל, עֶרֶב וִידַעְתֶּם כִּי יהוה
הוֹצִיא אֶתְכֶם מֵאֶרֶץ מִצְרָיִם.

Chazal (*Shemos Rabbah* 25:5) tell us that because Avraham said, "*Hineini,* Here I am," when Hashem called him (*Bereishis* 22:1), his children received the *mahn* directly from Hashem: "*Hineni mamtir lachem lechem min haShamayim* — Behold, I will cause bread to rain down on you from heaven." Working and making a living is not easy; it is challenging, it is grinding, it is pressurizing, it seeks to control our life and our identity, and it can be scary and dispiriting. But our commitment to announce "*Hineini* — Hashem, I am here with You and prepared to do Your will" engenders significant *berachah.* I will try my best not to let my career, my money, my success, and my struggles blind me to my essence. I will try my best to put my efforts into my priorities. What is true, what is eternal, what is a worthwhile investment of energy. Every day is a test. Every day is a challenge. But the story of the *mahn* gives me an injection of *bitachon.* I know that I am not alone and that You are with me, You are providing for me. I know that You are holding my hand and I can trust that You will help me overcome these tests. Tests in honesty, in jealousy, in managing my time appropriately, in setting priorities, tests in what I look at, what I hear, how I speak, how I dress, and how I think.

The Beis HaLevi met a former student and asked him what he was doing. The student replied that he was in business. The Beis HaLevi asked again what he did. Thinking his rebbi did not hear or understand, he repeated his answer, describing what he did in more detail. The Beis HaLevi interrupted and said, "Until now you have

[5]*And it will be on the sixth day that they will prepare what they will bring; for there will be double what they will gather day by day."* [6] *Moshe and Aharon said to all the Children of Yisrael: "This evening you will know that Hashem removed you from the land of Egypt.*

explained to me what Hashem is doing for you and your parnassah. I asked you what **you** *are doing. You are here on This World to grow in learning and mitzvos."*

עֶרֶב וִידַעְתֶּם כִּי ה׳ הוֹצִיא אֶתְכֶם מֵאֶרֶץ מִצְרָיִם —
This evening you will know that Hashem removed you from the land of Egypt (16:6).

◆§ *Never Despair*

Klal Yisrael looked around and saw nothing but an arid Wilderness in which nothing grew. How was a nation of millions going to survive? It looked hopeless. But Hashem provided *mahn*, showing that even when matters look bleak, even when it is evening and we do not see any possible way out, Hashem is there and provides for us. The greatest proof of this is that Hashem redeemed us and adopted us as His nation at a time when we were devoid of spirituality; we were like a barren desert. Hashem's love for us is unconditional. Rav Tzadok HaKohen (*Pri Tzaddik, Pesach*) writes that this is why there is a daily mitzvah to recall our redemption from Egypt. We must never despair; Hashem's help, guidance, and *berachah* are there for us at all times. Despair has no place in the Jewish people's vernacular.

◆§ *A Holy and Elevated People*

When they were slaves in Egypt, the Jews had no set time to eat meals; they were like chickens who peck at garbage at all hours (*Yoma* 75b). Once Hashem provided *mahn*, Moshe taught them to schedule regular mealtimes, as is appropriate for a holy and elevated nation.

The Sforno explains that when Hashem said, "You will know that I took you out of Egypt," He was conveying the information that once the *slav* began to fall that evening, meals would be on schedule. "I took you out of Egypt" not just physically, but also in removing you from the base practices they imposed on you, so I could transform you into a priestly and holy nation.

The Sforno is teaching us something so important. Knowing who we are translates into behaviors that reflect our princely status. We are required to speak in a refined way, dress appropriately, and dine with dignity; we must conduct ourselves in a way that reflects our elevated status.

Rabbi Abraham J. Twerski M.D. writes, "Our self-image — how we see ourselves — is the major determining factor in whether we succeed in life. I have been accused of having a one-track mind, and I plead guilty as charged. All psychological disorders are due at least in part, and sometimes entirely, to low self-esteem" (*Letters to My Children*, p. 16).

He cites Rav Shlomo Wolbe's insight about self-esteem. Rav Wolbe points out (*Alei Shur,* Vol. 1, p. 168) that the Hebrew word for self-esteem is *chashivus,* which means importance or value. Rav Wolbe says that without an awareness of *chashivus,* there is no *avodah*. Before giving the Torah, Hashem told Bnei Yisrael, "You shall be unto Me a kingdom of Kohanim" (*Shemos* 19:6), which Rashi translates as *sarim,* high-status officers. Hashem stresses the prestige of every single Jew; one who feels insignificant cannot achieve what Hashem wants him to accomplish. Rav Wolbe insists, "One must have a sense of personal *chashivus.*"

On the Shabbos before Rosh Chodesh, we ask Hashem to grant us *kavod,* honor. Yet, *kavod* is one of three things that remove a person from the world (*Avos* 4:28). So why are we asking Hashem to shower us with it? Rav Shmuel

Wosner answers that the honor we are asking Hashem for is not honor given to us by others; we are davening for a sense of self-worth. We have to realize that we are intrinsically special and have unlimited potential.

◆§ *Krias Yam Suf and the Lessons of Parnassah*

Chazal tell us, "Providing man's sustenance is as difficult as splitting the Yam Suf" (*Pesachim* 117a). Rashbam explains that Hashem's giving us *parnassah* is as great a miracle as splitting the Yam Suf. So one must continuously daven for financial success, and not take it for granted.

Why is the miracle of splitting the sea compared to the miracle of *parnassah*? Several beautiful and practical explanations are given.

✧ ***Thank You, Hashem!*** Rav Shimshon Pincus tells us something very special. Imagine leaving Mitzrayim after a lifetime of unbearable servitude. You get to the sea, but the impressive Egyptian army is in hot pursuit. Then, at the very last moment, just before Pharaoh's army catches up with you, Hashem does the unexpected: miracle of miracles, the sea splits in the most grandiose way. Certainly, the response to this is unrestrained song and praise to Hashem for the unbelievable miracle.

This is what occurred in Egypt. The Gemara is telling us that *parnassah* is a miracle on par with that!

When you come home to a fully stocked fridge, an overflowing pantry, a dinner table, a home filled with what you and your family need, this is like the awesome miracle of splitting the sea! Next time you open your fridge or your paycheck, take a moment to gaze at it all and ask yourself, "Who gave me all this? Look at all the love and care Hashem is showering on me and my family! How blessed we are!" Think about how much you need to thank Hashem, and sing to Him for the *berachah* He is showering on you and your family (*She'arim BaTefillah,* p. 60).

✧ ***Bitachon: the ultimate segulah.*** After witnessing the Ten Plagues, including a night of watching Hashem wreak vengeance on Egypt's firstborn, Bnei Yisrael arrive at the Yam Suf, where they are surrounded by danger on all sides. In front of them — the treacherous sea; on both sides — the foreboding and ominous desert; and behind them — the savage Egyptian army, out for blood. Bnei Yisrael cry out to Hashem to save them, and Hashem asks Moshe, "Why do you cry out to Me? Speak to Bnei Yisrael and tell them to go forward" (*Shemos* 14:15).

The Ohr HaChaim asks the obvious question: Haven't we been told to always daven to Hashem, and certainly at a time of enormous need and great national desperation?

He cites the *Zohar* to answer his question. The *Zohar* tells us that at the moment the Jewish people were cornered, the Heavenly Court passed judgment, declaring that they did not warrant to be helped because their sins were too numerous. That is why Hashem asked Moshe, "Why do you cry out to Me? I can no longer help! The Heavenly Court says that Bnei Yisrael are so impure that nothing can be done to save them. However, there is one thing they can do. Tell them to travel [into the sea]. The *emunah* and *bitachon* that requires shows how much they trust in Me. That will make them deserving of My love and protection."

When all else fails, *emunah* and *bitachon* in Hashem are the only things that can bring about salvation and *berachah*, and the same is true for *parnassah*. *Bitachon* and reliance on Hashem opens the gates of *parnassah*. When we feel the pressure, the anxiety, the walls closing in, the bills mounting, the expenses growing, what do we do? Travel into Hashem's hands, travel into the world of *bitachon*.

✧ ***When it is hard for you.*** Chazal compare the difficulty of providing *parnassah* with the difficulty of splitting the Yam Suf. They say the same about shidduchim (*Sotah* 2a). Rav Leibel Eiger asks how the term "difficult" applies to Hashem; is anything difficult for Hashem? (*Toras Emes, Parashas Beshalach*).

He answers that the word "difficult" applies not to Hashem, but to us; when *we* struggle with *parnassah* or with shidduchim, we should draw inspiration and direction from the splitting of the sea. Bnei Yisrael merited to be saved because, when they were in a desperate situation, they threw themselves into Hashem's hands — plunging into the ocean, literally immersing themselves in *emunah*.

When *parnassah* or shidduchim are difficult for you, when you are struggling, take direction from the Jews at the sea, and totally immerse yourself in *emunah*. This is our life raft in the sea of life.

✧ ***It is hard when it's me.*** The Klausenberger Rebbe (*Shefa Chaim*, pp. 203–204) explains that when a person feels it is difficult to earn *parnassah*, when he feels the full weight of supporting himself and his family weighing down his shoulders, then truly *parnassah* is as hard to come by as the splitting of the sea. A lack of *bitachon* prevents the *berachah* of *parnassah* from flowing. This is why Chazal use the word *adam,* a person, when they say, "*Kashin mezonosav shel adam k'krias Yam Suf* — Providing man's sustenance is as difficult as splitting the Yam Suf." When you think that it is up to the *adam*, the person, to control your financial destiny, then yes, it will be difficult.

✧ ***Hashem provides in surprising ways.*** Rav Simchah Bunim of Peshischa (*Kol Mevaser,* p. 48) says that when the Jews were trapped, with the Yam Suf in front, the Egyptian army behind, and the desert on each side, they must have thought about various ways Hashem could save them. They most likely never thought that Hashem would split the sea for them. That was so far-fetched that it probably never crossed their minds.

When we think about how we'll earn a *parnassah*, we think Hashem will use regular channels — a parent, a bonus, a relative, the client we have been pursuing... Yet all too often, money appears out of nowhere from an avenue we never even contemplated. This is the similarity between splitting the sea and *parnassah*.

Rav Yehudah Aryeh Dunner from Bnei Brak spoke about a man he knows whose business took an extreme turn for the worse and he had to declare bankruptcy. He was stuck with warehouses filled with medical supplies that no one was interested in buying. He spent years unsuccessfully trying to sell these supplies at cost price. Finally, he decided that it was time to just throw out the merchandise, so at least he wouldn't have to pay warehouse fees. But Hashem had other plans. Covid-19 took the world by storm, and three-ply surgical masks became a high-demand item. Out of the blue and in no time, his worthless masks became as valuable as gold and he earned an enormous profit.

Rav Dunner said something so special. He noted that people ask "*lamah* — why?" about the past. Why did that happen like this, and why did this happen like that? People ask "*mah yihyeh* — what will be?" about the future. What will be with the economy? What will be with my job? What will be with my expenses? How will I afford things in the future? The numerical value of both לָמָּה, *lamah*, and מַה יִּהְיֶה, *mah yihyeh*, is seventy-five. The numerical value of בִּטָּחוֹן, *bitachon,* is also seventy-five. One who has *bitachon* does not need to ask *lamah* or *mah yihyeh. Bitachon* is the answer to both; it removes all doubts, questions, and fears.

After two hundred and ten years of forced slave labor in Egypt, it was finally time for the Jewish nation's redemption. But not before Hashem took retribution against the Egyptians in the form of the Ten Plagues. The fourth plague was a Heaven-sent swarm of wild beasts that attacked and terrorized the Egyptians all the while the Jewish people were left unharmed and safe. Regarding this plague the Torah writes (*Shemos* 8:19), "I shall make a distinction between My people and your people — tomorrow this sign will come about." Rav Avraham Simchah Horowitz homiletically explains as follows: The ultimate distinction and differentiator between My people, the Jewish nation, and your people, the non-Jewish nation, is "tomorrow." What is our perspective about tomorrow? A Jew understands that he need not worry about tomorrow, he need not be concerned about what the future may or may not bring, as he has *bitachon* and the knowledge that Hashem is there with him every step of the way. לְמָחָר יִהְיֶה הָאֹת הַזֶּה — the true sign of who we are is how we view tomorrow.

✧ ***Hashgachah pratis.*** The splitting of the sea demonstrated absolute *hashgachah pratis*. The sea split into twelve channels, one for each of the twelve tribes. It supplied fresh water and delicious food for everyone throughout the journey.

Parnassah demonstrates the same absolute *hashgachah pratis*. Hashem provides for every one of His children exactly what he needs (*Ksav Sofer, Vayechi*).

The *Sfas Emes* (*Beshalach*) says that not only did the sea split into separate sections for each of the twelve tribes, it also split individually for every Yid, evincing the importance of every individual Jew. This is another way in which splitting the sea parallels *parnassah*: There's an exclusive, individual path through which each person receives the exact *parnassah* that's coming to him. Hashem provides each Yid with precisely what he needs; no one can take away from you even the smallest thing if it is meant to be yours (*Yoma* 38b).

✧ ***Feeling Hashem in every dollar.*** Scientists often try to show that the splitting of the Yam Suf was not a miracle, and come up with all sorts of unlikely meteorological possibilities for it. We all know this is hogwash and a means of negating God, which allows people to shirk all ethical and moral responsibility. But perhaps we do the same when it comes to *parnassah*. The Gemara says that *parnassah* is a miracle on par with that of splitting the Yam Suf. How often do we collect a paycheck, earn a commission, receive a gift, or get a return on an investment, and totally ignore the fact that it is Hashem Who is actively distributing our *parnassah*? We attribute the money in our bank accounts to our intelligence, our networking, our hustle, our timing of the market, our relationships, and our marketability. Learn from the splitting of the Yam Suf, which we know clearly was Hashem's work. Understand that the food in our fridges, the money in our bank accounts, and the roofs over our heads are gifts from Hashem.

✧ ***Kedushah: the common thread of parnassah, shidduchim, and parting the Yam Suf.*** The Gemara compares both *parnassah* and marriage to parting the sea. What is the connection?

Rav Chanoch Henoch Karelenstein tells us something so important. He points out that Yosef HaTzaddik was given the title of "*tzaddik*" because he successfully overcame the immense challenge of Potiphar's wife trying to seduce him. That was why he became the second-in-command in Egypt and the one who was the conduit for the entire world to be supported during the famine. This shows a direct connection between *kedushah* and *parnassah*.

"The sea saw and it fled" (*Tehillim* 114:3). Chazal ask, "What did the sea see? It saw Yosef's coffin" (*Yalkut Shimoni*). It split in deference to Yosef, who overcame overwhelming challenges to his holiness. A person's attentiveness to matters of *kedushah* is directly related to his finding a shidduch. A life of *kedushah* is rewarded with *parnassah* and shidduchim, which require miracles as great as that of splitting the Yam Suf.

Rav Mordechai Leiner (*Mei HaShiloach, Likkutim, Yoma*) asks why the details about the *mahn* are described in *Masechta Yoma*, in the chapter that describes the five afflictions of Yom Kippur. He explains that when a situation looms and a person afflicts himself for Hashem in one way or another, Hashem will shower bounty on him that sustains him like the *mahn*. Think about that when it is time to look away from things that shouldn't be seen; when it is hard not to indulge; when it is hard to say no. When you do this for Hashem, Hashem will sustain you with the food of angels!

☙ *Freedom*

Yetzias Mitzrayim plays a prominent role in the life of a Jew. The *Zohar* writes that it is mentioned in the Torah no fewer than fifty times, and there are mitzvos that require us to recall the Exodus each day: when donning tefillin, throughout davening, in *Bircas HaMazon*, and during Kiddush every Shabbos and Yom Tov.

Rabbi Avraham J. Twerski M.D., in the introduction to his book, *Haggadah: From Bondage to Freedom* (p. 9), writes, "I am indebted for the inspiration for the themes of this Haggadah to a young man who underwent treatment for a severe drug problem. At his first Seder at home, his father began reciting the Haggadah. He read, 'We were slaves unto Pharaoh.' The young man interrupted. 'Father,' he said, 'when were you ever a slave? I can relate to having been a slave. I was a slave to drugs, and there has never been so demanding and inconsiderate a taskmaster, so absolute an enslavement, as addiction to chemicals. I had no choice whether to use them or not. I did things in my addiction that I swore I would never do, because a slave must do as he is directed. If there ever was a slave in the world, it was me. I know what it means to be a slave and I know what it means to be free.' In brief, anyone who loses control over any kind of behavior is a slave. We should be proud to be free people, and the concept of slavery should be repugnant to us. Like our forefathers in Egypt, we should cry out to God to deliver us from enslavement to self-destructive behavior. The Haggadah is a beacon of hope. If we pray sincerely and truly wish to be free, God will answer our prayers."

People are shackled in so many ways: shackled by doing things they don't want to do, doing things that are not good for them and their families, and shackled by feeling the need to spend money they don't have in an effort to artificially inflate their standing. Internalizing the Exodus's message — that we were all slaves once, but that you can be free, you can change — it takes work, it takes discipline, it takes commitment, but no one is ever too stuck to change.

Each morning, we recite a *berachah* thanking Hashem, "Who did not make me a servant." A servant has no freedom

ז וּבֹקֶר וּרְאִיתֶם אֶת כְּבוֹד יהוה,
בְּשָׁמְעוֹ אֶת תְּלֻנֹּתֵיכֶם עַל יהוה,
וְנַחְנוּ מָה, כִּי תַלִּינוּ עָלֵינוּ.
ח וַיֹּאמֶר מֹשֶׁה, בְּתֵת יהוה לָכֶם בָּעֶרֶב
בָּשָׂר לֶאֱכֹל וְלֶחֶם בַּבֹּקֶר לִשְׂבֹּעַ,

of choice; he is totally controlled. Rav Wolbe (*Alei Shur*, Vol. 2, p. 351) explains that when reciting this *berachah* one should think, "I was born free, but am I truly free? Or am I indentured to certain things? Do I act in an unnatural way so that others will admire me? Am I a slave to my phone, to work, to money, to the pursuit of the next best thing?" When we forfeit control, we are no longer free.

The word "Mitzrayim" is from the word "*meitzar,* straits." In Mitzrayim, we were enslaved both physically, by the servitude, and spiritually, by its pervasive impurity. When Hashem took us out of Egypt, all generations of Jews gained the ability to attain freedom. That includes freedom from our personal slavery.

וְנַחְנוּ מָה — *For what are we?* (16:7).

Humility

The greatest leader of Klal Yisrael, Moshe Rabbeinu, spoke directly to Hashem. Yet he never allowed his stature, fame, or accomplishments to inflate his ego. He was truly humble and modest. Moshe understood that all that he had was a gift from Hashem for the purpose of redeeming Klal Yisrael. Even when blamed for the lack of food in the Wilderness, Moshe and Aharon did not resort to reprimanding, or ignoring; instead, they explained that it was not up to them, they were not in control.

The Gemara (*Chullin* 89a) tells us that the world continues

[7]And in the morning you will see the glory of Hashem when He hears your complaints against Hashem; for what are we, that you complain against us?" [8]Then Moshe said, "[This will occur] when Hashem gives you meat to eat in the evening and bread in the morning to satisfaction,

to exist because of Moshe and Aharon's humility. Just as birds flap their wings downward to fly higher, man can elevate himself with a healthy dose of humility.

Some of the greatest Jewish philanthropists demonstrated genuine humility. They refused to be involved in questions of *chinuch* or how a yeshivah should be run, saying, "Just because I was given the gift of wealth does not mean that I have *daas Torah*. We need to look to our rabbanim for *daas Torah* and guidance in matters of *ruchniyus*."

> *Dr. Yosef Walder was a man who many never heard of, and that is the way he wanted it to be. Dr. Walder was a biochemical researcher who started a company called Integrated DNA Technologies. Residing in Chicago, he was a benevolent philanthropist but remained purposefully under the radar. He gave and gave but in the quietest way, often through others. After his passing in March 2024, Shalom Goodman wrote in The Wall Street Journal, "Dr. Walder was one of the most unassuming men you'd ever encounter. If I were to show you a lineup of men, you'd never be able to identify the philanthropist. He didn't show off. He didn't boast. In fact, he lived in quite a modest house, considering his means, and drove his famous ol' Buick for many years. Dr. Walder never made it about himself. As you'll notice, there aren't any magazine profiles of this philanthropist, nor is there any news of extravagant purchases after his company was sold. When I asked a rabbi*

today about Dr. Walder's generosity and if there was more information online about his history, the rabbi responded, 'I don't know of anything like that. I worked closely with him for the [school] dinner and it was never about him; to him, it was all about the success of the school. He never demanded respect, even though he could have asked for it and gotten about thirty times the amount of respect.'"

— בָּעֶרֶב בָּשָׂר לֶאֱכֹל וְלֶחֶם בַּבֹּקֶר לִשְׂבֹּעַ
Meat to eat in the evening and bread in the morning to satisfaction (16:8).

☙ *Wants or Needs?*

There are two kinds of food mentioned in this verse: meat, which they should not have asked for; and bread, which was an acceptable request. Rashi explains that the request for meat was inappropriate, as it is a luxury, and they could have slaughtered their own animals for food. So the meat was given to them at night, when it was dark and difficult to prepare. Bread, which is a staple, was a suitable request, so they received it in the morning, in the form of *mahn.*

We see from here that Chazal distinguish between needs and wants. In our age of excessive consumerism and consumption, these lines can become dangerously blurred. Categorizing expenses as needs or wants can help to curb unnecessary, and at times harmful, unhealthy spending. If we do not want our children to succumb to peer-pressure purchasing, this is something we need to work on as well. Remember, our luxuries become our children's necessities.

☙ *Visual Satiety and the Shabbos Candles*

Mahn was eaten in the morning and resulted in satiety. The Midrash learns from here that a prerequisite full satiety involves seeing the food (*Lekach Tov*). With daylight, the Jews were able to see their food, enjoy it, and feel full.

In an enigmatic statement, the Midrash comments on the

Jews' complaint about the *mahn*. They asked, "Who will feed us meat? We remember the fish we ate in Mitzrayim free of charge; the squash, melons, leeks, onions, and garlic, but now... there is nothing; we have nothing but the *mahn* to look at" (*Bamidbar* 11:4-6). On which the Midrash comments, "'We remember the fish': From here we know we have to light Shabbos candles." What is the connection between longing for fish and lighting Shabbos candles?

To answer this, we need to understand why the Jewish people had a longing for fish. Were they not eating *mahn*, which tasted like anything they desired?

Although the *mahn* could assume any flavor, it always looked the same. It did not look the same as the food that it tasted like. The Jewish people longingly recalled the sight of the fish, which added to its taste. So, we light candles before the onset of Shabbos to enable us to see the food and optimally enjoy our Shabbos meals (*Taamei HaMinhagim* 160, *Kuntres Acharon*).

וּבַבֹּקֶר — *In the morning* (16:8).

☙ *The Power of Morning*

Rashi (*Beshalach* 16:7) writes that it was acceptable for Bnei Yisrael to ask for bread, as it is essential for survival, so when they received it, "the glory of the radiance of His countenance" shone on them and it was given "lovingly, in the morning."

Rav Wolbe writes that we see from this something exceptional. He cites this as proof that there is a special light, a Heavenly illumination and Godly endearment, in the morning. The morning hours, when the world is still asleep, the air is pure, and the mind is untainted by the day's distractions, is an auspicious time for spiritual accomplishment and Torah study. In the morning hours, a special closeness to Hashem and His love and mercy is accessible.

Rabbeinu Bachya (*Shemos* 16:3) tells us that morning is the

בְּשָׁמְעַ יהוה אֶת תְּלֻנֹּתֵיכֶם
אֲשֶׁר אַתֶּם מַלִּינִם עָלָיו, וְנַחְנוּ מָה,
לֹא עָלֵינוּ תְלֻנֹּתֵיכֶם, כִּי עַל יהוה.
ט וַיֹּאמֶר מֹשֶׁה אֶל אַהֲרֹן,
אֱמֹר אֶל כָּל עֲדַת בְּנֵי יִשְׂרָאֵל,

time that Hashem exhibits the *middah* of *rachamim,* mercy, and it is the time at which He allocates *parnassah.* (Of course, we know that *parnassah* is decided on Rosh Hashanah, but through *tefillah* one can increase what was allotted to him.)

Rav Wolbe writes that nearly all of his magnum opus, *Alei Shur,* was written in the early hours of the morning when his head was clear and that special light of Hashem shines down. The parts that were written at other times of the day needed editing. Take advantage of the early morning hours for Torah study; they will create a *berachah* for the rest of your day.

Just as one's actions on Rosh Hashanah affect the rest of the year, one's first thoughts and deeds in the morning set the tone for the rest of the day. Rav Chaim Volozhin writes that upon waking, one should resolve to dedicate himself to Torah and mitzvos; this is a *segulah* for a good day (*Keser Rosh*).

The first halachah in *Shulchan Aruch* describes how to get up in the morning: "[One should] rise like a lion in the morning to serve his Creator." To this, the Rema adds, "And when he gets into bed at night, he should know in front of Whom he lies down." Rav Zusha of Anipoli asks why this comment is here. It is not related to the laws of getting up in the morning, but to the laws and customs of going to sleep, which are enjoined later in the *Shulchan Aruch.* They explain that the Rema is telling us something so important: If you want to get up in the morning like a lion — fresh, energized, and totally prepared to serve Hashem — then you need to consistently go to bed at a time that is beneficial to your health.

when Hashem will have heard your complaints that you charge against Him; for what are we? — not against us are your complaints, but against Hashem!"
[9] Moshe said to Aharon, "Say to the entire congregation of the Children of Yisrael,

To serve Hashem properly in the morning, you need to serve Him properly at night, as well. This is alluded to in the words of the verse, "[In the] evening, you will know that Hashem brought you out of the land of Mitzrayim. In the morning, you will see Hashem's glory" (*Shemos* 16:6–7). If, in the evening, you know Hashem — by having a scheduled and reasonable bedtime — then in the morning, you will see Hashem's glory (*Beis Pinchas*).

☙ *Modeh Ani: Hashem Believes in Me!*

Each morning, upon arising, we recite the *tefillah* of *Modeh Ani*, in which we thank Hashem for returning our souls to us. The very first thing a Jew does upon waking up in the morning and being granted a new day is thank Hashem and acknowledge that all life comes from Him. When we start our day with such a mindset, it can inspire us to understand that Hashem likewise orchestrates all the subsequent events of our day.

The last words of *Modeh Ani* are somewhat perplexing. We say, "*rabbah emunasecha* — abundant is Your faithfulness." The simple understanding of this phrase is that we have great faith in Hashem that He will return our souls to us each morning. Yet if this were the intent, we would say, "abundant is *my* faith [in You]" — *rabbah emunasi*. What is the meaning of "abundant is Your faithfulness," referring to Hashem? The answer is life-changing and immensely empowering. Each morning that Hashem returns our soul to us He is demonstrating that

He has abundant faith in us to fulfill His will and impact this world in our own unique way. By waking us each morning and giving us a renewed spirit, Hashem shows that He has faith in us to work on the lifelong mission of becoming a better and more elevated person.

Never doubt the special role you play in this world. Never undermine your impact. Each morning you are granted another day. Hashem is telling you, "Get up, My child. Open your eyes. Today is a new day in which your family, your community, those around you, and My world need you and all the special attributes that you contribute. *Rabbah emuna-secha* — My faith in *you* is abundant!"

> *Rav Shlomo Freifeld said, "I faced many obstacles, and I triumphed over all of them. I faced difficult hurdles, but they never overwhelmed me. Do you know why? Because I had one chassid who never stopped believing in me — myself."*

קִרְבוּ לִפְנֵי ה׳ כִּי שָׁמַע אֵת תְּלֻנֹּתֵיכֶם — *Draw near before Hashem, for He has heard your complaints* (16:9).

◆ *Complaining and Appreciating*

Moshe instructed Aharon to tell the Jewish nation to "draw near before Hashem, for He has heard your complaints." They had to be told to "draw near" because they had distanced themselves from Hashem by complaining (*Abarbanel*).

All too often, complaints arise because the complainer only considers a minuscule part of the overall picture. This happens in *Parashas Behaaloscha,* after the Jews have been eating the *mahn* for some time. The *eirev rav's* detrimental influence affects the rest of the nation, who complain about the *mahn's* lack of variety. They say, "Our bodies are parched; there is nothing; we have nothing but the *mahn*" (*Bamidbar* 11:6).

'Draw near before Hashem, for He has heard your complaints.'"

The Torah then goes on to refute the complaint about the *mahn* by describing it: "The *mahn* was like coriander seed, and its color was like the color of *bedolach* [a gem identified as a crystal]" (ibid. 11:7). Hashem responded to their complaints, "See, inhabitants of the world, what My children complain about! The *mahn* is precious in these and those ways!" (*Rashi*).

Rav Pam says that at times, we are guilty of complaining about the magnanimous gifts we receive from Hashem (*Atarah LaMelech,* p. 128). A husband comes home to what looks like the aftermath of a tornado. The living room is a wreck and the couch is covered with books and toys. The kitchen table top is not visible under all the sippy cups and homework. He might be annoyed at his wife and complain, "How come the house is so disorganized?" When he says that, a voice in Heaven says, "See, inhabitants of the world, what My children complain about!" Toys on the floor? Homework and dirty dishes? Do you know how many people would give every dollar in their bank accounts to have children? How many people would give anything to have a home strewn with toys?

We must be sure that we're not like the *eirev rav,* complaining about Hashem's enormous gifts. We have to appreciate the food on our tables, our homes, spouses, jobs, community, family, children, and more. All that may be overwhelming and challenging, but we must not let that obscure our appreciation for the *chesed* and goodness that Hashem has bestowed.

Rav Dessler held up a large white paper with a small black circle drawn in the center of it. He asked every student what he saw, and all of them said that they saw a black circle. Rav Dessler asked, "Isn't it unbelievable that all of you only saw the small black circle, and not the abundance of white? You automatically focused on the tiny amount of black, and ignored the vast swath of white."

This is human nature. Our brains and eyes focus on the black,

י וַיְהִי כְּדַבֵּר אַהֲרֹן אֶל כָּל עֲדַת בְּנֵי
יִשְׂרָאֵל, וַיִּפְנוּ אֶל הַמִּדְבָּר, וְהִנֵּה כְּבוֹד
יהוה נִרְאָה בֶּעָנָן. יא וַיְדַבֵּר יהוה אֶל מֹשֶׁה
לֵּאמֹר. יב שָׁמַעְתִּי אֶת תְּלוּנֹּת בְּנֵי יִשְׂרָאֵל,
דַּבֵּר אֲלֵהֶם לֵאמֹר, בֵּין הָעַרְבַּיִם תֹּאכְלוּ
בָשָׂר, וּבַבֹּקֶר תִּשְׂבְּעוּ לָחֶם,

on the difficulties and the challenges. Perhaps we too often disregard the bountiful *berachah* and good with which we've been blessed and instead hyper-focus on what is not going well. Likewise, we often think more about the faults and negative traits of our family members than about their good points. We may pay more attention than necessary to a spouse's inability to carry on an engaging conversation or deal with the children; to a child's spaciness, an in-law's obtuseness, or a neighbor's lack of appreciation for a favor we did. Sure, we can find negative traits in anyone. The question is, what is our focus? Is it the white dominating the paper, or the small black dot? This is a question we must ask ourselves each day.

Rav Yaakov Yosef Twersky, the previous Skverer Rebbe, recounted the following story about his special father:

When I was a child, I was quite mischievous, and I was fascinated by my father's inkwell and feather. Oh, how I wanted to draw with them. But Father did not allow me to touch them. Knowing how badly I wanted them, he placed them high up in a locked cabinet whenever he wasn't using them.

Yet, I was determined, and waited for my chance. One day, while in the middle of writing, Father was called for some emergency. He put the inkwell high up in the cabinet, but did not take the time to lock it. This was my opportunity. Now I could get my hands on it. But

[10] And it happened that when Aharon spoke
to the entire congregation of the Children of
Yisrael, they turned toward the Wilderness and
behold! — the glory of Hashem was seen in a
cloud. [11] Hashem spoke to Moshe, saying,
[12] "I have heard the complaints of the Children
of Yisrael; speak to them, saying: In the after-
noon you will eat meat and in the morning you
will be sated with bread;

how was I going to get to the top shelf of his closet? Summoning all my strength, I pushed Father's large, heavy wooden desk to the closet. I was a small child, but my determination made up for my lack of strength. I climbed up, only to realize that I was still too short to reach the ink. So I took my father's heavy wooden chair and again used strength I never knew I had to push the chair onto the desk. The inkwell was finally in my reach! I jumped onto the chair and reached up, but at that very moment, Father's office door opened. Frightened, I dropped the inkwell and it crashed to the floor, splashing ink all over the floor, the furniture, my clothing, and — worst of all — Father's sefarim! I cannot describe to you the scene I created. And there I was, standing on Father's chair, on his desk, covered in ink! I could not imagine the punishment I was about to receive.

To my surprise, Father gave me a wide smile, kissed me on my forehead, and said, "Yankele, you have the willpower to change the world. You'll be able to accomplish anything you decide to do!"

The Rebbe's father had every right to be upset at his son. But he chose to see the positive side, the good within the larger picture, and the outcome was a son who became a Rebbe to tens of thousands.

וִידַעְתֶּם כִּי אֲנִי יהוה אֱלֹהֵיכֶם.

— וִידַעְתֶּם כִּי אֲנִי ה׳ אֱלֹהֵיכֶם
You shall know that I am Hashem, your God (16:12).

⸙ *What Is Emunah?*

The goal of life is to continuously work on knowing Hashem. Not just knowing in some abstract way that Hashem exists, but coming to the realization that it is Hashem Who loves us, looks out for us at every moment, and is involved in our lives in the most intricate ways. It is easy to talk about *emunah*, but it is a totally different experience to feel and to live with *emunah*.

One of the best ways to connect to Hashem is to notice His hand in your life. The Brisker Rav said that the greatest *mussar sefer* on *emunah* is your own life! Look at how Hashem has guided you and provided for you. Thinking about your job, your shidduch, and other incidents of *hashgachah pratis* in your own life will enable you to continue trusting in Hashem in the future.

The first of the Ten Commandments is to believe that "I am Hashem, your God, Who took you out of the land of Egypt" (*Shemos* 20:2). We hear about the concept of *emunah*, we read about *emunah*, and we try to strengthen our *emunah*, but what does it mean to have *emunah*? What does it mean to live with *emunah*? Rav Shamshon Raphael Hirsch explains that *emunah* is not merely philosophically believing that Hashem created the world and continues to take charge of its functioning; *emunah* means understanding that Hashem is **my** God, involved in **my** life, guiding **me** and watching over **me**! True *emunah* means understanding that Hakadosh Baruch Hu is not only the King over the galaxies and universes, but is deeply involved in every aspect of **my** life, **my** challenges, **my** successes, **my** destiny. It is bringing Hashem into every facet of life — at work, at home, and on vacation (*Chorev,* Ch. 1).

and you shall know that I am Hashem, your God."

Rav Tzadok HaKohen writes, "Just as one is obligated to believe in Hashem's omniscience, he is obligated to believe that Hashem has a personal connection with him... and Hashem is pleased when he does His will" (*Tzidkas HaTzaddik* §154).

Rav Shlomo Wolbe asked Rav Chatzkel Levenstein for advice regarding a student. When Rav Wolbe stood up to leave, Rav Chatzkel asked, "Rav Shlomo, do you know if there is a God?" Rav Wolbe was taken aback by the question. What was Rav Chatzkel trying to say? Rav Chatzkel repeated the question and Rav Wolbe answered that of course Hashem exists. Rav Chatzkel then said, "Make sure to teach this to all your students. We can learn, go to shul, give tzedakah, and go through all the motions of being a good Jew. But what is most important is bringing Hashem into your life and connecting with Him in the most personal way."

The Kotzker Rebbe said, "Where does Hashem dwell? Wherever you let Him in."

☙ *What Should I Do? Keeping Your Eyes Trained on Hashem*

When one is at a crossroads, unsure about what to do; when one lacks clarity and is confused; when one is struggling and does not see any way out — what should he do? Sometimes money is the problem. A person is out of a job, or his expenses have increased and he cannot make his money stretch to the end of the month; the credit card bills are mounting, his child needs special help, and the roof needs repairing — what can he do?

In the *Tachanun tefillah*, we recite the following *pasuk*: וַאֲנַחְנוּ לֹא נֵדַע מַה נַּעֲשֶׂה כִּי עָלֶיךָ עֵינֵינוּ, *We do not know what we should do; rather, our eyes are upon You* (*II Divrei HaYamim* 20:12).

Rav Yaakov Emden (*Siddur Beis HaKapores* §13) explains, וַאֲנַחְנוּ לֹא נֵדַע מַה נַּעֲשֶׂה — in life one does not need to know what to do. Why? כִּי עָלֶיךָ עֵינֵינוּ, because our eyes are set upon You, Hashem. Sometimes, we are not meant to know what to do. When we face a challenge, Hashem is prodding us, saying, "Look toward Me, connect to Me, know that I am Hashem, your God! Transfer your worry from your shoulders to Me."

When we lack clarity about how to proceed, we should internalize Rav Yaakov Emden's insight and say, "Hashem, I do not know how to continue. I do not know the next steps to take. I feel lost. But that is okay, because my eyes are on You. I know that when I rely on You, You will ensure that I am taken care of."

Rav Shimshon Pincus illustrates this with a beautiful parable:

> *In the middle of the night, six-year-old Chaim calls, "Mommy, Mommy!"*
>
> *Mommy, exhausted from a long, hard day, calls from her room, "Chaim, what do you need?"*
>
> *"Mommy, I need a cup of water."*
>
> *"Chaim, go to the kitchen and get yourself a cup of water."*
>
> *When Chaim was a month old and he cried out at night, Mommy jumped up to see what he needed. Why doesn't she do this now? Because six-year-old Chaim isn't as dependent on her as was one-month-old Chaim. Since his mother was aware of how fully baby Chaim relied on her, she answered his cries. But a child of six has his own opinions, can dress himself, and goes to school. He can help himself* (*Haggadah Tiferes Shimshon, p. 390*).

The same principle applies to *tefillah*. When we show absolute reliance on Hashem, when we daven, "Hashem, I cannot do anything without Your help, I am like a one-month-old child, please help me, please guide me, I am totally reliant on You," then Hashem takes care of us like a mother caring for her baby. "I calmed my soul like a nursing child on its mother... Yisrael, look to Hashem" (*Tehillim* 131:2–3).

◆§ *Ladder of Life*

סוּלָם (*sulam*), a ladder, has the same numerical value as מָמוֹן (*mamon*), money, as well as עוֹנִי (*oni*), poverty. The numerical value of each of these words is 136 (*Baal HaTurim, Vayeitzei* 28:12). Just as a ladder goes up and down, one's financial status goes up and down.

Perhaps the connection between money and a ladder is that a ladder must lean against something. A Yid must know that he needs to rely on Hashem in all areas of life with complete *emunah* and *bitachon,* especially when it comes to *parnassah*. "Throw your burden on Hashem and He will sustain you" (*Tehillim* 55:23). Lean on Him and He will provide for you, He will see to it that you can take the steps necessary to successfully scale the ladder.

Additionally, by using money in the right way — by giving *tzedakah*, supporting your family, and helping fellow Yidden — the money itself climbs to Heavenly heights and becomes uniquely spiritual (see *Baal Shem Tov al HaTorah*). כֶּסֶף (*kesef*), money, has the same numerical value as צֶלֶם (*tzelem*). Both equal 160. *Tzelem* can mean either "a Godly form," as in *tzelem Elokim,* because when money is used in a meaningful way, one's *tzelem Elokim* is expressed, or it can mean "an idolatrous figure." The question we need to ask ourselves is, "Are we using our money in a holy way that elevates us, or is our use of money causing a spiritual descent?"

◆§ *The Power of Bircas HaMazon*

Moshe Rabbeinu initiated the first blessing of *Bircas HaMazon* when the *mahn* fell (*Berachos* 48b), as the verse says, "In the morning, you will be satisfied with bread, and you will know that I am Hashem, your God." How did eating *mahn* teach them to "know that I am Hashem, your God"? Because they recited *Bircas HaMazon* (*Rabbeinu Bachya*).

The *mahn* was provided by Hashem, with no human intermediary. There was no possibility of thinking that it was the product of mortal labor or intelligence. And even though we purchase and prepare the food we eat, we recite the same *berachah* that the Jews in the Wilderness recited after eating *mahn*. We remember that our sustenance is provided by Hashem. It is a present-day manifestation of the *mahn* that came directly from Heaven (*Sfas Emes, Eikev,* 5747; *Likkutei Sichos,* Vol. 16, p. 178). Moreover, the Sfas Emes explains that when one eats to have the strength to keep mitzvos, and concentrates on *Bircas HaMazon*, he is tasting *mahn* (even more so on Shabbos)!

> *A young man whose family had suffered several tragedies asked Rav Shach what he could do to protect them. Rav Shach told him, "Commit to one small improvement, but make sure that you do it consistently."*
>
> *"What should I commit to?"*
>
> *"Reciting Bircas HaMazon from a bentcher!" answered Rav Shach (Haggadah Kinyan Torah, p. 124).*

This was a proposal that Rav Shach made to many people who came to him for advice with regard to challenging situations. Reciting *Bircas HaMazon* from a *bentcher*, slowly and carefully, is a small but powerful practice that each of us can implement.

The reward for concentrating while reciting *Bircas HaMazon* is protection from illness (*Midrash Alfa Beisa*). One who recites *Bircas HaMazon* carefully reaps Heavenly blessings and financial security, and will be spared from harsh judgment (*Sefer HaChinuch* §430).

The reason that the reward for internalizing the teachings of *Bircas HaMazon* is so great is that it strengthens one's *bitachon* that it is Hashem Who provides sustenance, and the greatest blessings go to those who strengthen their *bitachon,* as it says, "Blessed is the one who trusts in Hashem" (*Yirmiyah* 17:7).

Shlomo HaMelech said, "The blessing of Hashem makes wealth, and *etzev* (toil) will add nothing to it" (*Mishlei* 10:22). The word *etzev* appears in *Parashas Bereishis* after Adam sins, when mankind is cursed, "*b'itzavon tochelenah* — through suffering shall you eat of it." When one recites *Bircas HaMazon* carefully, word for word, he is spared from Adam's curse of having to toil for *parnassah*! (*Sefer Chaim V'Shalom* 37:15). Wow!

☙§ *Berachah on the Mahn?*

There is a fascinating discussion among the commentators about whether a *berachah* was recited prior to eating *mahn*.

- ✧ Rav Yehudah HaChassid writes that the blessing of "*Hamotzi lechem min haShamayim* — Who brings forth bread from the Heavens" was recited (*Sefer Chassidim, Kisvei Yad* 1640).

  Rema MiPano agrees and adds that when Mashiach comes and the *tzaddikim* gather to eat a meal, Adam HaRishon will recite this *berachah* on the *mahn* that was stored for future generations.
- ✧ The Ben Ish Chai writes that the blessing on *mahn* was "*Hamamtir lechem min haShamayim* — Who rains bread from the Heavens."
- ✧ *Sefer Mirkeves HaMishneh* writes that the *berachah* depended on the thoughts you had when eating the *mahn*. If one thought he was eating bread, the *mahn* then tasted like bread and the *berachah* of *Hamotzi* was recited. If one was thinking about chocolate, the *mahn* tasted like chocolate and the *berachah* of *Shehakol* was recited.
- ✧ Rav Chaim Palagi writes that if one had a set meal when eating the *mahn* the *berachah* was *Hamotzi*.
- ✧ *Sefer Gan Raveh* writes that the *berachah* was *Mezonos*, since the Torah describes the *mahn* as tasting like a waffle in honey (*Beshalach* 16:31). This is the Chayei Adam's opinion as well.
- ✧ *Sefer Chemdas Yisrael* opines that since one had to pick up the *mahn* from the ground, the *berachah* was *Borei pri ha'adamah*.

יג וַיְהִי בָעֶרֶב, וַתַּעַל הַשְּׂלָו וַתְּכַס אֶת הַמַּחֲנֶה, וּבַבֹּקֶר הָיְתָה שִׁכְבַת הַטַּל סָבִיב לַמַּחֲנֶה.

✧ The *Bnei Yissaschar* (*Maamarei HaShabbasos* 3:3) writes that after the sin of Adam all foods have both good and bad spiritual matter. A *berachah* removes the bad spiritual matter. But the *mahn* was pure and holy; it was the food of angels and therefore, it had no bad part. So no *berachah* at all was needed on weekdays. On Shabbos, the *berachah* was "*Le'echol seudas Shabbos* — Blessed... Who has commanded us to eat the meal of Shabbos."

✧ *Sefer Sdei Chemed* writes that since saying a *berachah* before eating is Rabbinic, *berachos* were not yet instituted. Therefore, no *berachah* was recited before eating *mahn*.

✧ *Sefer Duda'ei HaSadeh* writes that the source for reciting a *berachah* before eating is the Gemara (*Berachos* 35a) that states that it is forbidden to benefit from This World without making a *berachah*. Hence, the *mahn* did not require a *berachah* as it is not food of *This* World, but rather, food from Heaven.

✧ *Responsa Beis Yitzchak* writes that no *berachah* was recited on the *mahn* because no *berachah* is made on something that comes from an obvious miracle (*Yoreh Dei'ah,* Vol. 1, *se'if* 84).

✧ Chazal tell us that when Mashiach comes, the Jewish nation will once again eat *mahn* (*Chagigah* 12b; *Midrash Bamidbar* 11:2; *Igra D'Kallah, Beshalach*). At that time Eliyahu HaNavi will teach us which *berachos* to say. May it be speedily and in our days.

[13] ***And it happened in the evening that the quails came up and covered the camp, and in the morning there was a layer of dew surrounding the camp.***

— **וּבַבֹּקֶר הָיְתָה שִׁכְבַת הַטַּל סָבִיב לַמַּחֲנֶה**
In the morning there was a layer of dew surrounding the camp (16:13).

◈§ *The Mahn Was Provided With Love*

Before the *mahn* fell, a northern wind flattened the ground (*Yoma* 75b). It then rained, which cleaned the ground. Then dew fell (although usually there is no dew in a desert). The dew protected the *mahn* from dust and dirt. Then the *mahn* fell, and then another layer of dew on top of the *mahn*, to protect it from bugs and flies. Hashem provided *mahn* in the optimal, cleanest, freshest, and most loving way.

We should always be on the lookout to notice the love and care with which Hashem provides for us.

Rav Avigdor Miller saw Hashem's kindness in everything. From the banister in his home, to the hard tip of his shoelace and reinforced buttonholes. Every aspect of his life revolved around seeing Hashem and His boundless kindness. He picked up an apple and said, "Hashem, this apple is so beautiful. It is such a tantalizing red! You even gave it a nice scent! And You did this all for me! You did it all with kindness because You love me. How can I begin to thank You for all this?" Then he slowly and deliberately made a *berachah*.

Rav Miller also thought of something specific to be grateful for when he said *Modim*, because, as he said, "Thanking for everything is thanking for nothing." He kept a list of misfortunes that happen to other people so that he could read it and thank Hashem that these things did not happen to him (*Rav Avigdor Miller: His Life and His Revolution*, p. 265).

יד וַתַּעַל שִׁכְבַת הַטָּל, וְהִנֵּה עַל פְּנֵי הַמִּדְבָּר
דַּק מְחֻסְפָּס, דַּק כַּכְּפֹר עַל הָאָרֶץ.

In *Bircas HaMazon* we say that Hashem sustains us and nourishes us with *chein,* favor. What does that mean? Rav Yechezkel Sarna explains that an orange is sweet and juicy, delicious and nutritious. Clearly, we would enjoy an orange even if it came wrapped in an unappealing black skin. But Hashem not only provides us with delicious and nutritious foods, He sends them to us with *chein* — "gift wrapped" in an aesthetic and appealing way that increases our enjoyment. Moreover, Hashem designed the orange with small, individual segments, to make it easy to eat. Food is much more than just nourishing. It is full of appeal and beauty. Take a moment to think about how Hashem expresses His love for you and your family every day. Open the fridge, the pantry, the bedroom closet, and the door of your home, and notice the abundance, the *chein*, the *berachah*, the *mahn,* and Hashem's love within your home and your life.

◆ *Hiding the Berachah*

Berachah is only found when something is hidden from sight (*Taanis* 8b), when one hides his blessings and does not flaunt them, especially in matters of *parnassah*. When the *mahn* fell, it was covered by dew on both the bottom and top. And the *mahn* that Hashem instructed Moshe to keep in a container in the *Kodesh HaKodashim* for all eternity was also hidden from the eye.

Do not flaunt your *berachos.* Do not post about them. Do not gossip about them. Do not feel the need to regale people with them. Thank Hashem internally for your *berachah* and be happy. "He has told you, O man, what is good, and what Hashem demands of you; to do justice, to love *chesed*, and **to walk modestly** with your God" (*Michah* 6:8).

14 The layer of dew evaporated and behold! — upon the surface of the Wilderness was revealed something thin, exposed, as thin as frost upon the earth.

וְהִנֵּה עַל פְּנֵי הַמִּדְבָּר דַּק מְחֻסְפָּס — ***Behold! — upon the surface of the Wilderness was revealed something thin, exposed*** (16:14).

☙ *Parnassah From Hashem: Anytime, Anywhere*

It is hard, if not impossible, for the human mind to imagine how a nation of millions can survive for decades in the arid desert. Yet Hashem showed the Jewish nation that He is not bound by human understanding or the laws of nature. Hashem can provide for us in any place and at every time. When we think it is impossible, Hashem shows us that it is not.

At the end of his *Peirush al HaTorah,* the Ramban writes about coins minted in Eretz Yisrael. On one side was engraved a picture of a staff with almonds, and on the other side was a depiction of the flask of *mahn.* The intent was for all to know that the money in their hands was from Hashem.

Rav Shmuel Halpern, a chassid of Rav Yisrael Friedman, the Chortkover Rebbe, met a man who told him that the Chortkover had saved his life. Here is his story:

Living in Vienna, parnassah was difficult. I struggled to support my family and decided that, like many others at the time, I would make the trip to America, the land where the streets were paved with gold. It was a tough decision. I knew that America was a spiritual wasteland, and traveling there was a spiritual risk, but we needed the money. I bought a ship ticket and went to get a berachah from the Rebbe of Chortkov. I told the Rebbe of my plan and why I was traveling, and he smiled at me and

טו וַיִּרְאוּ בְנֵי יִשְׂרָאֵל, וַיֹּאמְרוּ אִישׁ אֶל
אָחִיו, מָן הוּא, כִּי לֹא יָדְעוּ מַה הוּא,
וַיֹּאמֶר מֹשֶׁה אֲלֵהֶם, הוּא הַלֶּחֶם
אֲשֶׁר נָתַן יהוה לָכֶם לְאָכְלָה.

said, "Ah, I have been waiting to meet someone traveling to America for some time now. Can you carry an important message for me?"

"Of course I can. Anything for the Rebbe."

"Excellent," said the Rebbe. "Please send my regards to the God of America."

"The God of America? What does that mean? Is there a different God in America than here in Vienna?" I asked.

"Exactly," said the Rebbe. "The same Ribbono shel Olam Who is here, is there; His honor fills the entire world. So why are you traveling to America at the risk of your ruchniyus? Is the God Who will support you there not able to support you here?"

Right then and there I decided to cancel my ticket and remain in Vienna. I was fortunate to have canceled, as it was a ticket on the... RMS Titanic.

A man told the Rebbe of Lelov that he was struggling with *parnassah* and was thinking of traveling to America so he could support his family from there. The Rebbe told him this story:

A rabbi in a small city struggled to support his family. Most of the other people in his city were impoverished as well. One day, two wealthy men from a nearby city came and asked the rabbi if he could serve as an advisor for them in an upcoming din Torah they had in their hometown. They would pay him a large sum for his assistance.

[15] ***The Children of Yisrael saw and said to one another, "It is mahn!" — for they did not know what it was. Then Moshe said to them: "This is the food that Hashem has given you to eat.***

"Please give me a few minutes to decide," the rabbi said. He then went to daven Minchah and when he returned, he told the men that he was unable to travel with them.

The rabbi's wife was perplexed and incensed, and after the men left, she asked her husband why he did not accept their generous offer. The rabbi told her, "I went to daven Minchah, and I came to the berachah of 'Bareich aleinu es hashanah hazos' — the berachah in which we ask Hashem for sustenance. I thought, 'From where does Hashem send this sustenance? Directly from His Heavenly Throne! The distance from there to our home is enormous. If Hashem is sending us parnassah from so far away, He does not need me to travel a few miles away to the city where these two men live; He can send it directly to us here.'"

That is what happened. The two men returned a little while later and arranged to have the din Torah in the rabbi's home.

וַיִּרְאוּ בְנֵי יִשְׂרָאֵל וַיֹּאמְרוּ אִישׁ אֶל אָחִיו מָן הוּא כִּי לֹא יָדְעוּ מַה הוּא — ***The Children of Yisrael saw and said to one another, "It is mahn!" — for they did not know what it was*** (16:15).

◆§ *Emunah in Hashem: Parnassah Is From Hashem*

The Bas Ayin explains that the word "*mahn*" is from the word "*emunah,*" since, when the *mahn* fell, the Jews said "מָן הוּא" (*mahn hu*), which is comprised of the same letters as the word "אֱמוּנָה" (*emunah*). The *mahn* strengthened their absolute belief in Hashem and their realization that they owed their sustenance and continued existence to Hashem.

Whenever one realizes that his *parnassah* is from Hashem, he is ingesting *mahn*.

A wagon driver came to the Chofetz Chaim in tears. "Rebbi, help me! In the past few days, the horses on which I was dependent for earning a living all died."

"You were dependent on horses to earn a living? Have you forgotten that it is Hashem Who supports you?" the Chofetz Chaim asked. "When you realize that it is Hashem Who sustains us all, then you will experience Hashem's largesse and chesed, 'for His kindness is eternal.' But if you think it is horses that provide you with parnassah, it is no wonder that they died."

Rav Ephraim Wachsman recounted that one shemittah year he was in Eretz Yisrael and was offered the opportunity to see firsthand the fields that were left fallow. The vast fields, the farmers' source of parnassah, lay unplanted and overgrown.

Before leaving the farm, Rav Wachsman saw a man sitting on a chair and learning from a sefer. It was one of the shomer-shemittah farmers. The man was serene and happy. Rav Wachsman asked him, "Are you not concerned about the long-term state of your fields?"

The farmer pointed to the fields and said, "They are not mine. They all belong to Hashem, so there is nothing to be worried about."

Chesed in the Midbar, Chesed Today

For forty years, in the Wilderness, all the Jews' physical needs were miraculously provided by Hashem. Food was supplied in the form of *mahn*. Clothing never wore out; it grew along with its owner, and it always remained clean and crisp.

The *Ananei HaKavod*, Clouds of Glory, provided protection from the elements (*Shibbolei HaLeket*).

It sounds ideal, but it raises a question: If everyone's physical needs were fulfilled, how could the Jewish people fulfill the mitzvah of *gemilas chasadim,* a foundation stone of Jewish existence and identity?

✧ ***Smile, encourage, and make peace.*** Even with all their material needs provided for by Hashem, Jews could do *chesed* by helping those needing encouragement, attention, and a simple smile. (See *Dibros Moshe, Bava Basra* 12:49, where Rav Moshe Feinstein explains that *chesed* performed in the Wilderness involved making peace between friends, and also between husband and wife.) *Sefer HaChinuch* explains that the mitzvah of *chesed* and *tzedakah* is fulfilled by helping one's friend with whatever he needs (Mitzvah §479). A friend may require emotional support as much as financial help. Acknowledgment and a comforting word are essential components of the mitzvah of *chesed.*

The Gemara tells us, "One who shows the whites of his teeth (i.e., he smiles) to his friend is better than one who serves him milk" (*Kesubos* 111b). Sometimes a person needs a smile more than a cup of refreshing milk. Milk is cooling, nourishing, and contains protein, but a smile can change a person's entire perspective.

One who gives charity to the poor receives six blessings, while one who gives charity and blesses the poor receives eleven blessings (*Bava Basra* 9b). The Maharal explains that the food or money given to one in need suffices only a short time. But a blessing, warm words of encouragement, or a smile can make a difference that will last forever, and that is why the one who bestows them is rewarded with additional blessings (*Nesivos Olam, Nesiv HaTzedakah* §4).

"I am Hashem, your God... open your mouth wide, and I will fill it" (*Tehillim* 81:11). How does one widen his mouth? By smiling. Hashem is telling us that if we widen our mouths by smiling at others, He will fill them with *berachah.*

Rabbi Benji Levin, a grandson of Rav Aryeh Levin, recounted the following story:

Someone once told me that as a young man, he rebelled and stopped wearing a kippah. Until the day he saw my grandfather, Rav Aryeh, walking toward him. Remembering that Rav Aryeh was at his bris and his bar mitzvah, and ashamed to be seen bareheaded, he tried to sneak down a side street so the rav would not see him. But he was not quick enough, and my grandfather called, "Tell me, did I ever do anything to hurt you? Because I noticed you were trying to avoid me."

The young man admitted that he did not want Rav Aryeh to see him without a kippah.

"Your grandfather took my hands in his," he told me, "and said, 'I am a very short person; I cannot see what's on top of your head. But I see what's in your heart.'

"Everyone else was telling me that I was a disgrace, that I was embarrassing my family. But Rav Aryeh never said anything negative. Your grandfather's sweet, sincere words convinced me to put my kippah back on my head."

When visiting a friend in the hospital, I was impressed by the staff member who was emptying the containers in which used needles and other biohazards were placed. It is not an especially respectable job, but this man was all smiles and seemed as happy as could be. He greeted us and asked my friend how he was feeling that bright sunny morning. He was truly interested and engaged. I walked him out of the room and commented on his upbeat personality. He told me, "Every day, while emptying the bins, I have an opportunity to cheer up patients. I choose to make the best of my job and make as many people as possible smile and be happy."

Regardless of our job, position, or rank, we have the opportunity to do chesed.

✧ ***Thinking for another.*** Chazal tell us that the *mahn* tasted like anything one desired. The Chiddushei HaRim explains that this presented a *chesed* opportunity. Those who were impoverished in Mitzrayim had never tasted any culinary delights. Therefore, when they ate the *mahn*, they were able to think only of the few basic foods they had previously consumed. Someone who had had rich culinary meals, who had tasted and enjoyed food, could tell his friend, "Come, give me your *mahn*. I'm going to think *for you* that it should taste like the most tasty cuts of meat prepared in the best way." The impoverished person was then able to taste these exceptionally delightful delicacies. Thinking about what someone else is missing, acting to provide it, and helping them enhance their experiences was the *chesed* that could be performed in the *Midbar*.

Today, there are many opportunities to do *chesed* without money. Each of us has some form of ability, each of us has something we can use for another's benefit — technical skills, Torah knowledge, medical information, connections, ideas, experiences, advice, or insights. Everyone has something to offer, everyone can help another Jew, his shul, his community, or Klal Yisrael.

Rav Naftali of Ropshitz writes that we are all soldiers in the army of Hashem. What is the worst thing a soldier can do? To desert his position, to abandon his job and responsibility as a soldier. Hashem has given everyone, every Yid, a special means whereby he can benefit others, and as a soldier in the army of Hashem, those are his orders. Not using that gift, that talent, that ability to help others, is to be derelict of one's duty.

From the verse "*Kabeid es Hashem meihonecha* — Honor Hashem with your wealth" (*Mishlei* 3:9), we learn that one should honor Hashem by spending money to beautify mitzvos. *Sefer Chassidim* (129) learns an additional point from this verse. Instead of reading the last word *"meihonecha,"* he reads it "*mimah shehana'acha* — from what He has bestowed upon you." If you have a beautiful voice, be the chazzan, join a choir, lead a *kumzitz*, or help a bar mitzvah boy learn to *lein*. Whatever skills you have were not given to you for your own sake, but to be shared with others.

Tanna D'Vei Eliyahu (28:15) writes, "Hashem says to the Jewish people, 'My beloved children, am I missing anything, that I need you [to do something on My behalf]? What do I ask from you, other than that you love each other and honor each other!'"

> *On October 7, 2023, two middle-aged brothers, Elchanan and Menachem Kalmanson from Otniel, both in the IDF reserves, were celebrating Simchas Torah. When Elchanan heard that something horrific was happening in the south, he packed his army gear and went to get his brother. "**Klal Yisrael needs us, our brothers need us**." They drove to Kibbutz Be'eri and for the next sixteen hours they went from house to house, rescuing over one hundred people, all the while facing terrorist gunfire. To convince Be'eri residents holed up in their safe rooms that they were there to help and were not terrorists dressed in IDF uniforms (as many Hamas terrorists were), Elchanan and his team went from house to house singing Simchas Torah songs and saying "Shema Yisrael."*
>
> *On October 8, a terrorist who was hiding fired on Elchanan and Menachem. Elchanan died in his brother's hands.*
>
> *"Klal Yisrael needs us! Our brothers need us!" was the call to which they responded. This was the expression of their essence.*
>
> *Reach out, support, encourage, and do chesed for your brothers and sisters in any way you can.*

The *Rambam* (*Matnos Aniyim* 10:7) writes that helping others find a job or coaching them to help them get a better job is the highest level of *tzedakah*. If you hear about an opening in your company, think about who you know who is looking for a job and tell them. Coaching and mentoring others in work-related skills is also a significant form of *chesed.*

> *After davening on Yom Kippur night, the congregation lined up to wish the Chazon Ish a gemar chasimah tovah. The Chazon Ish pulled one man close and asked him how he was doing with parnassah. The man was surprised — the Chazon Ish was asking about parnassah on the holiest night of the year?*
>
> *"For **you**, tonight is not the night to be concerned with your parnassah," said the Chazon Ish. "But for **me**, tonight is the night to be concerned about **your** parnassah! When the Kohen Gadol left the Kodesh HaKodashim on Yom Kippur, he davened for financial success for all the Yidden" (Maaseh Ish, Vol. 1, p. 194).*

✧ ***Protecting their honor.*** Where the *mahn* fell depended on one's mitzvah observance. It fell right outside the tent of a *tzaddik*, so he did not need to walk far to collect his portion. It fell a little further away for a *beinoni,* and outside the camp for a *rasha.*

Some people proclaim their righteousness and make a show of looking especially holy, although they are not. Such people faced a predicament. The *mahn* fell with exactitude. What a great embarrassment when there was no *mahn* waiting at the entrances to the tents of these prestigious people. How could they trek toward the outskirts of the encampment in front of everyone and gather their *mahn* from outside the camp? That would ruin their holier-than-thou persona. So they stayed home. They did not go out to gather their *mahn.* It was better to remain hungry than to ruin their reputations.

This is where a *chesed* opportunity arose. There were groups of people, a *gemach* of sorts, who went to gather the *mahn* for the people who were too embarrassed to go to the outskirts of the camp to retrieve their own (*Yafah Sichaseinu,* p. 9).

✧ ***Thinking of others.*** The *mahn* remained fresh until the fourth hour of the day. At the fourth hour, the sun began to melt it and it began to spoil. If one was delayed in gathering his *mahn*, his friends did *chesed* by going to retrieve it for him (*Rabbeinu Bachya* 16:21).

Next time you have to run to the grocery store on Erev Shabbos, ask your neighbor if he needs anything. What an easy *chesed* opportunity!

Along with the *mahn*, valuable stones fell, which were later dedicated to the Mishkan (*Yoma* 75a). Among the stones that fell were the two *avnei shoham,* precious stones that were placed on the *Eiphod,* and the *avnei miluim,* the twelve stones placed on the *Choshen*, each inscribed with a *shevet's* name. Rav Shmuel Berenbaum asks why the Torah calls these stones *avnei miluim* — literally, "stones that fill" (they filled the empty spots carved out for them on the *Choshen*). Each of these stones was exquisite and priceless; they were not just stones filling in gaps!

Calling them *avnei miluim* teaches us that the most valued feature of an item is not necessarily its value or even the item itself, but its ability to help someone else, to fill their needs, to compensate for what another is lacking. That is even greater than beauty and value (*Ohel Moshe, Terumah*, p. 619).

> *Chaya Salomon was a beloved teacher in the Noam Meiri school in Lod, Israel, until she was taken from us in a terrorist shooting in 2017. At the end of each school year, Morah Chaya wrote the following in her students' report cards: "When I give out report cards at the end of the school year, I'm always reminded of another report card, the one given by our Father in Heaven. Instead of giving grades for the usual subjects — halachah, Torah, grammar, and math — Hashem gives grades in the following subjects: friendliness, patience, understanding, love, kindness, responsibility, humility, and gratitude. His report card is more significant than any other. Life is so busy that sometimes we forget that developing good middos is the test that's really worth grading."*

◆§ *The Test of Staying in Growth Mode*

The *mahn* was so holy and pure that each time it was consumed, it transformed the person into a higher spiritual being, to the point that the next day his countenance was nearly unrecognizable to his friends (see *Igra D'Kallah, Beshalach*). This is the meaning of the verse, "They said to one another, 'It is *mahn*,' — "for they did not know what it was," referring to the visible change in the one who had eaten the *mahn*.

The *mahn* affected the spiritual constitution of the consumer daily; we, too, must see how we can change in some small way every day, so that today we are different than we were yesterday. Do not compare yourself to other people; compare yourself to who you were yesterday.

At times, those pursuing a career negate their spiritual growth, reasoning that they are working to support their children's yeshivah education. They claim to have already passed the torch of learning and growth to the next generation. In their minds, such a claim absolves them from Torah study and spiritual growth.

The Yid Hakadosh of Peshischa said that he asked a father why he was working so hard that he had no time to study Torah. The father said that he was doing it so that his son could study Torah. Years later, the Rebbe of Peshischa asked that man's son why *he* was working so hard that he could not work harder on spiritual advancement. The son said the same thing his father had said, that he was working so that his son could study Torah. Generation follows generation and, the Yid Hakadosh said, "I'm still waiting to see the son of this family who will devote himself to Torah study."

Rav Shimshon Pincus bemoaned this phenomenon as an American tragedy.

The Torah writes, "These are the children of Noach, Noach..." In other words, Noach treated himself like one of his own children; he made sure that he cared for his own spirituality as carefully as he cared for his children's.

Someone asked the Brisker Rav if he should move, because the environment in his neighborhood had changed and he was concerned about the *chinuch* of his children. The Brisker Rav asked, "And what about yourself? Is there no reason for you to be concerned about living in this neighborhood, no concern for how it affects your *neshamah*, your outlook, and growth?"

A wealthy man offered Rav Shmuel Berenbaum $250,000 as his share in a Yissachar-Zevulun partnership. Rav Shmuel told the man to keep the money and make a Yissachar-Zevulun partnership with himself. "You need to learn. Carve out time in your daily schedule and dedicate it to learning."

When Rav Shmuel was collecting for his yeshivah, a baal habayis gave him $5,000, a very large sum at the time. Rav Shmuel asked, "How long does it take you to earn $5,000?"

"One week."

Rav Shmuel gave the money back to him and told him to take a week off from work to learn. Rav Shmuel always asked baalei batim about their learning and ensured that even the wealthiest supporters were learning and growing.

A *malach* is called an "*omeid*," something that is stationary, because an angel remains in its spiritual position indefinitely. A righteous person, on the other hand, is called a "*mehalech*," something that moves, because he constantly takes strides to improve himself and grow in his *avodas Hashem* (*Kedushas Levi*, *Bechukosai*).

The Gemara tells us, "Whoever learns halachos each day is guaranteed that he will receive a place in the World to Come" (*Megillah* 28b). The Kedushas Levi says that *shoneh,* the word used for "learns," can also mean "changes," and the word halachos can also mean "*halichosav* — his ways," so that

Chazal are telling us, "Whoever changes his ways each day (by taking the opportunity to become better, even in some minuscule way) is guaranteed that he will receive a place in the World to Come."

Everyone, no matter their current situation, can climb the ladder of *ruchniyus.* Even one who does not learn in the *beis midrash* all day can grow. Everyone can do more *chesed,* or give more *tzedakah. Nisyonos* at work can make one more resilient in *avodas Hashem.* Time spent in Torah study can be more focused. One can take advantage of the time in the car, or on the bus or train, to learn. My cousin Shloime lives in the Five Towns and works in Manhattan. He learns the *daf* four times every day — before Shacharis with a *chavrusa,* then a *chazarah* on the train into the city, again on the way home, and a fourth time at night! Shloime is dedicated to growth. Every day he climbs a little higher on the ladder of Torah. He is a *mehalech*!

The Torah exhorts us (*Devarim* 16:32), "Do not establish for yourself a *matzeivah* (a monument used for *avodah zarah*)." The Kotzker Rebbe says that the Torah is saying, "Do not establish for yourself (turn yourself into) a *matzeivah* — an immobile, stonelike lifestyle that precludes you from growing as a person and in your *avodas Hashem.*"

When Sodom was being destroyed, the angel warned Lot's family, "Do not look back." Lot's wife could not restrain herself; she looked back at Sodom and turned into a pillar of salt. The Tolna Rebbe explains that the angel was telling the family not to look back because behind them was Sodom, representing evil and spiritual depravity. One who wants to be saved needs to commit to change and growth, to moving on from the evil that Sodom represented. One needs to extricate oneself from Sodom, not just physically, but also spiritually. But Lot's wife could not part from Sodom; she could not bring herself to change, to look ahead, and move forward. As such, her punishment was to turn into a pillar of salt. Salt is what preserves an item in its present state. Our job is to wake up

טז זֶה הַדָּבָר אֲשֶׁר צִוָּה יהוה, לִקְטוּ מִמֶּנּוּ
אִישׁ לְפִי אָכְלוֹ, עֹמֶר לַגֻּלְגֹּלֶת, מִסְפַּר
נַפְשֹׁתֵיכֶם, אִישׁ לַאֲשֶׁר בְּאָהֳלוֹ תִּקָּחוּ.

in the morning and ask, "What can I do today, even something so small that it will make me just a little bit better than I was yesterday?" Over time, these minuscule steps become transformative.

זֶה הַדָּבָר אֲשֶׁר צִוָּה ה׳ לִקְטוּ מִמֶּנּוּ אִישׁ לְפִי אָכְלוֹ עֹמֶר לַגֻּלְגֹּלֶת מִסְפַּר נַפְשֹׁתֵיכֶם אִישׁ לַאֲשֶׁר בְּאָהֳלוֹ תִּקָּחוּ — ***This is the thing that Hashem has commanded, "Gather from it, for every man according to his consumption — an omer per person — according to the number of your people, everyone according to whoever is in his tent shall you take"*** (16:16).

Ohel: Prioritizing

When we move from the comfort of our homes into the succah, we recall the time we spent under the *Ananei HaKavod's* protective shield during our forty-year sojourn in the Wilderness. It reminds us that This World is only temporary, so we must prioritize that which is to our eternal benefit over that which is only temporal.

Rav Yonasan Eibeschutz reminds us that the lessons of the succah do not merely apply for the eight days of Succos, but throughout the year (*Ya'aros Devash*, Vol. 1, *Derush* 6). Avraham, Yitzchak, and Yaakov always built tents; temporary housing, not permanent homes. They understood the transience of This World and the need to pay attention to bigger things. When Bilam saw the Jews' living arrangements, he said, "How beautiful are the tents of Yaakov." Even he could see the beauty of living in temporary dwellings, with the understanding that This World is but an antechamber.

Take time today to assess your priorities. Make sure that

[16]This is the thing that Hashem has commanded, 'Gather from it, for every man according to his consumption — an omer per person — according to the number of your people, everyone according to whoever is in his tent shall you take.'"

your behaviors and lifestyle choices match your priorities and will help you achieve your goals.

☙ Supporting the Family: Honoring One's Wife

"Gather from it... everyone according to whoever is in his tent shall you take" teaches us that a man is obligated to support his wife and family (*Mechilta D'Rashbi*). "Tent" refers to one's wife. The *kesubah* obligates a husband to support and honor his wife. The husband was responsible for gathering and bringing in the daily *mahn* for his wife and family (see *Malbim* 16:16).

With a full-time job — and many also have a second job — it is easy to lose sight of the importance of our spouse and family.

There was no one as busy as Rav Dovid Feinstein. Rav Dovid was a *gadol hador* and a world-renowned *posek,* yet his wife and family were always a priority for him.

> *Rav Dovid vacuumed on Erev Shabbos, set the table, and helped by making a salad or a salt-and-pepper kugel. He shopped for toys for his grandchildren in Amazing Savings. When asked what to look for in a chassan, he replied, "The most important thing to look for is a bachur who does not think that a wife is meant to be his shifchah kenaanis (maidservant). A wife is not a servant who stands at the ready to answer every beck and call" (Reb Dovid: The Life and Legacy of Rabbi Dovid Feinstein).*
>
> *Rav Zalman Leib Teitelbaum, the Satmar Rebbe, asked*

Rav Dovid if they could learn together on Thursday nights. Rav Dovid apologized, saying that he was unavailable at that time, as that was when he did the Shabbos shopping for his rebbetzin! (ibid. p. 61). When a video circulated of Rav Dovid shopping for Shabbos, some felt it was an embarrassment and a lack of kavod haTorah. When they offered that someone else do the shopping due to the video, Rav Dovid laughed and said, "Farkert, to the contrary — the video is a zechus for me, because now more people will know that they should help their wives prepare for Shabbos" (p. 132).

A popular daf yomi maggid shiur asked Rav Dovid for guidance. Attendance at his shiur had grown exponentially, and he wanted to know what his responsibilities were: Should he add halachah or perhaps, sometimes, raise money for important causes? Or was it his responsibility just to give the shiur?

Rav Dovid said, "Your responsibility is not to your shiur. Your responsibility is only to your wife. That is what it says in the kesubah — she is your responsibility. Everyone and everything else comes afterward."

For the last twenty years of his life, Rav Dovid had a chavrusa named Eli Berkowitz. They started learning together when Eli was single. After Eli married and his second child was born, Rav Dovid told him that they would no longer be learning together on Sundays, as "Sunday is a family day, and now you have two children to spend time with, so we will resume learning on Monday" (ibid. p. 95).

A young man asked Rav Avraham Genachowsky, the rosh yeshivah of Tchebin, what he could resolve to improve that year that would warrant his being inscribed for a good new year. Rav Avraham responded, "Resolve to be extra sensitive and caring to your wife. This is a substantial resolution that will put you in good stead on the Day of Judgment!"

Rav Avraham expounded on the seven key components for a successful relationship as enumerated by the *Rambam* (*Hilchos Ishus* 15:19). He told young couples that if they abided by the Rambam's guidelines, they would have a great marriage and a great life. These are the Rambam's guidelines:

(1) ***Honor.*** Honor your wife more than yourself. Avraham pitched Sarah's tent first, before his own. Prioritize your wife, assist your wife, and show her respect and honor, in action and thought.

(2) ***Love.*** As it says, "He (Yitzchak) loved her (Rivkah)" (*Bereishis* 24:67). Thinking about your wife's good points and how she complements you will inspire love.

I have a friend who is always anxious before a flight. If it was up to him, he would be at the airport five hours before departure. His wife, on the other hand, is more laid-back. If it was up to her, they would be at the airport thirty minutes before takeoff (which is not enough time). As a married couple, they came to a compromise; they arrive at the airport exactly two and a half hours before takeoff.

(3) ***Support.*** A husband is obligated to provide for his wife's daily needs. He should not be too frugal or overbearing when it comes to money. All financial *berachah* in the home comes from one's wife. As such he should be as generous with her as finances allow.

(4) ***Do not intimidate.*** There is no room in a home for too much fear. Create an atmosphere of calm, serenity, and joy. A home is not a dictatorship, so don't be a dictator.

(5) ***Speak gently.*** How do you speak to your wife? Always use a calm tone and soothing voice. Never raise your voice at your wife. Speak to her with respect and honor. Compliment her frequently.

(6) ***Create a pleasant atmosphere.*** Fill your home with happiness, joy, and laughter. A continuous heartfelt smile plays a significant role in creating a pleasant atmosphere.

יז וַיַּעֲשׂוּ כֵן בְּנֵי יִשְׂרָאֵל, וַיִּלְקְטוּ הַמַּרְבֶּה
וְהַמַּמְעִיט. יח וַיָּמֹדּוּ בָעֹמֶר, וְלֹא הֶעְדִּיף
הַמַּרְבֶּה, וְהַמַּמְעִיט לֹא הֶחְסִיר,
אִישׁ לְפִי אָכְלוֹ לָקָטוּ.

(7) ***Avoid anger.*** Keep the emotional temperature in your home low-key. How you respond to irritations has a direct effect on your wife and family. The Admor of Lelov said that reading *Iggeres HaRamban* is a *segulah* for overcoming anger. But for it to work, **study** and **internalize** *Iggeres HaRamban* (*Agan Hasar,* Vol. 1, p. 89).

Rebbetzin Freifeld was speaking to some friends while her husband, Rav Shlomo, walked a few steps ahead of her. He stopped short and said, "I almost forgot. I gave my wife a kesubah that says that I will honor her and wait for her."

When talmidim asked Rav Shlomo if they should grow a beard, or put on a frock, or make any change to their outer appearance, he always asked, "What does your wife say? Does she like it? Does she approve?"

The Maharil writes that one should fold his tallis immediately after Shabbos in order to start off the week with a mitzvah (see *Magen Avraham, Orach Chaim* 300). Some say that it is a *segulah* for *shalom bayis* (see *Taamei HaMinhagim* 647, *Kuntres Acharon*). Rav Itzikel of Pshevorsk added, "And I say that rolling up your sleeves and helping wash the dishes right after Shabbos is a *segulah* for *shalom bayis*!"

A *chassan* asked the Kotzker Rebbe, "Rebbe, for how long does the *chassan* retain the status of a king? Is it just the day of the *chuppah*? The seven days of *sheva berachos*? The first year of marriage?"

[17]The Children of Yisrael did so; they gathered, he who took much and he who took little. [18]Then they measured in an omer, and whoever took more did not have extra and whoever took less was not lacking; each one gathered according to his consumption.

The Rebbe said, "As long as you treat your wife as a queen, you retain the status of a king."

וַיִּלְקְטוּ הַמַּרְבֶּה וְהַמַּמְעִיט. וַיָּמֹדּוּ בָעֹמֶר וְלֹא הֶעְדִּיף הַמַּרְבֶּה וְהַמַּמְעִיט לֹא הֶחְסִיר אִישׁ לְפִי אָכְלוֹ לָקָטוּ — ***They gathered, he who took much and he who took little. Then they measured in an omer, and whoever took more did not have extra and whoever took less was not lacking; each one gathered according to his consumption*** (16:17,18).

☙ *Hishtadlus*

No matter how much time was spent gathering the *mahn* or how large the quantity of *mahn*, upon arriving home, everyone had the same amount, no more and no less. We see from here that one's *parnassah* is not a result of his *hishtadlus*, it is not a result of hustle, effort, time spent working, or the type of job; it is all Divinely orchestrated. There are people who work sixty-five hours a week and barely make ends meet, and there are those who work just a few hours a week and are comfortable.

The *mahn* showed us for all eternity that yes, you have to go out and gather the *mahn*, but there is no connection between your efforts and what you bring home. One of the most difficult questions that we must ask ourselves (or our rav) is, "Is the *hishtadlus* I am doing too much, or just right?"

Hishtadlus, explains the *Mesillas Yesharim* (Ch. 21), is a tax that we all pay since Adam HaRishon ate from the *Eitz HaDaas*. *Hishtadlus* is a box that Hashem requires us to check off before He provides *parnassah*; it is not the source of *parnassah* itself. Rav Mattisyahu Salomon points out that no one wants to pay more taxes than they are required to. Moreover, many people hire accountants and tax experts to figure out how to minimize their tax bills. The same should be true for the tax of *hishtadlus*. One should actively figure out a way to balance *hishtadlus* appropriately (*Matnas Chelko*, p. 282).

The Alter of Novardok pointed out something so striking but true: *Hishtadlus* and working for *parnassah* is a curse that was levied against man, as it says, "Accursed is the ground because of you... by the sweat of your brow shall you eat bread" (*Bereishis* 3:17,19). *Bitachon*, on the other hand, is a wellspring of blessing, as the verse tells us, "Blessed is the man who trusts in Hashem" (*Yirmiyah* 17:7). Yet man runs after *hishtadlus* day and night without a stop, convinced that it is his salvation, although the Torah deems it a curse. And man only employes *bitachon* sparingly, although it is the wellspring of *berachah* and prosperity.

It is a life's work to change this.

Rabbeinu Bachya (16:4) tells us something so amazing. He points out that the *mahn* fell at night, when everyone was sleeping. When they awoke in the morning the *mahn* was ready for them. It was clear to see that Hashem provided it, and that *hishtadlus* is not what generates *parnassah*, but is merely a technical formality that must be employed to access it.

> *The rosh yeshivah of Chevron, Rav Moshe Mordechai Epstein, told a student, "Listen to something fascinating: I travel to London to raise money for the yeshivah, and money comes in from Switzerland. I try to raise money from America, and I receive money from London. Hashem is showing me clearly that it is not from my hishtadlus that the money comes. Yes, I am obligated to do hishtadlus, but I see so clearly that the salvation comes from Hashem!"*

Rav Tzvi Elimelech Shapiro writes that when one believes that his *parnassah* comes from his job, his boss, his schooling, his career choice, his investment prowess, his intelligence, or any other source, he transgresses a form of *avodah zarah,* as he is ascribing powers and control to other entities. "Many are the thoughts in man's heart, but only Hashem's decisions are fulfilled" (*Mishlei* 19:21; *Igra D'Kallah, Parashas Lech Lecha*). The ideas that enter our minds are all a product of *hashgachah pratis.* Hashem sends us the ideas He wants us to have.

The Torah commands showing honor to one's father and mother, as well as fearing them. A practical example of fearing one's parents would be not standing in their places and not sitting in their places (*Kiddushin* 31b). The Torah also equates the honor that must be shown for one's father and mother with the honor that must be shown for Hashem (ibid. 31a).

The Sfas Emes says that just as the halachah of revering parents states that one may not stand or sit in their place, one may not attempt to "sit in Hashem's place" — to question why things happen; we should not doubt why Hashem orchestrates certain events. A Yid with *bitachon* understands that Hashem is the One in control of his life, and he does not attempt to "sit" in Hashem's place, so to speak, by thinking that he controls his own destiny, or by worrying about the future. Reb Moshe Reichman, the noted *baal tzedakah*, often said, "A person must allow himself to be led by Hashem."

The Imrei Chaim of Vizhnitz recounted that his great-grandfather, Rav Kopel Chassid (who served as the chazzan in the Baal Shem Tov's *beis midrash*), was a businessman. The non-Jews whom he encountered in the marketplaces referred to him as the "*Shivisi'nik*," because throughout the day, while busy buying and selling, he could be heard whispering under his breath, "*Shivisi Hashem l'negdi samid*—I have set Hashem before me always" (*Tehillim* 16:8).

The Pittsburgher Rebbe, Rav Yosef Leifer, was offered a ride in an unusual car: it had a steering wheel on the passenger's side, just like the one in front of the driver's seat.

The driver explained, "You see, Rebbe, I have a young child who is quite rambunctious, to put it mildly. My sweet young boy is hyperactive and he loves to control the steering wheel. There have been many times that I was driving and he tried to take control of the steering wheel! It became dangerous to have him as a passenger, until I came up with this idea: I had the car dealership install the exact same wheel on the passenger's side. Now my son sits in his seat and 'drives around town,' turning here and turning there. He enjoys his 'driving' and has not attempted to take control of the real wheel since. This is the reason, Rebbe, you find yourself sitting in front of a second steering wheel."

The Rebbe said, "Hashem distributes steering wheels to each and every person. We all think that we are the drivers, turning this way or that, slowing or stopping. But the steering wheels we are given are just for pretending. We think we are making decisions, that we oversee our destinies, that we are the ones who make the decisions that guarantee our success. However, only Hashem controls the real steering wheel. He guides us and is in control of the directions we take. This is our ultimate test — to see that it is Hashem Who is guiding every aspect of our lives and to act accordingly."

לֹא הֶעְדִּיף הַמַּרְבֶּה וְהַמַּמְעִיט לֹא הֶחְסִיר אִישׁ לְפִי אָכְלוֹ לָקָטוּ —
Whoever took more did not have extra and whoever took less was not lacking; each one gathered according to his consumption (16:18).

"Lo Sachmod — Do Not Covet"

For forty years the Jewish nation was provided with *mahn*. During this time there was no place for monetary jealousy as everyone received the exact same amount of *mahn*. However, the prohibition of jealousy has been a test for every generation since then, and is most certainly a challenge in ours.

We live in a time of extreme consumption and consumerism. There is, *baruch Hashem*, so much available to us. Clothing, watches, jewelry, cars, vacations, food, homes, vacation homes, and so much more. We may become jealous of a friend who is building a new home, or a coworker with a new watch or expensive jacket.

This can cause a few things to occur. We can become dissatisfied with our lot; our home may suddenly seem much smaller, our car more dated, our watch less handsome, and our jacket less stylish. We may become upset at our friend, or upset at Hashem, questioning, "Why does he deserve a new house and not me?" This may lead to an overwhelming desire to live up to our neighbor's standards, or the community's, and lead one to assume unbearable financial obligations. In our tight-knit communities, the issue is intensified a thousand-fold.

The last of the *Aseres HaDibros*, the guidebook to what it means to be a Jew, is "*Lo sachmod* — Do not covet." A brief glance at the *Aseres HaDibros* makes it look as if the list started with the most important and then worked its way to the least important; the commandments and prohibitions about idolatry, Shabbos, honoring parents, and killing or stealing seem vital to the sustainability of society and the Jewish nation, and not coveting seems less so. Yet, the *sefarim* tell us that the entire Torah can be found in the *Aseres HaDibros* and that all ten of them are included, in essence, in one commandment: *Lo Sachmod* — Do not covet! (*Igra D'Kallah*, *Parashas Vayechi,* based on *Pesikta Rabbasi* 21:17). Moreover, each of the *Aseres HaDibros* corresponds to one of the Ten Days of Repentance, so "do not covet" corresponds to none other than that holiest of holy days — Yom Kippur.

The Vilna Gaon writes that all *aveiros* stem from transgressing the prohibition of coveting (*Even Shlomo* 3:2).

Jealousy stems from a lack of faith in Hashem. Like the *mahn* that was Heaven-sent in precise measure, our *parnassah* and all that we have is apportioned with Divine precision. Being content with what we are given — not coveting what is not ours — is the practical application of *emunah*. It is the essence of what it means to be a Jew. So next time we feel envious, or feel an urge to buy something or make some change in our life because that is what everyone is doing, let's gird ourselves internally with *emunah* and remember that what we have is exactly what we are Divinely ordained to have.

Rav Aharon Kotler writes, "The pursuit of materialism is only to quell the sadness that comes from the darkness of our physicality" (*Mishnas Rabbi Aharon*, Vol. 1). Thinking that materialism will provide happiness is like a dehydrated person drinking salt water. The coolness of the water on his lips initially feels good, but the salt water will intensify his thirst. Our souls crave the light, joy, and satisfaction that come from spiritual accomplishment and character growth.

Jealousy also comes from an internal lack of self-worth. When the yardstick of your success is income, the size of your home, the age of your car, or the style of your clothing, then money has total control over you. You are on a hamster wheel that goes nowhere. This prompts irrational, immature choices and provides no long-term joy. Joy and success come from being oneself, and doing what is best for oneself and one's family. Financial standing has no bearing on one's intrinsic self-worth. Rav Kook writes, "There are free men with the spirit of a slave, and slaves whose spirits are free. One who is true to his inner self is a free man, while one whose entire life is merely a stage for what is good in the eyes of others is a slave." The well-known adage enforces this idea: "Be yourself; everyone else is already taken." Contentment and happiness come from Torah study, davening, spiritual accomplishments, family, *tzedakah*, the good one does for others, and self-improvement.

> *Gerontologist Karl Pillemer, who wrote the book, "Thirty Lessons for Living," interviewed more than one thousand elderly Americans to glean lessons that can be transmitted to younger people. He writes:*
>
> *No one — not a single person out of a thousand — said*

that to be happy you should work as hard as you can to make money to buy the things you want. No one — not a single person — said it's important to be at least as wealthy as the people around you, and if you have more than they do, it's real success. Looking back on fully lived lives, these elderly people are telling us what truly matters, and it's not a life steeped in money, externalities, and things. Rather, it's a life of meaning, relationships, doing good for others, and family.

I had the pleasure of knowing Mr. Friedman from Monsey. He was a kind man who was one of the earliest Jewish builders in the tristate area. He told me that when his house was nearing completion, he spoke to his neighbor across the street, who was also building. "Listen," he told him, "the landscaping that I am going to plant in front of my house is really to impress you. And the landscaping that you are going to plant is to impress me. Let's make a deal; neither of us will do anything to impress the other. That's not what life is about."

Rabbi Abraham J. Twerski M.D. tells of two friends. When they grew up, one became the owner of a huge laundry chain, and the other became a grocer. The owner of the laundry chain was extremely wealthy but suffered from painful ulcers (for which there was no cure in those days). He could not eat anything but milk and crackers. One day, the laundry owner asked his friend how he was doing. "Not too good," answered the grocer. "I have to get up at four in the morning to go to the market, and then I have to stand on my feet until nine o'clock at night, and all I earn is enough for me to eat rye bread with radish." To which the businessman replied, "You are so lucky! You do not know what you have! If I could eat rye bread with radish, I would give you all my laundries!"

יט וַיֹּאמֶר מֹשֶׁה אֲלֵהֶם, אִישׁ אַל יוֹתֵר מִמֶּנּוּ עַד בֹּקֶר.

☙ *Hashem Has Provided Me With All That I Need*

The essence of a Yid is his *emunah* and *bitachon* (see *Makkos* 24a). He knows that Hashem orchestrates everything down to the smallest detail. Everything is determined by Hashem. Chazal tell us that whatever you have — your home, your watch, your suit, your job, your car, your everything — is meant for you, and no one can take away from you even the most insignificant thing (*Yoma* 38b). Hashem supplies each person with all the tools needed to fulfill their unprecedented mission.

It is so easy, almost automatic, for us to look at what others have and say, "Well, if I had that skill, talent, intelligence, spouse, paycheck, or those children, looks, and opportunities, then I could do what I need to do." This is wrong and dangerous. Each morning we thank Hashem because He "provided all my needs — *asah li kol tzorki.*" This is the moment to think about Hashem having given you all you need to actualize your potential (see *Alei Shur,* Vol. 1, p. 36). This is transformative. It means that at every moment of your life you are missing nothing, not spiritually, physically, or financially.

Rav Kook writes something that each of us should print out, display on our fridge, place by our desks, and read to our families on a regular basis:

"The thought that our happiness is dependent on some external factor is an offensive, evil, and foolish idea that haunts a person and arouses all the bad *middos* that are the basis of evil — forgetting Hashem and all His goodness, light, salvation, wisdom, *chesed*, and might. Therefore, honest people are always happy, as it says (*Tehillim* 32:11), 'Exult, righteous ones, and all those of upright heart, sing praise' " (*Oros HaKodesh* 3:105).

We need not wait until we have the house of our dreams,

19 ***Then Moshe said to them, "Let no one leave over from it until morning."***

the children of our dreams, or millions in the bank. At this moment, it is in us to be happy and enjoy our successes and our ability to be close to Hashem. When we feel pangs of dissatisfaction or unhappiness, it is often our *neshamah* that is desperately crying out for fulfillment.

> *World-famous violinist Itzhak Perlman was performing when one of his violin's strings snapped. The sound of the snap was audible to all; the conductor ceased his motions, the orchestra stopped playing, and all eyes were on Itzhak. He closed his eyes, lifted his violin — which now had only three strings — and signaled to the conductor that he was ready to continue. He played stunning music with just three strings, a highly improbable feat. When he concluded, the audience rose to its feet with deafening applause. After a few minutes, Itzhak said to the crowd, "A true artist is someone who can make beautiful music* ***with what he has****."*

וַיֹּאמֶר מֹשֶׁה אֲלֵהֶם אִישׁ אַל יוֹתֵר מִמֶּנּוּ עַד בֹּקֶר —
Moshe said to them, "Let no one leave over from it until morning" (16:19).

◆§ *Bitachon: The Antidote to Worry*

Bnei Yisrael were instructed to finish all the *mahn* and not leave over any for the following day; so each day, they looked to Hashem for sustenance and learned to trust and constantly rely on Him. This paved the way for all future generations to place their trust in Hashem (*Abarbanel*).

Worry, fear, stress, and anxiety, are at an all-time high, and many of these stressors are directly related to money. How can we combat this? How can we enjoy a more joyful, serene existence? The *Chovos HaLevavos* tells us that the *only* way to be free from worry and anxiety is to trust in Hashem. That is the singular vehicle for a worry-free life. More money in the bank, a larger house, more clothing — none of these equal less worry. *Bitachon* — living with Hashem and trusting in Him — is the only means of attaining *simchah* and calm.

Hashem led the Jewish nation through the Wilderness on a forty-year journey and provided them with the miraculous *mahn*. This is the prototype, showing us how Hashem has and will continue to provide for His children under any and all circumstances. Hence, there is no reason to worry. Place your trust in Hashem (*Rav Hirsch Commentary on Chumash* 16:3).

One of the most common physiological symptoms of anxiety is tension in the back and shoulders. Dovid HaMelech tells us how to deal with it: "Throw your burden on Hashem and He will sustain you" (*Tehillim* 55:23). The weight of worry that sits on your shoulders and makes your mind circle endlessly around the same dilemmas — give it to Hashem. Take a deep breath, release the tension from your shoulders, clear your mind, and say, "Hashem, here are my worries, this is what is concerning me, this is what I need Your help with. Please take it from me. Hashem, please, I'm trusting in You. Help me and guide me."

The *Kedushas Levi* (*Beshalach*) writes that when one has *bitachon* that Hashem will provide for him, that creates a flood of abundance. But the opposite is true as well. Worrying about *parnassah* creates a barrier. True *emunah*, *emunah* that's been internalized, is trusting that I, as a child of Hashem, will be taken care of by my loving Father.

Rav Moshe of Kobrin explains the verse, "*Atzabeihem kesef v'zahav, maasei yedei adam* — Their idols are silver and gold, the work of man's hands" (*Tehillim* 115:4), as follows: "*Atzabeihem* — their idols" is from the root *etzev*, sadness. People are sad and anxious when they think that "*kesef v'zahav maasei yedei adam* — gold and silver (*parnassah*) is a human product." They worry, "What will be, what will happen, how will I afford this and that? The markets are so volatile, interest rates are so high, inflation is ruining us." Worry and anxiety are the lot of those who think that *parnassah* is in their dominion. But fortunate, blessed, and calm is the one who places his full trust in Hashem. He has nothing to worry about; he has a Father in Heaven Who controls it all.

In a letter to a student struggling with parnassah, the Bobover Rebbe, Rav Ben Tzion Halberstam, wrote, "From the words of your letters I sense that your heart is filled with concern about the future. Although it is the responsibility of man to make appropriate efforts to provide for his family, he is not permitted to worry, which accomplishes nothing. Worrying has never generated any amount of money. On the contrary, it causes one to be confused and misdirected. Making an effort to earn a living is avodas hakodesh — it is doing the will of Hashem — but worry is not permissible."

A huge fire broke out in Rav Avraham Genachowsky's apartment building. Everyone was evacuated safely, and they all stood watching the flames leap from the windows and the firemen working to douse the fire. Many students gathered around Rav Genachowsky, the venerable rosh yeshivah of Tchebin in Yerushalayim, offering their help and support. The rav was smiling and serene, even though his apartment, home to all his family's possessions, sefarim, and hundreds upon hundreds of precious Torah novella and notebooks, was being destroyed.

A student asked how the rav could be so calm, and not בִּדְאָגָה*, filled with worry. Rav Genachowsky replied, "Worried? The word* בִּדְאָגָה *is mentioned in the Shulchan Aruch in only one place, where it deals with the order of cutting the fingernails on the right hand (*בדאג״ה*, fingers 2,4,1,3,5; Orach Chaim 260, Rema). Apart from that, there is no mention anywhere in halachah of the word "worry" — so I am not worried!"*

The next day, the rav and his family were allowed to enter their apartment and, miracle of miracles, the apartment was in good condition, despite the smoke, fire, and water. The rav's notebooks and sefarim were in excellent condition. There was truly no reason for worry (Vayomer Hineni, p. 207).

◆§ *Bitachon: Relying on Hashem*

When asked to describe *bitachon*, the Vilna Gaon cited the verse, "I calmed my soul like a nursing child on its mother... Yisrael, look to Hashem" (*Tehillim* 131:2–3). A nursing baby is totally content and at peace, with no worries about where his next meal will come from. This is the level of *bitachon* one should strive to attain: complete reliance on Hashem, faith that makes one serene and unworried about the future (*Divrei Eliyahu, Tehillim* 131; see also *Malbim*).

The more a child nurses, the more milk is produced; the less a baby nurses, the less milk is produced. Rav Pinchas HaLevi Horowitz, the author of *Sefer Haflaah*, uses this analogy to explain the seemingly redundant phrases in the verse, "Blessed is the man who trusts in Hashem; Hashem will be his trust" (*Yirmiyah* 17:7). He explains that the verse is telling us that Hashem's protection over us comes directly from the level and depth of our *bitachon* in Him. The more we trust in Hashem, the more Hashem protects us and provides for us. "Blessed is the man who trusts in Hashem," and according to his level of *bitachon,* "Hashem will be his trust" (*Panim Yafos, Shemos* 16:6).

Sefer HaIkarim writes something so amazing about the power of *bitachon*: "Hoping and trusting in Hashem is greater than all the praises in the world with which one can praise Hashem! This is why Dovid HaMelech writes, 'As for me, I will always hope, and I will add to Your praises' (*Tehillim* 71:14). Trusting in Hashem is the greatest song we can sing to Him. It is like the most elevated sacrifice offered in the Beis HaMikdash!"

Dovid HaMelech's comparison of a person's level of trust in Hashem to that of a nursing baby can help us better understand our relationship with Hashem and what it means to have *bitachon*. A baby depends totally on his mother. He relies on her to change him, bathe him, feed him, and do whatever else is necessary. Our reliance on Hashem is also absolute; one who has complete *bitachon* knows he is totally dependent on Hashem to supply him with all his needs. Moreover, a nursing baby has no desire for food other than milk; he is totally satisfied with the milk provided by his mother. The same is true of one who has *bitachon* in Hashem. He has no desire for more than Hashem provides for him. He is content and satisfied with his lot, knowing that this is what is best for him (*Beis HaLevi, Chovas HaBitachon*).

A young man came to Rav Chaim Halberstam, the Rebbe of Sanz, with a worried look on his face. "Rebbe, I need help. I am worried about how I will be able to support my family."

The Rebbe responded, "There are three times when a person cries: The first is when he emerges from his mother's womb — he cries to Hashem, 'Hashem, until now You miraculously supported me in my mother's womb. Who will support me now?' Hashem tells him, 'Do not worry; Just as I miraculously supported you while you were in utero, I will support you now as well.' And Hashem miraculously supplies the baby's mother with the milk he needs, containing the exact nutrients that he needs to thrive.

"The second time a child cries is when his mother weans him. He cries to Hashem, 'Hashem, who will feed me now? Who will provide for me?' Hashem responds, 'I have supported you until now and I will continue to do so.'

"The third time he cries is under the chuppah. 'Hashem, until now my parents supported me. Who will support me now?' Hashem tells him, 'Do not worry, My child. It is I Who gave your father the means to support you until now. Just like I cared for you and supported you in your mother's womb, while you were nursing, and in your parents' home, I will continue to care for you now. Do not worry, My child.'"

כ וְלֹא שָׁמְעוּ אֶל מֹשֶׁה, וַיּוֹתִרוּ אֲנָשִׁים מִמֶּנּוּ עַד בֹּקֶר וַיָּרֻם תּוֹלָעִים וַיִּבְאַשׁ, וַיִּקְצֹף עֲלֵהֶם מֹשֶׁה.

— וַיִּקְצֹף עֲלֵהֶם מֹשֶׁה
Moshe became angry at them (16:20).

Anger and Its Downside

Moshe was angry at the Jews who put aside *mahn* for the next day, in defiance of Hashem's orders. Chazal tell us that because of his anger, Moshe forgot to let Klal Yisrael know that a double portion of *mahn* would fall on Friday (*Vayikra Rabbah* 13:1).

Anger has many detrimental side effects: It causes rash behavior, poor judgment, and all too often, irrevocable physical, monetary, and emotional pain to others. Families, spouses, companies, relationships, neighbors, and communities have been ripped apart due to poor anger management. When an unpleasant situation involves money, anger and tempers intensify one-hundred-fold.

Chazal teach us that when one becomes angry, it is as if he served idolatry (*Shabbos* 105b; *Rambam, Hilchos Dei'os* 2:3). The Baal HaTanya writes that anger comes from a lack of *emunah* in Hashem (*Igros HaKodesh* 25). I am angry because I believe that *you* wronged me, *you* hurt me, *you* caused me a loss — when in truth Hashem is controlling everything. When I live with Hashem and understand and internalize that He is the One Who is in control of all aspects of my life, there is no place for anger at others. Therefore, Chazal compare anger to serving a foreign god, because one who becomes angry excludes himself from seeing Hashem as the true orchestrator. The *Meor Einayim* writes that just as one is prohibited from benefiting from idolatry, one must not benefit from anything that comes from anger.

We all want to be close to Hashem. We want Hashem to love

[20] ***But they did not heed Moshe, and some men left part of it over until morning and it bred worms and became putrid, and Moshe became angry at them.***

us. How do we gain Hashem's love? The Gemara (*Pesachim* 113a) tells us that Hashem loves one who does not get angry! Speaking calmly to all those we encounter (and most certainly our immediate family), and working on ourselves to temper our anger, is the catalyst for Hashem to love us.

The students of Rav Adda bar Ahavah asked him what he had done to be granted a long life. He responded that he never became angry at his household. His home was warm and serene (*Taanis* 20b). *Sefer Chassidim* (72) writes that controlling one's anger is the most beautiful and elevated *middah* of all the *middos*! A person never loses by not responding with anger (*Sefer HaYashar L'Rabbeinu Tam*).

Reb Shabsi Frankel, a Holocaust survivor, established a kollel that was dedicated to reprinting the Rambam and indexing his myriads of sources and textual variations. Today we have the Shabsi Frankel Rambam edition, which is the edition found in any beis midrash, shul, or home in the world.

One day, Reb Shabsi and another talmid chacham were poring over an extremely rare and valuable manuscript of the Rambam that he had purchased for an exorbitant sum after much investigation and hard work. As they were working, his fellow scholar's coffee spilled on the priceless manuscript, causing an immense financial and historical loss. Reb Shabsi got up, went to the kitchen, and returned a few minutes later with another cup of coffee. "Here is another cup of coffee for you," he said.

What restraint! What tremendous ability to control his anger!

Some say that it was because of this story that the

כא וַיִּלְקְטוּ אֹתוֹ בַּבֹּקֶר בַּבֹּקֶר,
אִישׁ כְּפִי אָכְלוֹ, וְחַם הַשֶּׁמֶשׁ וְנָמָס.
כב וַיְהִי בַּיּוֹם הַשִּׁשִּׁי, לָקְטוּ לֶחֶם מִשְׁנֶה,
שְׁנֵי הָעֹמֶר לָאֶחָד, וַיָּבֹאוּ כָּל נְשִׂיאֵי הָעֵדָה,
וַיַּגִּידוּ לְמֹשֶׁה.

Frankel Rambam enjoyed such enormous success and widespread acceptance (Devarim Areivim, Vol. 4, p. 280).

Rav Ben Tzion Kook was traveling in a taxi with a few students. When they entered the cab, they gave the driver the address of their destination, which was only about ten minutes away. The cab driver smiled and started the meter. Thinking that the students were not familiar with the way, the cab driver took a circuitous route to make a few extra shekels. The bachurim, who knew the route well and saw exactly what the driver was doing, became upset and were about to accuse the driver of stealing from them. But Rav Ben Tzion told them to restrain their anger and not say anything. "The driver is a good man and knows the best way to get us to our destination," he said.

When they reached their destination, the meter showed fifty shekels, but the driver said, "I went a longer way than I needed to, so only pay me forty-five shekels."

Rav Ben Tzion said, "No, I am paying you the full fifty. Your car was clean and the ride was pleasant, you deserve the full fifty."

The driver said, "You should know, we have three children and my wife wants to send them to a chareidi school, but I refused, wanting them to stay in the state-sponsored schools. Now that I see how you behaved — even when I wronged you, you were so kind and did not

[21] ***They would gather it every morning, everyone according to his consumption, and when the sunlight grew hot it would melt.***
[22] ***It happened on the sixth day that they gathered a double measure of food, two omers for each one; and all the leaders of the congregation came and told Moshe.***

get angry at me — I agree with my wife that it is time to send our children to the chareidi schools."

"Look what we acquired with a mere five shekels and by restraining our anger: the neshamos of three Jewish children and their future progeny!" Rav Ben Tzion told his students.

לֶחֶם מִשְׁנֶה —
A double measure of food (16:22).

☙ *Lechem Mishneh*

As a remembrance of the double portion of *mahn* that fell on Friday in honor of Shabbos, the halachah says to recite the *berachah* of *Hamotzi* at each Shabbos meal on two loaves of bread (*Shabbos* 117b). The challah is likewise covered both on top, with a challah cover, and on the bottom, by the challah board, to recall the dew that protected the *mahn* from top and bottom (*Rashi* 16:7; *Tur*; *Shulchan Aruch, Orach Chaim* 271:9).

The *Tur* cites another, seemingly unrelated, reason for covering the *challos*. Halachah mandates that *berachos* be recited in a certain sequence; the *berachah* on bread is made before the *berachah* on wine. Since we change the order on Shabbos and make a *berachah* on wine before bread, in order to avoid "embarrassing" the bread, we cover it when reciting Kiddush on wine. The idea is that showing sensitivity toward an inanimate object, such as bread, trains us to be more sensitive in our interpersonal relationships.

כג וַיֹּאמֶר אֲלֵהֶם, הוּא אֲשֶׁר דִּבֶּר יהוה, שַׁבָּתוֹן שַׁבַּת קֹדֶשׁ לַיהוה מָחָר, אֵת אֲשֶׁר תֹּאפוּ אֵפוּ, וְאֵת אֲשֶׁר תְּבַשְּׁלוּ בַּשֵּׁלוּ, וְאֵת כָּל הָעֹדֵף הַנִּיחוּ לָכֶם לְמִשְׁמֶרֶת עַד הַבֹּקֶר.

The *mahn* taught us to rely only on Hashem, Who is the sole Decider of what we get and what we do not. The people around us — bosses, employers, the markets, clients, customers, vendors, and others — are mere messengers carrying out Hashem's will. When we understand this and internalize it (no easy feat by any stretch of the imagination), there is no reason for anger, jealousy, hatred, *lashon hara*, annoyance, or disputes. When there is harmony, the Shechinah dwells among us, which is a conduit for *parnassah*. There is no greater receptacle for *berachah* than peace (*Mishnah Uktzin* 3:12). Discord, on the other hand, diminishes the conduit for *parnassah*. The Shelah writes, "One disagreement destroys one hundred people's livelihoods" (*Yoma* §197).

When Yosef's brothers asked their father for permission to bring Binyamin to Mitzrayim, Yaakov said, "*Vayeitzei ha'echad mei'iti va'omar, 'Ach tarof toraf'* — One went away from me and I said, 'He (or, alternatively, his food) has been torn to pieces'" (*Bereishis* 44:28). The Chasam Sofer interprets the verse this way: "One went away" — the unity was gone — and "his food has been torn to pieces." When the *achdus* dissipates, one's sustenance is torn to bits. One disagreement destroys a hundred livelihoods.

Baron Rothschild once made a gala kiddush in honor of a family simchah. Hundreds of people were invited, including the gedolei hador. To the surprise of many, the tables were only set with Kiddush cups and wine. There didn't seem to be either bread or other mezonos on the table, which is mandated by halachah.

[23] He said to them: "This is what Hashem spoke of; tomorrow is a day of rest, a holy Shabbos to Hashem; what you wish to bake, bake; and what you wish to cook, cook; and whatever is left over, put away for yourselves in safekeeping until the morning."

Baron Rothschild made his way to his seat, next to Rav Chaim Ozer Grodzinski, took his Kiddush cup, made Kiddush, and drank. To the crowd's amazement, while still holding the becher, he recited the berachah of Mezonos and bit off a piece of the cup. Lo and behold, the Kiddush cup was edible! After this the baron honored Rav Chaim Ozer with saying Kiddush. Rav Chaim Ozer filled the cup but then paused for some time, deep in thought. After several moments, he lifted the cup, made Kiddush, and then said "...borei minei mezonos" on the cup itself.

After the kiddush, several of Rav Chaim Ozer's students asked why the rav had paused before making Kiddush; what was the rav thinking about at that moment? "I was caught up in a halachic quandary," Rav Chaim Ozer explained. "Halachah mandates that bread, as well as mezonos according to many opinions, needs to be covered when one makes Kiddush, since the berachos of Hamotzi and Mezonos are to be recited before the berachah of HaGafen, and we don't want to 'embarrass' the foods that are more significant than the wine. All the more so when I am holding the mezonos in my hand while I make Kiddush! But then I thought, 'If I do not make Kiddush, the Baron will be embarrassed, and I decided that it is better for the mezonos to be embarrassed than for the Yid'" (Be'er HaParashah, Devarim, p. 25; Kovetz Yeshurun 5672; see also V'haarev Na, Vol. 1, p. 41, for the halachic ramifications of making Kiddush on such a cup).

כד וַיַּנִּיחוּ אֹתוֹ עַד הַבֹּקֶר כַּאֲשֶׁר צִוָּה מֹשֶׁה,
וְלֹא הִבְאִישׁ, וְרִמָּה לֹא הָיְתָה בּוֹ.
כה וַיֹּאמֶר מֹשֶׁה, אִכְלֻהוּ הַיּוֹם, כִּי שַׁבָּת
הַיּוֹם לַיהוה, הַיּוֹם לֹא תִמְצָאֻהוּ בַּשָּׂדֶה.

אִכְלֻהוּ הַיּוֹם כִּי שַׁבָּת הַיּוֹם לַה׳ — *Eat it today for today is a Shabbos to Hashem* (16:25).

⊛§ *Fish on Shabbos*

There is a nearly universal custom to eat fish at the Shabbos meals (*Shulchan Aruch HaRav* 242:7; see *Bnei Yissaschar, Maamar Shabbos* 1:11). In addition to the central reason — that fish is a prestigious food, the eating of which honors the Shabbos — other reasons are given. The Apter Rebbe explains that the *mahn* tasted like anything one desired, except for fish (or onions or garlic, which is why many eat these foods on Shabbos as well; *Taamei HaMinhagim* 367). By eating fish we honor Shabbos with every possible taste, even those that were not found in the *mahn*.

Fish do not have eyelids; their eyes are always open. This is a form of *tefillah* for Hashem to always have His eyes on us, never removing His *hashgachah* from upon us even for a moment (*Ramak*, *Tefillah L'Moshe*).

Fish are not susceptible to the evil eye, as they live below the surface of the water, hidden from human sight. We eat fish and daven that we, too, should not be affected by the evil eye.

The Biala Rebbe pointed out that the very first course we eat at the Shabbos *seudah* is fish. Fish make no audible sounds; we, too, should work on keeping quiet, as the Mishnah tells us, "I have found nothing better for a person than silence" (*Avos* 1:17). The Kotzker Rebbe used to say, "Silence is the most powerful of voices."

[24]*They put it away until the morning,*
as Moshe commanded; and it did not become
putrid and there were no worms in it.
[25]*Then Moshe said, "Eat it today*
for today is a Shabbos to Hashem;
today you will not find it in the field.

The *berachah* that Yaakov gave Yosef was that his children should multiply like the fish in the sea (*Bereishis* 48:16). Rav Kook explains that this was because fish live in their own underwater ecosystem, totally disconnected from the world above them. A Jew, likewise, lives in This World ("*b'kerev ha'aretz*") but remains totally separate, elevated beyond and impervious to the world around them.

Rav Itzikel of Pshevorsk explained that salmon (and lox) are often the fish of choice for Shabbos because salmon swim upstream against the current. The job of a Jew is to not just follow the current norms of society but to do what the Torah demands. The Jew is exhorted to swim against the current.

◆§ *Spending for Mitzvos*

Rav Hirsch (16:5) says that the double portion of *mahn* that fell for Shabbos shows us that obeying the Torah never causes a financial loss. On the contrary, Hashem never asks us to do something without providing the *berachah* that enables us to do it. Refraining from work on Shabbos brings about the *berachah* of a double portion of *mahn* on Friday. Refraining from working the land in Eretz Yisrael during *shemittah* generates the *berachah* of the sixth year producing enough for three years. Adhering to the Jewish lifestyle entails expenses and imposes restrictions on our work schedules, but Hashem provides and showers on us the *berachah* that enables us to do His will.

The Gemara tells us that the amount of money a person will earn is decided each year on Rosh Hashanah (*Beitzah* 16a). Expenses for Torah, Shabbos, Rosh Chodesh, and Yom Tov are not included in this amount (a mnemonic is תשר״י, Tishrei — תורה, שבת, ראש חודש, יום טוב, **T**orah, **Sh**abbos, **R**osh Chodesh, **Y**om Tov). Hashem repays what is spent on those.

The word "שָׁלֵם, complete" forms the acrostic of שבת לימוד מועד, **Sh**abbos, *limud* (learning), and *moed* (Yom Tov) — because one remains financially whole even when expending funds for these. The Rishonim tell us that the same is true for *tzedakah* and mitzvos. One never loses from spending on mitzvos.

וַיֹּאמֶר מֹשֶׁה אִכְלֻהוּ הַיּוֹם —
Then Moshe said, "Eat it today" (16:25).

⁂ *Today Is the Day!*

Rav Tzvi Hirsch of Rimanov translates "*ichluhu hayom* — eat it today" as "eat today"; consume today, get all you can out of today, do not wait for tomorrow, because "today is the day that will not be found [again]."

The Torah writes, "וְעַתָּה — *V'atah...* — Now, Yisrael, what does Hashem, your God, ask of you?" (*Devarim* 10:12). Chazal tell us that the word "*v'atah* — now" signifies *teshuvah* (*Bereishis Rabbah* 21:6). The Chofetz Chaim asks, "What about the word '*v'atah*' signifies *teshuvah*?" He explains that the *yetzer hara's* primary tactic is to convince a person not to take charge of his life *now* (*Ahavas Chesed*). The *yetzer hara* is the procrastinator within us. It asks us, "Today to work on yourself? Today to daven better? Today to pick up the phone and apologize to someone you hurt? You are young, you can address this at a different time. You are so busy now."

The Torah writes, "*Mipnei seivah takum* — Rise before an old person" (*Vayikra* 19:32). Before you become an old person, rise! (*Raya Mehemna,* Vol. 2, p. 122). Before you get old, before it gets too hard to change, rise up and make changes.

Do not delay! Maturity comes from realizing that *now* is the best time to change.

The Mishnah says, "One should not say, 'When I have time I will learn,' because maybe you will never have time" (*Avos* 2:5). The Kotzker Rebbe explained the Mishnah this way: Do not say, "When I have time I will learn," because maybe you were sent to This World to learn when you do not have time. Hashem wants you to study Torah when it is hard, when you are pressured and have no time (*Emes VeEmunah* 4). That is what is precious to Hashem.

The first step to self-improvement is recognizing that the present moment is the time to step up to the plate and work on yourself. *Now* may be a challenging time. You may be exceptionally busy; you may be dealing with a specific struggle. But the first step to *teshuvah* is saying to yourself, "Enough! I am drawing a line in the sand and will address this issue *now*."

"You are standing *today*, all of you, before Hashem, your God" (*Devarim* 29:9). The *Sfas Emes* (§634) explains that right now, *today,* is the prime time for *teshuvah*. Today is the day to start changing. There is no greater feeling of accomplishment than taking the first strides of self-improvement and growth. Do not delay. There is no better time than the present.

> *A financial advisor told me, "I have the privilege of guiding my clients in retirement planning. A pattern I have picked up on is that many people have lofty goals for when they retire. 'When I retire, I will start learning daf yomi'; 'When I retire, I will commit more time to learning'; 'When I retire, I will start to daven with a minyan'; 'When I retire, I want to spend more quality time with my wife, children, and grandchildren'; 'When I retire, I want to volunteer at this chesed organization or that one.' So many people delay doing what they want to do until they reach retirement and are free from the rigors of work. But what often happens is that their dreams do not come to fruition because of health, financial, or family issues. Moreover, changing a habit after sixty years is challenging.*

כו שֵׁשֶׁת יָמִים תִּלְקְטֻהוּ, וּבַיּוֹם הַשְּׁבִיעִי
שַׁבָּת, לֹא יִהְיֶה בּוֹ. כז וַיְהִי בַּיּוֹם הַשְּׁבִיעִי,
יָצְאוּ מִן הָעָם לִלְקֹט, וְלֹא מָצָאוּ.

"So let me give an idea for anyone at any age: Build retirement into your work life. If one of your retirement goals is to learn more or have a steady chavrusa, then schedule a small amount of additional time for Torah study into your day or week now. Do not wait. If one of your retirement goals is to spend more time with your family, then make a schedule where you do this already. Build retirement into your work week. Schedule a monthly outing with each of your children. Take a day off once a month to go out with your wife. Why wait thirty years to spend time with your family when you can do it now and reap enormous, compounding rewards? If increased chesed and volunteering is something on your retirement bucket list, see what you can do today in some limited capacity for the project or organization you choose. As you get older, you can add more and more time to these dreams. Retirement can start when you are twenty-five. Build retirement into your work life."

— **וַיְהִי בַּיּוֹם הַשְּׁבִיעִי יָצְאוּ מִן הָעָם לִלְקֹט וְלֹא מָצָאוּ**
But it happened on the seventh day that some of the people went out to gather, and they did not find (16:27).

⟫ *Hakaras Hatov*

Moshe told Bnei Yisrael that a double portion of *mahn* would fall on Friday, because none would descend on Shabbos. That Friday night, Dasan and Aviram scattered *mahn* all over the camp, to undermine Moshe. But by morning, the birds had eaten all of it. Because of this, many have the custom of feeding the birds before Shabbos *Parashas Beshalach,* to show gratitude (*Taamei HaMinhagim;* see *Pardes Yosef,* p. 128).

[26] You are to gather it for six days; but the seventh day is Shabbos, there will be none on it." [27] But it happened on the seventh day that some of the people went out to gather, and they did not find.

Hakaras hatov, expressing sincere appreciation, is a foundational *middah* of a Jew. There are literally endless opportunities to show appreciation to others, from your spouse, parents, and neighbors, to that day's *shaliach tzibbur* and *baal korei*, someone at work who did a good job, the mailman, the *maggid shiur*, and Hatzalah volunteers.

The Alter of Kelm, Rav Simcha Zissel Ziv, would stand in his doorway for several moments each Friday night when returning home from shul. He spent the time admiring the beautiful Shabbos table, laden with all the different delicious Shabbos foods. He only went inside when he felt enough appreciation for his wife to express his *hakaras hatov* wholeheartedly.

> *When Shlomie Gross's youngest daughter was engaged, Shlomie went through her elementary school, personally thanking each of his daughter's teachers who had had a positive impact on her life. He understood that his daughter's development and growth was the result of the efforts of dozens of teachers and school staff, and he wanted to show his appreciation to each and every one of them (Shlomie!, p. 251).*

> *Rav Nosson Tzvi Finkel, the rosh yeshivah of Mir, suffered from debilitating Parkinson's, but did not allow the disease to stand in the way of building one of the world's largest Torah empires.*
>
> *A Mir student asked the rosh yeshivah if he could officiate at his wedding. Rav Nosson Tzvi gladly agreed. However, a few days before the wedding, a member of*

the rosh yeshivah's household phoned the chassan to tell him that the rosh yeshivah was too weak to come to the wedding, so the chassan asked another rosh yeshivah to officiate.

On the day of his wedding, the chassan attended Rav Nosson Tzvi's lecture. Hours later, in the middle of the wedding, the chassan was surprised to see none other than Rav Nosson Tzvi himself enter the hall! He ran to thank the rosh yeshivah and asked him why he had troubled himself to come when he was so weak. "I am extremely weak," Rav Nosson Tzvi admitted, "but when I saw how you exerted yourself to come to my shiur today, on the day of your wedding, I wanted to reciprocate and show my appreciation by coming here, despite the extreme difficulty involved!" (Bechol Nafshecha, p. 164).

Reb Eliyahu Tatel always brought a cake to the daf yomi siyum in Rav Shlomo Gissinger's shul. After one siyum, Rav Gissinger called to tell the Tatel girls that the cake they had baked for their siyum was so delicious that he wanted the recipe for his wife.

◆§ *Kibbud Av Va'eim: The Root of Hakaras Hatov*

Hakaras hatov is central to our relationship with Hashem. It is also the root of the mitzvah to honor one's father and mother (*Sefer HaChinuch* §33). One might think that we are obligated to honor our parents because of all the material support they provide: food, money, shelter, clothing, etc., and that once parents no longer provide all that, the obligation to respect and honor them is diminished. That is incorrect! The Ksav Sofer proves how mistaken such thinking is. After the Jews left Egypt, all their physical needs were provided miraculously by Hashem. They had *mahn* to eat, clothing that grew with the person and never wore out, and the *Ananei HaKavod* that provided protection from the elements. Yet Chazal tell us that at that point in time, even before the Torah was given, Hashem commanded the Jewish nation to honor their parents (*Sanhedrin* 56b). This demonstrates that honoring and respecting parents is an absolute obligation, irrespective of the parents' ability to provide material assistance for their children (*Ksav Sofer, Devarim* 5:16).

◆§ *Inviting Hashem Into Our Lives: The Ultimate Berachah*

The Gemara states that when one honors his father and mother, Hashem says, "It is as if I am dwelling among you and you are honoring Me" (*Kiddushin* 30b). We all want the presence of Hashem to dwell among us, as this is an incomparable *berachah*. When we honor our parents, we infuse our homes and our lives with the Shechinah; we open the door to allow Hashem to reside among us.

The *Meshech Chochmah* (*Shemos* 28:9) asks why the *Kodesh HaKodashim* was placed in Binyamin HaTzaddik's territory. What did he do to warrant the honor of hosting the holiest place on earth? He explains, Binyamin was not involved in selling Yosef and so did not inflict pain on his father. That was enough to give him the special distinction of providing a home for the *Kodesh HaKodashim*.

At times it may be difficult to honor parents properly. Unfortunately, sometimes parents have their own mental or emotional or even physical health issues, and they are unable to give their children what they need. Some adult children feel their parents were not there for them when they were young. As parents age, it can be even more difficult. One might think that in exceptionally challenging situations, one is not obligated to honor his parents. To dispel this notion, Rav Chaim Palagi explains why the Torah writes, "Honor your father and mother, as Hashem, your God, commanded you" (*Devarim* 5:16). He asks why the Torah adds the words "as Hashem,

כח וַיֹּאמֶר יהוה אֶל מֹשֶׁה, עַד אָנָה מֵאַנְתֶּם
לִשְׁמֹר מִצְוֹתַי וְתוֹרֹתָי.
כט רְאוּ כִּי יהוה נָתַן לָכֶם הַשַּׁבָּת,

your God, commanded you," and explains that this mitzvah is not an interpersonal mitzvah, a *bein adam lachaveiro* mitzvah; it is a mitzvah *bein adam laMakom*, between man and Hashem. It is like observing Shabbos and putting on tefillin. It must be done even if it is hard.

עַד אָנָה מֵאַנְתֶּם לִשְׁמֹר מִצְוֹתַי וְתוֹרֹתָי. רְאוּ כִּי ה׳ נָתַן לָכֶם הַשַּׁבָּת — ***How long will you refuse to observe My commandments and My teachings? See — because Hashem has given you the Shabbos*** (16:28,29).

❧ *Torah Study on Shabbos*

The Torah was given on Shabbos (*Shabbos* 86b). Shabbos, the day our minds are (hopefully) clear from the hustle and bustle of work, we dedicate time to Torah study. This is especially important for those who work all week (*Shulchan Aruch, Orach Chaim* 290:2). The Midrash writes, "The Torah said to Hashem, 'Hashem, when the Yidden enter Eretz Yisrael, this one will run to his vineyard and this one to his field (to work their fields, since they no longer have *mahn*). What will be with me? Who will study Torah when everyone is busy working?' Hashem said to the Torah, 'Do not worry, I have a *zug*, match, that I will pair with you, and its name is Shabbos. On Shabbos the Yidden are not working and can study Torah'" (*Tur* 290).

Shabbos's marriage partner is the Torah itself! On Shabbos, Hashem provides special assistance in Torah studies (*Sfas Emes, Yisro*). The *neshamah yeseirah* that we are given on Shabbos provides us with extra capacity for concentrating

[28] *Hashem said to Moshe: "How long will you refuse to observe My commandments and My teachings?*
[29] *See — because Hashem has given you the Shabbos,*

on Torah study and spiritual matters (*Shelah, Succah, Ner Mitzvah* 38).

The Ben Ish Chai writes that *divrei Torah* learned on Shabbos have one thousand times more worth than Torah learned during the week!

Rav Hillel Kalamai said, in the name of his rebbi, the Chasam Sofer, that it may be challenging for people who work to find a set time to study Torah, but when it comes to Shabbos, there is no excuse. He sees the verses of Parashas HaMahn as a dialogue. Hashem asks each of us, "How long will you refuse to keep My mitzvos and My Torah?" To those who answer, "Hashem, I'm busy working and supporting my family," the Torah responds, "See that Hashem has given you the Shabbos," a day of rest and joy that can be spent immersed in Torah study.

Rav Yissocher Frand knows a family of outstanding *talmidei chachamim* whose father was a hard worker employed in a simple job. He asked the sons what was it that inspired them to dedicate themselves to a life of Torah. The sons explained that their father spent long and strenuous hours at work. On Shabbos, he was exhausted. But he did not go to sleep or relax with a newspaper on the recliner after the meal. He took out a Chumash, read a *pasuk*, and fell asleep. He'd wake up a few minutes later, read a *Rashi*, and again his eyes would close. This went on for hours until he completed the *parashah*. "This was the sight we grew up with," they said, "the sight of our father dedicating himself to Torah despite his exhaustion."

עַל כֵּן הוּא נֹתֵן לָכֶם בַּיּוֹם הַשִּׁשִּׁי לֶחֶם יוֹמָיִם, שְׁבוּ אִישׁ תַּחְתָּיו, אַל יֵצֵא אִישׁ מִמְּקֹמוֹ בַּיּוֹם הַשְּׁבִיעִי.

רְאוּ כִּי ה׳ נָתַן לָכֶם הַשַּׁבָּת עַל כֵּן הוּא נֹתֵן לָכֶם בַּיּוֹם הַשִּׁשִּׁי לֶחֶם יוֹמָיִם
— See — because Hashem has given you the Shabbos, therefore He provides you on the sixth day with food for two days (16:29).

◆ *Shabbos*

Chazal debate exactly when Bnei Yisrael were commanded to observe Shabbos (see *Tosafos, Shabbos* 87b). Was it in Marah, or at this time, in Alush, when the nation began to receive the *mahn*? The Sfas Emes explains as follows: In Marah, the *laws* of Shabbos were given — the do's and don'ts. In Alush, when the *mahn* fell, they were informed of the *gift* that is Shabbos; "I have a good gift in My treasury and Shabbos is its name" (*Shabbos* 10b). Gifts are given with an *ayin yafah*, a spirit of total giving (*Bava Basra* 65a). The Sfas Emes, in the name of his grandfather, the Chiddushei HaRim, explains that when Hashem gave us Shabbos, which is a gift, He gave it with an *ayin yafah,* a benevolent spirit that tells us that the Shabbos is a gift of *berachah* and plenty (*Beshalach* 5743).

Shabbos is our expression of trust in Hashem and internalizing through action (or lack thereof) that Hashem is in total control of our lives, including our finances.

> *Kivi Bernhard is an internationally known business speaker and the author of Leopardology, a book on business strategy. Kivi received a phone call inviting him to give the opening address at a Microsoft conference that was to be attended by hundreds of industry leaders, vendors, and Microsoft CEO Bill Gates himself. This*

therefore He provides you on the sixth day with food for two days. Let every man remain in his place; let no man leave his place on the seventh day."

was a huge, once-in-a-lifetime opportunity for Kivi. But Kivi turned it down, because it was going to be held on Shabbos.

A few minutes later Kivi received a call from John, one of Microsoft's senior vice presidents, who offered to double and even triple Kivi's speaking fee. Kivi responded politely, "John, it's not about the money, it's about Sabbath observance."

Microsoft ended up changing the conference to Sunday so Kivi could deliver the opening remarks!

A few months later, John called Kivi and told him, "I was just with Bill Gates on his private jet, along with several other top Microsoft executives. We were discussing the conference and how you, Kivi, refused to speak on your Sabbath. Even though I threw money at you, you didn't budge, due to your Sabbath observance. When Mr. Gates heard about it, he said, 'That's what happens when you have something money can't buy.'"

Shabbos is an invaluable gift from Hashem.

שְׁבוּ אִישׁ תַּחְתָּיו אַל יֵצֵא אִישׁ מִמְּקֹמוֹ בַּיּוֹם הַשְּׁבִיעִי — *Let every man remain in his place; let no man leave his place on the seventh day* (16:29).

Shabbos: A Journey Inward

We think that to be successful in life we need to go out, travel, work, accomplish, influence, purchase, build, transact, network, and connect. But on Shabbos, we are told, "Do not leave your place." Happiness does not come from any external source. Shabbos is the time to turn inward; the root of the word "Shabbos" is שבת, which means "to return." Use the day to think about your relationship with Hashem, who you are, and who you can become, without all the distractions of the weekday.

This verse also tells us not to leave the place we are in right now. We often think that things would be better if only they were different: *If only* I had a better childhood, *if only* I was smarter or better looking, *if only* I was in better shape, *if only* I had more money, *if only* I had that specific talent, *if only* I had more confidence, *if only* I did not have this issue, *if only* I could be living in that house or in that community, *if only* I lived on that block or sent my kids to that school, *if only* I had more friends, *if only* I had that career.

Stop that thinking. Do not leave the place you are in right now. No matter what you are going through, the place you are in right now is the right place for you to be. You can shine here, you can grow here, you can become a better person at this instant, in this situation, in this place.

Shabbos is a chance to live with *bitachon*. It is about releasing ourselves to Hashem. "Hashem, I'm resting from all my work because I know that You are taking care of me. I'm in the right place, I can do Your will right here and right now. I can learn Torah right here and right now."

— אַל יֵצֵא אִישׁ מִמְּקֹמוֹ בַּיּוֹם הַשְּׁבִיעִי
Let no man leave his place on the seventh day (16:29).

⸎ *Boundaries: The Essence of a Jew*

The prohibition of gathering *mahn* on Shabbos was based on the laws of carrying. It is forbidden to leave the *techum* on Shabbos, and it is forbidden to carry from a *reshus harabim,* public area, to a *reshus hayachid,* private area.

30 *So the people rested on the seventh day.*

The laws of *hotzaah,* carrying from a private location to a public one or vice versa, are unparalleled. The other thirty-eight *melachos* of Shabbos cause a noticeable change in the world. For instance, weaving turns threads into a wearable garment. Cooking changes meat from inedible to edible. But *hotzaah* makes no physical difference. The item is the same item, unchanged other than for its location. That is why *hotzaah* is called a *melachah geruah*, a downgraded *melachah*. It is surprising that in spite of its being a "weak" *melachah,* the Gemara dedicates a significant space to its laws; large parts of *Masechta Shabbos* and the entirety of *Masechta Eiruvin.* Almost an entire volume of *Mishnah Berurah* and many more *simanim* of *Shulchan Aruch* are dedicated to these halachos. What is the reason for this?

Every Jew needs to know in his core what is a *reshus harabim* and what is a *reshus hayachid.* Boundaries and an acute awareness of "where I am right now" are critical. We need to know that matters that we see or hear in a *reshus harabim* are not to be brought into the home, our *reshus hayachid.* And matters of the *reshus hayachid* — private matters, about family, finances, and vacations — are not to be brought into the *reshus harabim* and shared with others. Appropriate boundaries are vital. Speech and behaviors that we may be exposed to at work should not be brought into the home. When we go on a vacation with our family or make a successful business deal, keep it confined to the *reshus hayachid.* Do not give free rein to the impulse to share with others; it may stoke jealousy.

Rav Zeira's students asked him what he did to be gifted with longevity. He said, "I did not think about Torah matters in an unclean alleyway" (*Megillah* 28a). Rav Zeira was always acutely aware of where he was; he was attuned to his surroundings and what they required from him. He understood his boundaries. This is why he was granted a long life.

לא וַיִּקְרְאוּ בֵית יִשְׂרָאֵל אֶת שְׁמוֹ מָן, וְהוּא כְּזֶרַע גַּד לָבָן, וְטַעְמוֹ כְּצַפִּיחִת בִּדְבָשׁ.

— וַיִּקְרְאוּ בֵית יִשְׂרָאֵל אֶת שְׁמוֹ מָן
The House of Yisrael called it mahn (16:31).

Mahn and the Home

Rav Shamshon Raphael Hirsch writes that "*beis Yisrael*" is a reference to the women of Klal Yisrael. It was they who named the *mahn*.

It is the women who set the tone in the home. They are their family's thermostats; women create the environment of respect for Torah and mitzvos in which their families are steeped. That is why Rav Yose referred to his wife as his "home" (*Shabbos* 118b). Since the women were the ones to intuit the *mahn's* significance and impart it to their families, they were given the opportunity to name it.

When a taxi driver asked Rav Aryeh Levin where his home was located, Rav Aryeh paused and then said, "From the day that my wife died, I do not have a home; I have an address, but not a home."

The Chofetz Chaim had exceptional *hakaras hatov* to his wife. She had been brought up to live simply and had no expectations of any kind of luxury. She supported him while he studied and required very little for herself and the family. Had he married someone wealthy, he would have been required to maintain her standard of living, which might have distracted him from his Torah. His wife's ability to make do with the little she had made it possible for the Chofetz Chaim to concentrate on his learning and his writings, without which he could not have had the extraordinary influence on Klal Yisrael that he did.

[31] ***The House of Yisrael called it mahn. It was like coriander seed, it was white, and it tasted like dough kneaded with honey.***

וְהוּא כְּזֶרַע גַּד לָבָן —
It was like coriander seed, it was white (16:31).

◆§ Supporting Others

The *Degel Machaneh Ephraim* tells us something so special. The word גַּד (*gad*), spelled with a *gimmel* and *daled*, is used to describe the *mahn*. This can be seen as a reference to the Gemara (*Shabbos* 104a) that explains that the letters *gimmel* and *daled* are next to each other in the *alef-beis*, to teach us גּוֹמֵל דַּלִּים — one should support the poor. The Gemara (*Shabbos* 151b) also tells us whoever has mercy on [Hashem's] creations, Heaven will have mercy on him. The *mahn*, described as "*gad*" — גּוֹמֵל דַּלִּים, demonstrates to us that when we are kind, sensitive, merciful, giving, and charitable to others, Hashem extends that same kindness and support towards us.

Moshe counted Bnei Yisrael by using the *machatzis hashekel*. Each Jew of age donated a half-shekel and Moshe then counted the half-shekels. The expression in Hebrew is "וְנָתְנוּ (*v'nasnu*) — and they will give" (*Shemos* 30:12). The *Baal HaTurim* points out that the word "וְנָתְנוּ" is a palindrome, a word that can be read both forward and backward. This teaches us that one who gives *tzedakah* will never lose because of it.

> *When Rav Moshe Sokolovsky of Brisk authored his seminal work, Imrei Moshe, a young bachur sent him a letter. The bachur was Yaakov Yisrael Kanievsky, the future Steipler Gaon, asking Rav Moshe to please send him a copy of his sefer. Although he wanted to buy it, he did not have the necessary funds. Rav Moshe sent young Yaakov Yisrael a copy of the sefer at no charge.*

It appeared that the Imrei Moshe was doing the favor for the Steipler. But World War II broke out a little while later and all copies of the Imrei Moshe were burned, except for the one copy that he had sent to the Steipler, who had already made his way to Eretz Yisrael. His was the last remaining copy. The sefer was subsequently reprinted from this copy and became available for all. The power of v'nasnu!

◆§ *Mahn and Money*

The word "גַּד" is also related to the word הַגָּדָה (*haggadah*), which means to tell or to reveal (*Yoma* 75a). The *mahn* revealed hidden truths. When there was a doubt about whether a slave was stolen or not, where his *mahn* fell told us to whom he belonged. Similarly, if a husband said that his wife had done something to forfeit her *kesubah* and she claimed she was innocent, the placement of her *mahn* would reveal the truth.

The way we relate to money can often reveal some deep truths about us. Some people totally lose themselves when it comes to money, while others have internalized that money is from Hashem; it is transient, it is a test. When financial challenges arise, they remain levelheaded, cool, and full of *emunah* that it is all from Hashem. Here are two stories of people with diametrically opposed attitudes to money.

I was speaking with a non-Jewish CEO of a large company over dinner at a popular kosher steakhouse. He mentioned that he had been near this restaurant before. "I was working for a different company then. I was asked to collect more than ten million dollars that a client owed us. The client was having obvious financial issues but was also ghosting us, and we needed answers and money. I managed to get him on the phone and arranged to meet him at a neighboring eatery.

"After ordering, I explained that my company was in a ten-million-dollar hole because of his severely delinquent

payments and lack of accountability. He listened as if he cared, but then he took the thick cloth napkin from the table, blew his nose into it, and threw it right on my plate! He smiled and said, 'Money? You and your company will never see a dollar of mine!'"

This is an example of how money reveals an individual's unpleasant core and the rot that sets in when he ceases to work on himself and develop his *emunah*.

Here's a more positive story, one that shows the righteousness and *emunah* of a Yid.

> *Pinchas learns until noon every day, even as he runs a large company. He's in the vending machine business and reached out to us to see if he could service a large portfolio of nursing homes we manage. We reviewed the situation and were told there was no provider contract in place, so we gave him the green light. The contract was for nursing homes spread out throughout the state of Texas. Pinchas sent a team of people to personally visit each of the forty-five nursing homes and see which machines they required. It is not simple to have a team travel to so many places, each quite a distance from the other, and it entails considerable expense.*
>
> *After about a month of work, plans were made for each site and the switchover was about to happen. Then, at the eleventh hour, we received a letter from the current vending machine provider. He had heard that we were looking to terminate his service and produced a signed contract, obtained from someone who had worked in the company previously. Legal counsel told us that the current vendor had another three years on his contract, and any attempt to break the contract could result in penalties.*
>
> *I called Pinchas to tell him the news. His reaction, after a month of work and expense, was calm and controlled,* ***"This is what Hashem wants, so that is what I want.*** *Im yirtzeh Hashem, in three years we will get the business."*

לב וַיֹּאמֶר מֹשֶׁה, זֶה הַדָּבָר אֲשֶׁר צִוָּה יהוה,
מְלֹא הָעֹמֶר מִמֶּנּוּ לְמִשְׁמֶרֶת לְדֹרֹתֵיכֶם,
לְמַעַן יִרְאוּ אֶת הַלֶּחֶם אֲשֶׁר הֶאֱכַלְתִּי
אֶתְכֶם בַּמִּדְבָּר בְּהוֹצִיאִי אֶתְכֶם מֵאֶרֶץ
מִצְרָיִם. לג וַיֹּאמֶר מֹשֶׁה אֶל אַהֲרֹן, קַח
צִנְצֶנֶת אַחַת וְתֶן שָׁמָּה מְלֹא הָעֹמֶר מָן,
וְהַנַּח אֹתוֹ לִפְנֵי יהוה, לְמִשְׁמֶרֶת לְדֹרֹתֵיכֶם.

לְמַעַן יִרְאוּ אֶת הַלֶּחֶם אֲשֶׁר הֶאֱכַלְתִּי אֶתְכֶם בַּמִּדְבָּר בְּהוֹצִיאִי אֶתְכֶם מֵאֶרֶץ מִצְרָיִם — ***So that they can see the food that I fed you in the Wilderness when I took you out of the land of Egypt*** (16:32).

Bitachon Is for Everyone, No Matter What Level

The Meshech Chochmah tells us something so powerful. He points out that Hashem provided the miraculous *mahn* when Bnei Yisrael went into the Wilderness, before they accepted the Torah. Although they were still tainted by the spiritual impurity of Egypt, Hashem provided them with *parnassah*. This teaches us that even when one is far from Hashem, even when one has not done what Hashem wants him to do, he can and should have *bitachon* that Hashem will provide. Even one who does not yet abide by Torah law but is striving to grow and working to improve himself can have *bitachon* that Hashem will provide for him. *Bitachon* is not reserved for *tzaddikim*. *Bitachon* is for everyone. It is for the one who has done wrong, the one who has strayed, and the one who is distant. There is no Yid on earth who cannot reach out to Hashem for help. The *mahn* fell even on the day that Bnei Yisrael worshiped the Golden Calf! (*Rashi*, *Yechezkel* 16:19). Hashem's *chesed* is boundless and unceasing.

32 Moshe said: "This is the matter that Hashem commanded: An omerful of it is to be a keepsake for your generations, so that they can see the food that I fed you in the Wilderness when I took you out of the land of Egypt." 33 Moshe said to Aharon, "Take a single earthenware jar and place in it an omerful of mahn, and set it down before Hashem as a keepsake for your generations."

Regarding the verse, "One who trusts in Hashem, kindness surrounds him" (*Tehillim* 32:10), the Midrash says that "even an evildoer is surrounded by the kindness of Hashem when he has *bitachon*!" (*Yalkut Shimoni, Tehillim* §719). The *mahn* teaches this vital lesson. Each and every one of us, no matter our level of observance or what we may have done in the past, can have a relationship with Hashem and can trust Him and rely on Him. His mercy extends to all His creations (see *Ramban, HaEmunah V'HaBitachon; Igra D'Pirka* 163; *Sefer Nefutzos Yisrael,* Ch. 8).

קַח צִנְצֶנֶת אַחַת וְתֶן שָׁמָּה מְלֹא הָעֹמֶר מָן וְהַנַּח אֹתוֹ לִפְנֵי ה׳ לְמִשְׁמֶרֶת לְדֹרֹתֵיכֶם — ***Take a single earthenware jar and place in it an omerful of mahn, and set it down before Hashem as a keepsake for your generations*** (16:33).

◆§ *The Message of the Container*

Moshe told Aharon to take one *tzintzenes* and put a full *omer* of *mahn* in it. The word *tzintzenes* connotes a small receptacle. A full *omer* is 3.4–3.9 lb. How could a small receptacle hold a full *omer* of *mahn*?

Rav Meir of Premishlan explains that this was the lesson Hashem was imparting for all generations. Take a small container — do a small *hishtadlus* — and you will see that it will miraculously hold a great deal of *mahn* and *berachah*. Witness how a small, seemingly negligible opportunity can contain exponential *berachah*. Look into your past and notice Hashem's hand; how seemingly small opportunities blossomed into *berachah*.

My friend was in his upper twenties when he began working. Lacking work experience, he took an entry-level job at a financial management company. At lunch time, he said to himself, "What have I done? I took a job that pays minimum wage, even though I have a family to support. All the other folks in the department are in their late teens and early twenties. I am in the wrong place. This is totally not for me and there is no opportunity for me here. I need to get a job that pays more and that is geared toward my age and skill set." He was thinking of walking out and not coming back, but that was too unprofessional. So, he did return after lunch, and several years later holds a senior position at the company.

Hashem showed him so clearly how from the smallest tzintzenes, immense berachah was generated.

◆§ *The Message of the Mahn Today*

The *mahn* was placed in the *Kodesh HaKodashim*, the place with the greatest concentration of the Shechinah. Rav Moshe Sternbuch says that we see, from where the *mahn* was placed, how important it is for Hashem Himself to see that His children are sustained, like a father who loves his children and wants nothing more than to care for them. This is why in *bentching*, when we speak of Hashem as the One Who supports us — "אֱלֹהֵינוּ אָבִינוּ, רְעֵנוּ זוּנֵנוּ, our God, our Father, shepherd us, nourish us" — we refer to Him as our Father, a term of endearment.

When Yirmiyah saw a nationwide weakening in Torah study, he admonished those who were not learning. They said that they were unable to study because they were busy working to provide for their families. Yirmiyah showed them the jar of *mahn* and said, "Look, your forefathers were miraculously sustained by *mahn* in the Wilderness, and therefore you, too, should prioritize your Torah studies."

The generation of the *Midbar* was sustained by *mahn* and so they were able to dedicate themselves to studying Torah. But in Yirmiyah's time, people had to work to earn a living. So what was Yirmiyah telling them?

He was telling them that even today, the *berachah* of the *mahn* exists. Although the source of our sustenance is less obvious, as it is "dressed in *teva*, nature," it is still fully controlled by Hashem. Yirmiyah displayed the *mahn* to tell Klal Yisrael, "Do not abandon the Torah, do not sacrifice Torah study for the pursuit of *parnassah*. Hashem will provide for you."

The *mahn* was placed in the *Aron HaKodesh*, which represents the Torah, to convey the information to all generations of Jews that their *parnassah* is dependent on their dedication to Torah study and adherence to the Torah. The *Ohr HaChaim* (*Vayikra* 26:3) elucidates the Mishnah that says, "If there is no flour, there is no Torah" (*Avos* 3:21), by saying that "If one finds himself without flour, struggling for sustenance, it is because there is no Torah." Commitment to Torah study directly impacts one's *parnassah*. Consequently, when people came to the Kuzmir Rebbe to ask him for a blessing for *parnassah*, he told them to study Torah, as it says in *Kaddish D'Rabbanan*, "May all Yisrael… and all those who study Torah… enjoy abundant sustenance… from their Father in Heaven."

> *After World War II ended, as the boat carrying the Mir Yeshivah from Shanghai, China, to the United States, came in sight of the Golden Gate Bridge, many bachurim rushed to the decks to see it. Rav Shmuel Berenbaum was learning at that time. When he was urged to come look, as it was a once-in-a-lifetime opportunity, he said, "It is also a once-in-a-lifetime opportunity to learn while I have the desire to see the Golden Gate Bridge!"*

לד כַּאֲשֶׁר צִוָּה יהוה אֶל מֹשֶׁה, וַיַּנִּיחֵהוּ
אַהֲרֹן לִפְנֵי הָעֵדֻת לְמִשְׁמָרֶת.
לה וּבְנֵי יִשְׂרָאֵל אָכְלוּ אֶת הַמָּן אַרְבָּעִים
שָׁנָה, עַד בֹּאָם אֶל אֶרֶץ נוֹשָׁבֶת, אֶת
הַמָּן אָכְלוּ עַד בֹּאָם אֶל קְצֵה אֶרֶץ כְּנָעַן.
לו וְהָעֹמֶר עֲשִׂרִית הָאֵיפָה הוּא.

Rav Shmuel Berenbaum asked, "What is the purpose of a child learning Torah in his mother's womb if he's just going to forget it all when he's born?" He answered, "It gives him the experience of using his time for Torah study. Whenever we have time on our hands, we should use it to study Torah."

❧ *Seeing Hashem's Hand in Our Parnassah*

Hashem instructed Moshe to have *mahn* placed in the Beis HaMikdash for all generations. This enabled Yidden to internalize that although the actual *mahn* had ceased to fall, *parnassah* is still *mahn*, even though it is dressed up as *teva*, nature. The Klausenberger Rebbe writes that nowadays the *yetzer hara's* principal task is to blind us so that we cannot see Hashem's hand. It is easy to congratulate ourselves for our hustle, our innovative ideas, our connections, the clients we land, and our timely investments. Really, it is all miracles, it is the *mahn*, Hashem's hand in disguise. What people refer to as מִקְרֶה — *happenstance* — is really רַק מֵה׳ — only from Hashem.

The first question asked by the Heavenly Court on the Day of Judgment is, "Did you conduct business with integrity?" (*Shabbos* 31a). According to the *Bnei Yissaschar* (*Nissan* 4:4), the Gemara means, "Did you conduct business with the *emunah* and knowledge that it was not your *hishtadlus* that created

34 ***Just as Hashem commanded Moshe,***
so Aharon set it down before the Aron of
Testimony as a keepsake.
35 ***The Children of Yisrael ate the mahn for forty***
years until they arrived at a populated land;
they ate the mahn until they arrived at the
edge of the land of Canaan.
36 ***The omer is one-tenth of an eifah.***

the revenue?" It was not one's ideas that bore fruit; it was all from Hashem.

Once this realization has set in, the next question the Heavenly Court asks is, "Did you dedicate time to study Torah?" When a person shoulders the entire weight of *parnassah* on his back it is a struggle to think about anything else. But if he has *emunah* that Hashem provides, he can take the time to study Torah, to daven, and to do mitzvos, because he knows with utter clarity that the time spent will not detract from his earnings.

The Greeks decreed that all Jews write on the horns of their oxen that they do not have any connection to Hashem (*Bereishis Rabbah* 2:4). Why the horns of oxen? If the Greeks wanted to make it known that the Jews were denouncing Hashem, why not have them write it on the walls of their homes, on the streets, or in their shuls? Rav Yaakov Shayish (*Doresh Tov, Chanukah*, p. 11) explains that the ox was the source of *parnassah*; oxen powered their plows. The Greeks wanted to deny Hashem's role in providing for His people in their everyday lives — in business, in the fields, and in the marketplace.

Rav Yitzchok Dov Koppelman, rosh yeshivah in Lucerne, Switzerland, tells us something so unbelievable (*Sod HaParnassah,* p. 12): There is something even more remarkable than a nation following Hashem into the Wilderness,

סגולות לפרנסה

Segulos for Parnassah

Introduction

The Jewish nation is called the *am segulah*, Hashem's treasured nation (*Devarim* 7:6). *Segulos* are not vending machines where we drop in a coin and out rolls a heap of cash. The ultimate power of a *segulah* is working on ourselves, changing ourselves, and uplifting ourselves through our actions.

> *Rav Yehudah Aryeh Leib Alter, the Sfas Emes, told a man seeking a segulah, "I only know of one segulah. It is the most powerful of all segulos, and that is what Hashem says to the Bnei Yisrael, 'Vihyisem li segulah — be My treasure' (Shemos 19:5). This is what Hashem wants from us: that we be good Yidden, close to Him, safeguard the Torah... and be a treasure, a light to Him and to the world."*

The list below, of *segulos* for *parnassah,* is not an exhaustive list of *segulos* by any means.

A common theme that runs through nearly all *segulos* is strengthening our *emunah* and *bitachon.* One should be aware that the penalty for certain *aveiros* is a deleterious effect on one's financial standing. A *segulah's* efficacy may be impeded by misdeeds that block the flow of *berachah* (see *Shu"t Chasam Sofer*, Vol. 1, *Orach Chaim* 158; Rav Shimon Sofer, *Shir Maon Avos,* 4:22; *Ahavas Chesed,* Ch. 19). Through relying on and connecting to Hashem in a more profound and deep way, one merits the blessing of "Blessed is the man who trusts in Hashem."

Bitachon and Parnassah — The Ultimate Segulah

Chovos HaLevavos tells us that when one has *bitachon*, Hashem provides for his needs and those of his family. *Chovos HaLevavos* goes to great lengths to explain the *baal habitachon's* virtues and how he can live in serenity and security by tapping into the wellsprings of *bitachon*. It is no wonder that the Apter Rebbe said that learning *Chovos HaLevavos's Shaar HaBitachon* is a *segulah* for *parnassah* (*Yalkut Ohev Yisrael,* p. 116). Relinquishing anxiety and recognizing that you are not in control is the ultimate *segulah* for *parnassah*. We are called "יְהוּדִים — *Yehudim,*" which has the same numerical value as בִּטָחוֹן — seventy-five. *Bitachon* is the core of our genetic makeup.

The Gemara tells us that "*Berachah* is only found when something is hidden from sight" (*Taanis* 8b). *Berachah* is present when one does not openly flaunt his blessings. *Maor VaShemesh* explains that "*Berachah* only infuses one who has *bitachon* in Hashem, Who is hidden from the eye" (*Va'eschanan*). We cannot see Hashem, but we can perceive His loving hand. When we trust in Hashem and have faith that He provides for us, we will see much *berachah*.

The *pasuk* in *Tehillim* (37:5) says, "גּוֹל עַל ה׳ דַּרְכֶּךָ וּבְטַח עָלָיו וְהוּא יַעֲשֶׂה — Commit your way to Hashem, rely on Him and He will act." The word גּוֹל (*gol*), commit, is related to the word גַּלְגַּל (*galgal*), a wheel. There is an elementary difference between something that is square and something that is round. For example, a team of porters who need to transport a square package must carry it all the way to its destination. On the other hand, if they need to transport a barrel, all they need to do is place the barrel on its side and give it a little push; the barrel will roll the rest of the way on its own momentum. This is why, in describing how a Yid should transfer his burdens to Hashem, Dovid HaMelech uses the word "*gol,*" from the word "*galgal,*" a wheel. All a Yid needs to do in terms of *hishtadlus* is to roll his load a little bit; a small effort, a little push, is enough to pass the burden of his *parnassah* onto Hashem. Then he can "rely on Him and He will provide" (*Rav Chaim Volozhin; Maharil Diskin, Parashas Mikeitz*).

The Gemara (*Beitzah* 15b) tells us that one who wants to ensure that his assets remain viable should plant an אֲדָר (*adar*). Rashi explains that an אֲדָר is a type of grass. The Chiddushei HaRim writes that an אֲדָר is a reference to Hashem, who is called אַדִּיר בַּמָּרוֹם ה׳, *adir bamarom Hashem* (*Tehillim* 93:4). One who wants his assets and his financial standing to be firm should implant Hashem within his life and understand that every dollar, every idea and thought is from Hashem. Plant Hashem firmly in your life, see that it is He who is in total control. This is the ultimate merit for longstanding financial stability.

Sefer Mishpat Tzedek cites the Maharal of Prague, who says that one should recite *pesukim* of *bitachon* as a means of strengthening trust in Hashem. Reciting these *pesukim* before going to work or before a business transaction is a *segulah* for success and *parnassah*.

Honesty in Business: The Ultimate Expression of Bitachon

The first question one is asked in the Heavenly Court on the day of judgment is, "Did you conduct business with integrity?" (*Shabbos* 31a). Honesty in business is an expression of *bitachon*. It is no secret that money blinds, causing people to take actions that are not in accordance with halachah. The *Rambam* (*Hilchos Sechirus* 13:7) writes that Yaakov Avinu was given great wealth because he was always honest in his dealings with Lavan, even though Lavan swindled him many times.

The term "*tzaddik*" is reserved for those who are honest in money matters (*Rashi*, *Avodah Zarah* 6a; *Rambam*, ibid., refers to Yaakov Avinu as "Yaakov HaTzaddik" when praising his honesty). The *Meiri* (*Yoma* 22b) tells us that one who is honest in all his business dealings will have a successful business.

A Jew who was apprehended for fraud defended himself by explaining his halachic rationale. Rav Dovid Feinstein said, "I know the heteirim in Choshen Mishpat, but where is the emunah that Hashem sends money even if one doesn't engage in shady business?"

Several decades ago, a young man purchased a home in Brooklyn. One day his kids were jumping on the bed, and they heard a crash. Something had fallen out from inside the bed. They discovered a box containing diamonds, jewelry, and cash worth tens of thousands of dollars.

His contract clearly specified that his purchase of the home included all contents. Wanting to do the right thing in halachah and be one hundred percent honest, he consulted with Rav Moshe Feinstein. Rav Moshe told him that he should return the jewelry and cash, as people do not usually sell money. The young man phoned the house's previous owner, who said, "Our parents left money in the house, but we were never able to find it. We knew that a religious Jew like yourself would return it to us if it was ever found."

What a kiddush Hashem.

At the time, the young man, who was committed to doing what was right and honest, was just starting out in real estate. Today, he is the esteemed philanthropist, Mr. Ruby Schron.

Elisha Loewenstern was killed defending Israel. His wife, Hadas, recounted at his funeral that Elisha was a man of absolute honesty, which came from his sincere bitachon. Elisha worked for a credit card company and had access to the credit cards, financial histories, and transactions of millions of people. He was required to take credibility tests in which he was asked questions such as: Have you ever stolen? Have you ever lied? Have you ever used something that is not yours?

Elisha was told that he had failed the test. This was a shock to Elisha and his boss, as he was known to be extremely honest. When Elisha's boss asked how he had failed, the test administrator explained, "It is too good to be true. There is no way that a human being never stole, never lied, never took a pen or a piece of paper that was not his. It just cannot be. The test is not accurate, or else Elisha managed to trick the system."

Elisha's boss responded, "The test is correct. There are no errors here. Elisha is a man of absolute integrity."

Tefillah

The Gemara (*Niddah* 70b) tells us, Rabbi Yehoshua ben Chananya was asked what a person could do to be granted wealth. He ultimately answered, "Request mercy from He to Whom all wealth belongs, as it says (*Chaggai* 2:8), 'The silver is Mine and the gold is Mine.'"

The Maharsha explains that even if it was decreed before one was born that he would be impoverished, he can change the decree through *tefillah*. With *tefillah*, one can rise above one's *mazel* (*Panim Yafos*). Therefore, one should be sure to concentrate when reciting the *berachah* of *Bareich Aleinu* in *Shemoneh Esrei*. The *Magen Avraham* (*Orach Chaim* 119:1) quotes the *Zohar* and Arizal, who say that one should ask Hashem for *parnassah* in the *berachah* of *Shema Koleinu*. Consequently, a special *tefillah* for *parnassah* is included in nearly all siddurim, and should be recited. *Tefillah* is our declaration that we are powerless to control anything, including our financial plight. When we daven to Hashem, we declare our reliance on Him.

Tefillah is the key that opens the door of Heaven for whatever we need (see *Arvei Nachal, Va'eschanan*). *Tanna D'Vei*

Eliyahu (*Zuta* 6) writes, "Hashem says to Moshe, 'Moshe, I will reveal to you a fraction of My ways: When I see a Yid who does not have any Torah or good deeds, neither he nor his forefathers, yet he stands [before Me in *tefillah*] and thanks Me, blesses Me, praises Me, and makes requests of Me, I listen to him and double his sustenance!'"

Zohar Chadash (*Beshalach*) writes that when one davens each day to Hashem for sustenance, Hashem opens His storehouse of *parnassah*. Rav Moshe of Kobrin (*Imros Moshe,* p. 118) said that davening to Hashem for *parnassah* is itself a *segulah* for *parnassah*. By davening, one demonstrates his *emunah* and his *bitachon* that it is Hashem and only Hashem Who provides sustenance. This opens the gates of *parnassah*. A child relies on his father for support and looks to him in his time of need. When we daven to Hashem asking Him to support us and provide us with *parnassah,* we are like a son who understands that our Father in Heaven is the one to Whom we turn (see *Meor Einayim, Parashas Va'eschanan*).

"*Liyeshuascha kivinu kol hayom —* We hope for Your salvation all day"

When reciting these words in *Shemoneh Esrei*, one should long for the *yeshuas Hashem*, the ultimate salvation which will herald the coming of Mashiach. Rav Yaakov Tzemach writes that when reciting these words, one can also have in mind one's longing for Hashem's salvation from any of his personal challenges, "and many times I have been helped through doing this" (*Shaarei Teshuvah, Orach Chaim* 118). The Chofetz Chaim (*Machaneh Yisrael* 2:2) quotes the Arizal who says that sincerity in saying these words is a *segulah* for success.

Chazaras Hashatz

The Gemara (*Berachos* 32a) tells us, "What should a person do if his *tefillos* have not been answered? He should daven again, as the verse says (*Tehillim* 27:14), 'Hope to

Hashem, be strong and He will give your heart courage, and hope to Hashem.'" The Vilna Gaon says that "daven again" means that he should concentrate on the chazzan's repetition of *Shemoneh Esrei*, as doing so is the catalyst for exceptional *mazel* and *berachah*. Rav Shimshon Pincus (*She'arim BaTefillah*) explains that the individual *Shemoneh Esrei*, recited quietly, is like someone trying to transport diamonds; he hides them carefully, so as not to be robbed. *Chazaras hashatz*, on the other hand, is so great that there is no accusing angel who can stop it, and nothing can prevent it from going straight to Hashem. That is why it is recited out loud for all to hear!

Rav Shimshon compares this to someone driving a car with a stick shift. While in gear one, he steps on the gas and thinks that the car can only travel ten mph. "Well, it's better than walking," he says. We laugh and tell him, "Put the car into fourth gear and you can fly at sixty-five mph and more!"

Avudraham says that a person should know that Hashem sustains and provides for one who is careful about *tefillah*. The numerical value of "זָן (*zan*), feed," is fifty-seven. When a person davens *Shemoneh Esrei* he recites nineteen *berachos*. When he hears *chazaras hashatz* and answers *amen*, it's as if he said another nineteen. But Chazal tell us that answering *amen* is even greater than saying the *berachah* (*Berachos* 53b). So answering *amen* accrues another nineteen *berachos*, for a total of fifty-seven, the *gematria* of *zan*. Hashem provides for those who are particular about davening and listening to *chazaras hashatz*!

Davening to Hashem for Support to Fulfill Torah and Mitzvos

The Chozeh of Lublin writes that a *segulah* for *parnassah* is to daven to Hashem that He should bless you with *parnassah* so that you can learn Torah, pay for your children's Torah education, and do mitzvos. A request to be supported so we can live a life of *ruchniyus*, Torah, mitzvos, and *chesed* is likely to be accepted (*Zos Zichron* 56). *Sefer Chassidim* (131) writes that when one prays for spiritual goals, Hashem hears and is receptive, even when the person does only a limited number of mitzvos.

Having Intent When Reciting the Words, "Posei'ach es Yadecha U'Masbia L'Chol Chai Ratzon"

One should concentrate when reciting the words in *Ashrei*, "*Posei'ach es yadecha u'masbia l'chol chai ratzon* — You open Your hand and satisfy the desire of every living thing" (*Tehillim* 145:16), as it is these words that declare that Hashem is the One Who provides sustenance for every living creature (*Shulchan Aruch, Orach Chaim* 51:7; *Mishnah Berurah* 51:15). It is vital that one strengthen his *emunah* that it is Hashem and only Hashem Who provides our needs from His loving and giving hand. The key to *parnassah* is one of the three keys that Hashem Himself retains and does not give to any angel to handle. Every dollar and every penny comes to us through the *hashgachah pratis* of Hashem opening up His hand. The Sforno writes that the word "*ratzon*" here refers to Hashem, as Hashem's will is to provide for every living being.

If one recited this verse by rote, it should be repeated. Some have the custom to open their hands and lift them upward when reciting this verse as a means of demonstrating that we want Hashem to open His hands. Moreover, opening the hands shows that we are prepared to receive Hashem's abundant bounty (*Mekor Chaim* 51:7; see *Shu"t Tzitz Eliezer* 12:8 for additional sources). Lifting one's hands is a pose of *tefillah* and pleading (see *Bereishis* 14:22; *Shemos* 9:29, 17:11; *Ben Ish Chai, Lech Lecha*).

The Alter of Kelm (*Chochmah U'Mussar*, Vol. 2, number 40) writes that in this *pasuk*, we are asking Hashem to give us the ratzon, *will*, to make the right choices; to choose right over wrong, and to give priority to meaning over short-term hype.

At an Agudah convention, Rav Elya Brudny, rosh yeshivah of Mir Brooklyn, was on a panel discussing the issues facing Klal Yisrael. He was asked for some possible solutions to help struggling middle-class Jewish families. Rav Elya responded, "Concentrate on reciting 'posei'ach es yadecha' with all your heart. This is what Chazal tell us! Maybe it's old fashioned to have emunah peshutah, simple faith, but this is the truth!"

Reciting Parashas HaKetores

The Gemara (*Yoma* 26a) tells us that the Kohen who brought the *ketores,* incense offering, in the Beis HaMikdash would become wealthy. We do not have the Beis HaMikdash and cannot bring *ketores,* but we can recite the *parashah* of *ketores,* which is comparable to actually offering it (*Rema, Orach Chaim* 132:2). As such, reading Parashas HaKetores in the morning and afternoon is a *segulah* for wealth and an unceasing flow of *parnassah* and success (*Seder HaYom, Me'il Tzedakah*). Some have the custom to recite Parashas HaKetores from a *klaf* (see Rav Chaim Palagi *in Kaf HaChaim* 18:18; Rav Chaim Sofer in *Kaf HaChaim* 132:23).

Washing Netilas Yadayim With Care

Using plenty of water for *netilas yadayim* is a *segulah* for wealth, as Rav Chisda said, "I washed my hands with a full fist of water and Hashem gave me a full fist of *berachah.*" The Gemara (*Shabbos* 62b) says that a disregard for the halachos of *netilas yadayim* can result in poverty. *Kav HaYashar* (Ch. 13) writes that one should be careful with *mayim acharonim* as well.

Bircas HaMazon With Kavanah

Sefer HaChinuch (§430) writes, "Thus I have learned from my rabbis... whoever is careful about *Bircas HaMazon* will be given sustenance in an honorable way all his life."

The *Mishnah Berurah* (185:1) writes that it is preferable to use a *bentcher* when saying *Bircas HaMazon* as it improves concentration. *Seder HaYom* writes that *bentching* with concentration results in *berachah* for himself and his family.

The *pasuk* (*Mishlei* 10:22) says, "The blessing of Hashem enriches; sadness will add nothing to it." The Chida (*Nitzutzei Oros*) explains that when one blesses Hashem he will attain wealth — "The blessing of Hashem enriches" — provided that the blessing is not recited out of sadness, but with joy and appreciation.

The *Sifsei Kohen* (*Parashas Vayeishev*) writes that Yosef HaTzaddik was designated second-in-command to Pharaoh and was the one to support the entire world financially during the famine because he *bentched* with *kavanah*.

When reciting *Bircas HaMazon* one should have bread on the table so that there will be something upon which the *berachah* can apply, so to speak (*Shulchan Aruch, Orach Chaim* 180:2).

One of those killed in the Lag BaOmer tragedy in Meron was a twenty-four-year-old man named Reb Menachem Zekbach. On the door of the shivah house was a sign asking those coming to visit the mourners to resolve to bentch from a siddur, l'ilui nishmas Menachem. This was a stringency that Menachem had adhered to during the eight years before his death. If a bentcher was not available, Menachem did not eat bread.

A sofer who came to the Zekbach shivah was inspired to begin using a bentcher every time he said Bircas HaMazon. The sofer wrote a sefer Torah and showed it to a safrus merchant, who told him, "The sefer Torah is beautiful, but the way you finish each letter, the gimurim, needs improvement if you hope to earn a higher price."

The sofer ended up selling the sefer Torah for a minimal price, intending to spend time improving the way he finished letters before writing another sefer Torah. He decided to go to a safrus room, a quiet place where sofrim go to write without distractions. On his way, he bought a roll for lunch, but when he got to the safrus room, he realized that he could not wash for his roll until he was sure there was a bentcher he could use. He searched high and low, but there was no siddur or bentcher in sight. His hunger was getting to him, but he'd resolved never to eat bread unless he had a bentcher, in memory of Menachem Zekbach. He began looking at a pile of dusty parchments and noticed a parchment on which the entire Bircas HaMazon was written. He took a closer look and noticed that the handwriting was magnificent! The finishing touches were beautiful as well.

Now he didn't only have a bentcher from which to bentch; he also had the unknown sofer's handwriting to learn from.

He washed, ate his roll, and bentched from the klaf with the beautiful handwriting. He decided then and there to start writing another sefer Torah, in the style of the script of the klaf in front of him.

A few days later, the sofer received a phone call. Rav Shmuel Dovid Friedman, a talmid chacham and baal tzedakah, was commissioning the writing of forty-five sifrei Torah in honor of those who had been killed on Lag BaOmer. Rav Shmuel Dovid asked him to write one of them, and the sofer agreed. But he had one question: "When I write the sefer Torah, which name should I have in mind?"

Rav Shmuel Dovid said, "This sefer Torah is being written in memory of Reb Menachem Zekbach."

Wow! It was because of Reb Menachem Zekbach that the *sofer* resolved to always *bentch* from a *bentcher*! Because of that resolve, he'd found a way to improve his writing, and now he was writing a sefer Torah in memory of the man who'd motivated him to improve his *bentching*!

Reciting Berachos With Concentration

Saying *berachos* with *kavanah* is a source of blessing (see *Rabbeinu Bachya, Eikev*).

The Gemara (*Berachos* 40b) refers to the fixed text of *berachos* as a "*matbei'a,*" a word that also means "coin." *Sefer HaChaim* writes that the foolish place their trust in the coins in their pockets. But for those who have *emunah*, their "coins" are their trust in Hashem, Whom they are assured will provide for them with mercy. That is why Chazal refer to *berachos* as coins. Hashem decrees a good *parnassah* for one who recites *berachos* earnestly (*Selichah U'Mechilah,* Ch. 8).

Pele Yoetz (*Parnassah*) writes that one needs to concentrate when reciting *berachos* as it is through them that one is granted the lion's share of his *parnassah*. On the flip side, carelessness in *berachos* can result in poverty (*Mateh Moshe*).

Davening With a Minyan

The Torah (*Shemos* 23:25) says, "You will serve Hashem, your God, and He will bless your bread and your waters." The *Maor VaShemesh* writes, "You will serve" is a reference to *tefillah*, which is called "service of the heart." It is written as a plural — "*va'avad'tem*" — which implies that Hashem will bless the "bread and water" of one who davens with others, i.e., with a minyan! Therefore, one who davens with a minyan "is guaranteed to be able to earn a living." (See also *Chasam Sofer, Mishpatim* and *Ksav Sofer, Eikev*). Rav Aharon of Karlin said that *tefillos* davened with a minyan are as powerful as a *berachah* from the *gadol hador*!

> *In a letter written to a businessman, the Yismach Moshe, Rav Moshe Teitelbaum, wrote, "To strengthen the pillar of tefillah, I encourage those working to daven with a*

minyan, and if they must wait for a minyan to gather, they should use the time to study Torah. I guarantee them that they will never lose from davening with a minyan; on the contrary, they will be blessed with abundant berachah. And because of their dedication to tefillah, their children will follow in their ways. One who enters a perfume store carries the scent of perfume with him."

Rav Yosef Shlomo Kahaneman was in London collecting for his rapidly expanding yeshivah. He wanted to meet a particular philanthropist, someone who could truly improve the yeshivah's difficult financial predicament. The man was leaving the country the next morning but told the Ponevezher Rav to meet him at the train station at eight a.m. and they could speak there.

The next morning, the Ponevezher Rav awoke and realized at once that he had overslept. If he were to rush to the train station now, he could catch the man, but would miss davening with a minyan. What should he do? On the one hand, the yeshivah desperately needed the money and this was an opportunity of a lifetime. On the other hand, what about davening with a minyan? Hashem holds the keys to parnassah!

The Rav decided that, be it as it may, he was not going to pass up the opportunity to daven with a minyan.

After davening, he made his way to the train station, thinking that there was not much chance that the man he needed to see might still be there. But although he was an hour late, the philanthropist was there! He apologized for having missed the time they'd set for their meeting and explained that he had overslept. Rav Kahaneman smiled and explained that he, too, had come late. They spoke for a few minutes and the man gave the Rav an even larger check than he had expected.

When recounting the story, Rav Kahaneman said, "Imagine I had not davened with a minyan but rushed to the train station at 8:00. I would have found no one there and would have waited for perhaps thirty minutes and then left, with no check and no minyan. But I davened with a minyan and left with an even larger check than I had expected. No one loses from davening with a minyan!"

Tosefes Shabbos

The *Zohar* (*Shemos*) tells us that the *berachah* for the entire week comes from Shabbos. Shabbos is the *mekor haberachah*, the source of all blessing.

Bringing in Shabbos early taps into an additional source of *berachah*. Shabbos is a gift of the highest caliber (*Shabbos* 10b). When one accepts Shabbos early, he brings the blessings of this special gift into his life. It has the power to effect change in all areas of his and his family's lives, including *parnassah*.

The Gemara (*Pesachim* 112a) tells us, "Make your Shabbos [like a] weekday and do not rely on others." The simple understanding of this is that it is better to make the Shabbos meals inexpensive than to have to borrow money for them, or to ask others to finance them. But *Ateres Menachem* (40b) *darshens* that the Gemara is telling us that one who makes the Shabbos holy when it is still the weekday [by bringing in Shabbos early] will not need to rely on others for financial help, as Hashem will reward him with financial security.

When one accepts Shabbos early, he makes part of the workday holy. He is actively showing that he is confident that Hashem is the One Who provides him with everything he needs and therefore there is no concern about curtailing his workweek. This is itself a source of *berachah*. (See *Toras Avos, Shabbos* 17; *Mei HaShiloach*, *Parashas Behar*. See also *Ben Yehoyada, Shabbos* 118a, who explains why one who honors Shabbos by bringing it in early is worthy of a boundless inheritance.)

Rav Chaim and Rebbetzin Batsheva Kanievsky encouraged anyone who came to them with a dilemma, whether it involved health, finances, children, or shidduchim, to accept Shabbos ten minutes earlier. Rav Chaim explained, "It is within the power of accepting Shabbos early that one will be given children, health, financial stability, wealth, salvation from all pain and difficulty, a suitable marriage partner, and long life. The reward for accepting Shabbos early is immeasurable!"

Honoring Shabbos

The Gemara tells us that a boundless inheritance is the lot of whoever honors Shabbos (*Shabbos* 118a). Additionally, Chazal ascribed wealth to those who honor the Shabbos. Rabbi Chiya bar Abba visited a home, the tables of which were draped with expensive gold silk tablecloths in honor of Shabbos. Rabbi Chiya asked the *baal habayis* how he had attained such wealth. The man responded, "I was a butcher and each time I saw a good cow, I said, 'This is for Shabbos!'" (ibid. 119a).

Honoring Shabbos, which is the source of all *berachah*, is the way to open the flow of *parnassah*. *Tiferes Shlomo* (*Mikeitz*) says something so powerful: "What we give to the Shabbos, the Shabbos gives back to us throughout the week!" The *Sfas Emes* (*Beshalach* 5647; see *Likkutei Yehudah, Beshalach*) writes that when one honors and takes pleasure in the Shabbos, he taps into the *segulas hamahn* that was stored for all eternity!

Honoring Shabbos in Thought

One way of honoring Shabbos is not thinking about your business on Shabbos (even though thinking about business is permitted; see *Shulchan Aruch, Orach Chaim* 306:8). Rav Meir of Porisov said that a *segulah* for *parnassah* is to refrain from thinking about your business or any business-related dealings on Shabbos. Consider your work to be completed. When you are stressed about work, or in the midst of putting together a big deal, it is not easy to shut it out. But when Shabbos comes and you say, "Hashem, now I'm entering a different world. I'm entering Your world and Your home, the treasure house that is Shabbos," this is a *segulah* for success and *parnassah*.

Many women place a white kerchief on their heads Friday night when lighting candles. The Rebbe of Munkatch (*Divrei Torah* 6:68) pointed out that the numerical value of נֵר (*ner*), candle, is 250, which is the same numerical value as the word צָעִיף (*tza'if*), a kerchief. The letters *tza'if*, rearranged, are an acronym for "עַמְּךָ יִשְׂרָאֵל צְרִיכִין פַּרְנָסָה (**a**mcha Yisrael **tz**erichin **p**arnassah) — Your nation, Yisrael, needs *parnassah*."

Honoring Shabbos With Wine

Honoring Shabbos by reciting Kiddush on wine is a *segulah* for *parnassah*, as the Gemara (*Shabbos* 23b; see also *Megillah* 27b) tells us, "One who is careful with *Kiddush HaYom* will be worthy of barrels of wine." *Ben Yehoyada* (*Shabbos* 23b) writes that one should fill the cup to its brim as this is a *segulah* for wealth.

Likewise, *Pirkei D'Rabbi Eliezer* (20) writes that one who does not recite Havdalah on wine does not see *berachah*.

Tefillas V'Yiten Lecha on Motzaei Shabbos

There is a *minhag* to say the *tefillah* of וְיִתֶּן לְךָ on Motzaei Shabbos in order that one be blessed in his work (*Tur, Orach Chaim* 295). The Shinover Rebbe (*Divrei Yechezkel*) said in the name of his father, the Divrei Chaim, that he does not understand how a Jew can have *parnassah* if he does not recite the *tefillah* of *V'Yiten Lecha* on Motzaei Shabbos! The words "וְיִתֶּן לְךָ" have the same numerical value as "מָעוֹת (*maos*)," money — 516. Rav Menachem Mendel of Rimanov also said (*Ateres Menachem* 191) that reciting this *tefillah* is a *segulah* for *parnassah* for the upcoming week, and it should be said together with two or more people.

As part of this *tefillah* we recite Chapter 128 in *Tehillim.* The *perek* includes the words, "*Yegia kapecha ki sochel* — When you eat the labor of your hands." The Kotzker Rebbe (*Amud HaEmes,* p. 122) said that in business one needs to work with his hands but not his head. In other words, make sure that your business life remains somewhat external — on your hands — but does not totally infiltrate your head, distracting you from Torah study and mitzvos This is an important message as the new work week begins: Do not let work overtake you.

Melaveh Malkah

The *Ritz Geius* writes that if one eats *melaveh malkah,* his meals will be prepared for him (financially) for the entire week. Rav Yisrael of Ruzhin said that although many people are not stringent about eating this *seudah,* it is an especially holy one. The source for this is the verse, "*Sulam mutzav artzah, v'rosho magia hashamaymah* — A ladder was set on the ground, and its top reached heavenward" (*Bereishis* 28:12). The word סֻלָּם (*sulam*), ladder, is formed from the first letters of סְעוּדַת לְוָיַת מַלְכָּה (**s***eudas* **l***evayas* **m***alkah),* "a feast to escort a queen." The ladder is "*mutzav artzah,* set on the ground," because it is lowly, as people are not careful with it; however, *v'rosho magia hashamaymah,* "its top reaches to Heaven" — this *segulah* reaches to the Heavens. The *Baal HaTurim* writes that סֻלָּם has the numerical value of מָמוֹן *(mamon),* money.

Shem MiShmuel (*Mikeitz* §674) tells us something amazing: We know that all *berachah* comes from Shabbos. Shabbos is so holy that it needs a special conduit that can transport the *berachah* to the weekday. What can serve as this conduit? *Melaveh malkah.* When honoring this *seudah,* all the *berachah* that Shabbos generates is brought into the week!

It is fascinating to note that the *Shulchan Aruch* speaks about the halachah of *melaveh malkah* in *Siman* 300. There are three main reasons for the *melaveh malkah* meal.

1. Escorting her as she departs is an honor, a *kavod,* for Shabbos.
2. The *melaveh malkah* meal causes *refuah,* healing (see *Shabbos* 119b).
3. As per the *Ritz Geius*, the *melaveh malkah* meal supplies *parnassah,* livelihood.

The numerical value of the first letters of these three reasons for eating *melaveh malkah* — כָּבוֹד, רְפוּאָה, פַּרְנָסָה — equals 300, corresponding to the *siman* in which this halachah is taught in *Shulchan Aruch* (Rav Avraham Stern, *Shulchan Eish*).

Maaser, Tzedakah, and Supporting Torah

Rav Yochanan says, "Give *maaser* so that I [Hashem] will make you wealthy" (*Shabbos* 119a; see also *Taanis* 8b and *Shabbos* 32b). Although generally we are not permitted to test Hashem, when it comes to *maaser*, we are permitted to do so. (*Tosafos* here explains that *maaser* is referring to all types of *maaser,* including monetary.) Rebbi asked Rav Yishmael how the wealthy people in Eretz Yisrael became so wealthy. He answered that it was because they gave *maaser* in accordance with halachah (*Shabbos* 119a). Rav Yaakov Horowitz, the brother of the Shelah, writes, "It is clear to all that in the places where people are careful to give *maaser*, many became wealthy, and they passed this wealth down to their children and future generations" (*Yesh Nochlin*). Why did Hashem bless Avraham with everything? Because he gave *maaser* from all the blessings Hashem bestowed upon him (*Tanchuma, Chayei Sarah*). The Vilna Gaon said that the *berachah* of wealth comes from giving one-fifth of one's income (twenty percent) as opposed to just one-tenth (*Keser Rosh* 123; see also *Ahavas Chesed* 19).

The Gemara (*Bava Basra* 25b) tells us that one who needs *parnassah* should face north when davening, as the *Shulchan* was in the north of the Mishkan and was a source of financial blessing. Rav Tzvi Mendel, the son of Rav Zusha of Anipoli, said something very special. The difference between עֲשֵׂר (*aseir*), tithing, and עֹשֶׁר (*osher*), wealth, is the placement of the small *nekudah* (dot) on top of the *shin*. This is what the verse hints at when Avraham tells Lot, "אִם הַשְּׂמֹאל וְאֵימִנָה — If [you go] left, I [will go] right" (*Bereishis* 13:9). If you place the dot on the left side of the letter *shin*, which indicates *maaser*, then you will have the reward of "*v'eiminah*, going right"; you will have the *nekudah* on the right side of the letter *shin*, which makes it read "*osher*, wealth."

Meor Einayim (*Parashas Re'eh*) writes that the blessing that *maaser* brings is the blessing of being happy with what one has. Some people have so much but are never happy; they always feel that they are lacking, and they want more and more. And there are those who have so little but feel they have what they need and are happy. They are content with what they have.

It is not only the money that was given for *maaser* that becomes blessed and holy; all the money one has becomes sanctified and elevated. For example, if someone makes $1,000 and gives $100 to *tzedakah*, each of the one thousand dollars is part of the mitzvah, since they enabled it. The remaining nine hundred dollars are blessed and a vessel for additional *berachah*! (*Kedushas Levi, Parashas Re'eh*).

Many people set up a separate bank account for their *maaser*, so they can transfer *maaser* monies directly into it. This gives people an accurate, up-to-date read on their *maaser* standing.

The Blessing of Tzedakah

Rabbeinu Bachya (*Devarim* 15:10) notes that when the Torah speaks about *tzedakah*, it uses the seemingly double terminology of "*nason titein* — you will give," to teach us that the more you give (*nason*) the more Hashem will give you (*titein*).

Sifsei Kohen (*Shemos* 30:12) points out that throughout the

Torah, double terminologies are used in connection to *tzedakah*: *nason titein* (*Devarim* 15:10), *pasoach tiftach* (ibid. v. 11), *ha'aneik ta'anik* (ibid. v. 14). This drives home the idea that when we give, Hashem will give back to us.

"*Maaser* is a protective wall for wealth" (*Avos* 3:17). Rav Isaac of Kamarna explains that by giving *maaser*, one ensures that his assets are protected.

The *Aruch HaShulchan* (*Hilchos Tzedakah, Yoreh Dei'ah* 247) writes that collecting *tzedakah* for others provides a safety net for his own children, so that they will not need to collect charity for themselves.

Rabbeinu Bachya (*Kad HaKemach, Tzedakah*) explains that the one who gives *tzedakah* receives more than the one who receives the *tzedakah*. The one who receives *tzedakah* benefits in This World, while the one who gives *tzedakah* benefits for all eternity in the Next World.

In describing *mahn*, the Torah writes, "כְּזֶרַע גַּד הוּא, *k'zera gad hu*." *Degel Machaneh Ephraim* writes something so beautiful: "*Mahn*, sustenance, כְּזֶרַע גַּד — is a product of 'גַּד' — which stands for גוֹמֵל דַּלִּים, supporting the poor." One's financial security is a product of one's to bring kindness to his fellow in need.

Siddur HaGra (*Avnei Eliyahu*, p. 131) says something so powerful: Hashem created two doors. One is a door to Heaven and one is a door to the heart of a person. When you open your heart to a person in need, Hashem mirrors your action and opens the door in Heaven to shower blessing on you.

Supporting a Torah scholar generates a magnanimous *berachah* for *parnassah, nachas*, and success in all areas of life (*Tanna D'Vei Eliyahu* 20).

The Chofetz Chaim (*Shemiras HaLashon*, Ch. 5) writes that when one makes a Yissachar-Zevulun arrangement to support a *talmid chacham*, his business will be successful, as the verse says, "Rejoice, Zevulun, in your going out [to work]" (*Devarim* 33:18). Zevulun rejoices as he goes out to work, since he knows he will be successful, because he is supporting Torah.

Requests for *tzedakah* can be bothersome, and impinge on one's time. The *Zohar* tells us something so unbelievable. When Hashem wants to reward someone, when He wants to give someone a gift, He sends a poor person to his door so that he can do the awesome mitzvah of giving *tzedakah*. This protects him. Such is the power of *tzedakah*. Next time we are approached by a poor person in shul, are interrupted by a knock on our door, or an ad for a *tzedakah* campaign pops up, do not look at it as a nuisance, but as a gift of protection!

Rav Shimshon Pincus writes that This World is like a stormy sea. We are surrounded by rolling waves that pose a danger to our survival at every moment. Torah and mitzvos are the boat that allows us to successfully navigate the tempest. But when a person transgresses, or does not perform a mitzvah, it creates a crack in the boat; water seeps in and his life is jeopardized. He desperately needs a lifeboat. *Tzedakah* is the lifeboat. *Tzedakah* is exceptional among mitzvos in that it can save one's life. Therefore, when someone asks you for *tzedakah*, he is stretching out a hand to offer you a safety jacket.

The Segulah of Giving When It's Hard

The Gemara (*Yevamos* 63a) says, "Regarding one who lends a poor man money in his hour of need, the *Navi* states (*Yeshayah* 58:9), 'You will call and Hashem will respond; you will cry out and He will say: "Here I am!"'" What does it mean when it says, "One who lends money to a poor person in his hour of need"? Every poor person is in an hour of need! The *Ksav Sofer* (*Behar*) explains why Hashem gives such an awesome *berachah*, telling a person, "You will call and Hashem will respond; you will cry out and He will say, 'Here I am!' " It's because "in his hour of need" refers not to the poor person, but to the one who gives even in his own hour of need; the one who distributes *tzedakah* even though the timing is bad, the one who gives when he himself is short of cash. Giving when the financial situation is not that great is the ultimate display of *emunah*. That is why Hashem promises such a wondrous *berachah*.

"If a person sees that his sustenance is limited, he should use it for *tzedakah*" (*Gittin* 7a). Specifically when one is struggling financially, he should give *tzedakah*. The *Kedushas Levi* (*Aggados*) says that this seems counterintuitive; while his bank accounts are at an all-time low and he is struggling, he should give *tzedakah*? The answer is yes. Because the ultimate *segulah* for financial security is *bitachon* and there is no greater concrete demonstration of *bitachon* than giving when it is hard. When you give at a difficult time, you connect yourself directly to Hashem and experience all the fantastic *berachah* that comes along with that.

Tzedakah: Our True Investments

The Torah says, "Everyone's holy things will belong to him" (*Bamidbar* 5:10). In other words, everyone gets to decide to which Kohen to give his *terumah*. The verse continues, "Whatever a man gives to the Kohen will be his." The *Be'er Mayim Chaim* (*Mishpatim* §13) asks, what truly belongs to a man? What does it mean, that it "will be his"? What are man's eternal investments and assets? The answer is, "Everyone's holy things," those things that he has made holy — his Torah, his mitzvos, his children, his *tzedakah*, and the positive effect he has had on others. These things will remain with him forever.

> *When Sir Moses Montefiore was asked how much he was worth, he pondered the question for a while and named a figure. The questioner was confused. "But surely your investments are worth more than that!"*
>
> *"You did not ask me how much I own," Sir Moses said. "You asked me how much I am worth. So I told you how much money I have given to charity this year. We are worth that which we are willing to share with others."*

Shlomie Gross called a friend because he needed to talk. He had lost a lot of money because of a drastic downturn in the stock market. Shlomie said, "What a shame, what a waste! I invested this money and it went down the drain. Do you know how many yeshivos could have benefited from the money I invested?" (Shlomie!, p. 146). Shlomie understood that his true financial value was not what he had in the markets or in assets, but what he had distributed to charity.

Representatives of a Torah institution were unhappy with the donation that the philanthropist Reb Moshe Reichman gave them. They began to shout at him. The situation was unpleasant and Reb Moshe's wife, Lea, was hurt by their ingratitude. But Reb Moshe was tranquil. He turned to his son, Chesky, and said, "Chesky, this is a nisayon, a challenge, to see if I will give less tzedakah... but I won't. I'll give more!" (Building for Eternity, p. 216).

A poor man in a tattered old hat poured out his heart to the Kapischnitzer Rebbe. The Rebbe listened to him and said, "First things first. We need to get you a new hat. Here, I have a brand-new hat, still in the box. It will be perfect for you."

"Rebbe, we just bought this for you," his students said when he went into the next room to get the hat. "Why not give him your old hat, which is still in very good shape? It will be an immense improvement for him."

The Rebbe responded, "For how many years am I going to wear this new hat? Maybe three or four years. But when I give this hat to the poor man outside, I transform a transient physical hat into a precious crown. The kedushah generated by that lasts forever. Such is the power of tzedakah!"

A wealthy man died, leaving behind two wills, one to be opened after he died but before the funeral, and one to be opened after the burial. The lawyer presented the first will to the children, who tore it open to see what instructions their father left for them. It was a short but puzzling will, to say the least: "Please, my children, bury me with my socks."

The children looked at each other and were stunned. Their father had been a deeply religious man who certainly knew that a Jew is not buried in anything other than shrouds. But a will carries great weight in Jewish law, and they asked a leading posek if they were permitted to honor their father's request to be buried in his socks. The posek said no, it was not permissible to bury him in his socks.

The children followed the psak and their father was buried in the customary shrouds, without socks.

The next day, their father's lawyer came to deliver the second will. It read: "My dear children, I have left each of you a sizable amount of money; each of you is wealthy. But know that money and possessions will not go with you into the Next World. The only things that will go with you there are your Torah, davening, closeness to Hashem, chesed, tzedakah, and raising your families with Torah values. Look, I was not even able to be buried in my own socks."

Only Torah, mitzvos, and spiritual growth go with us to the Next World; these are our only true belongings, our true investments.

Rav Yaakov Galinsky recounted that while in Siberia, after a day of backbreaking labor, they would gather to talk. In his hut were the Punsky brothers from Kovno, who had been fantastically wealthy until they were exiled. "There are two people we cannot forgive," said the brothers. "The rav of Kovno, the Dvar Avraham, and the Ponevezher Rav!"

Rav Galinsky was bewildered. What did these two towering Torah luminaries do wrong?

The wealthy brothers said, "These rabbanim came to our homes to collect tzedakah, and we gave them generously, but they should have forced us to give more. They should have come with 'guns,' as the Communists did when they stole all of our money."

Years later, in Eretz Yisrael, Rav Galinsky told this story to the Ponevezher Rav, who recalled meeting the Punskys. He said that when he'd asked them for more, they'd said, "If we give more to Torah and tzedakah, what will be left for us?"

"I told them, 'On the contrary, what you ***give*** *is what you will have for all eternity," the Ponevezher Rav said, "but they just smiled..."*

Honoring One's Wife

The Gemara (*Bava Metzia* 59b) tells us, "*Berachah* is only found in one's home because of one's wife." Rava urged the townspeople of Mechuza to honor their wives so they would become wealthy. The Chida (*Pesach Einayim*) explains that when a couple lives in harmony, Hashem's Shechinah rests among them. Where the Shechinah is present, the channel of *berachah* and *shefa* is open. *Ben Yehoyada* (*Bava Metzia* 59a) writes that the numerical value of the word אִשָּׁה (*ishah*) equals that of בְּרָכָה לֶחֶם (*berachah lechem*), because the conduit of ample sustenance in a home comes through the woman of the home. Many who came to Rav Chaim Kanievsky for a *berachah* in *parnassah* were instructed to take extra care in treating their wives with respect and honor as a *segulah* for *parnassah*.

A Yid from Elad took a taxi, a red Skoda, and left his hat in the cab. He was distraught as it was a new hat and he did not have the money to buy another. He hung up signs, but knew that the chances of finding his hat were like his chances of finding a needle in a haystack.

Then he recalled the Chazal that says that the berachah in one's home comes from his wife, so he went to the bakery and bought her favorite pastry. When he saw the cashier, he was taken aback. "Are you by any chance a taxi driver, and do you drive a red Skoda?" he asked.

The cashier smiled. "Actually, no, but my brother who resembles me very much does." The Yid got his hat back thanks to his good shalom bayis!

Tznius and Parnassah

Related to the previous topic, how the *berachah* in one's home comes from his wife, the *Olelos Ephraim* (382) writes that when a woman excels in the mitzvah of *tznius,* she and her family enjoy tremendous *berachah* in all matters, including *parnassah.* The modest woman will be royally adorned: "All honor [awaits] the King's daughter who is within, adorned with golden chains" (*Tehillim* 45:14).

At the very first *Knessiah Gedolah,* in 1923 in Vienna, Torah luminaries, with the Chofetz Chaim at the helm, gathered to discuss pressing issues affecting the Jewish nation. Before opening the congress, the Chofetz Chaim assembled the rabbanim and said, "We are gathered here today to seek solutions to many pressing problems. What needs to be crystal clear is what the Torah writes: 'Hashem, your God, walks in your camp to rescue you... Your camp should be holy, so that He will not see a shameful thing among you and turn away from behind you' (*Devarim* 23:15). If there is a shameful thing, a lack of *tznius*, Hashem will turn His back on us, and all our plans and solutions will be futile. But when there is *tznius* within our communities and homes, then Hashem is with us, He protects us, and we will see His assistance in all that we do!" (*Meor Einei Yisrael,* Vol. 3, p. 643; see also *Chofetz Chaim, Geder Olam,* p. 111).

On the last Yom Kippur of the Chofetz Chaim's life, after *Kol Nidrei*, the elderly *gadol* spoke and, with tears pouring down his face, said, "One who wants closeness to Hashem, one who wants the presence of Hashem in his home, one who wants forgiveness from Hashem, needs but one thing: *tznius*. It is with *tznius* that one brings Hashem into the four walls of his home and into his heart." The Kaliver Rebbe said that when a woman takes upon herself even the smallest improvement in *tznius*, it weighs on the scales of judgment like a heavy bar of gold, tipping the scale toward life.

Rebbetzin Zahava Braunstein *a"h* said that many of us are big fans of *segulos*. People recite *Shir HaShirim* forty times in a row in hopes of finding a shidduch, make *shlissel challah* the Shabbos after Pesach, and daven Tefillas HaShelah on Erev Rosh Chodesh Sivan. Some wear a red *bendela* (string) from Kever Rachel. No one is disparaging any *minhag* or *segulah*, but the Torah tells us the ultimate *segulah*, a *segulah* that opens wellsprings of *berachah,* and that is: "Your camp should be holy." When we dress and act with *tznius,* "Hashem, your God, walks in your camp." Hashem will walk with us, protect us, and rest His presence within our homes, our families, and ourselves.

The *Zohar* writes that women who are careful to cover their hair according to halachah will raise highly distinguished children (cited in *Mishnah Berurah* 75:14). Additionally, her husband will be blessed with all *berachos,* including wealth, children, and grandchildren. "*Berachah* is only found when something is hidden from sight" (*Taanis* 8b). Moreover, "*Berachah* is only found in one's home because of one's wife" (*Bava Metzia* 59b). When the fountain of *berachah* within the home is adorned with *tznius,* exceptional *berachah* can flow unceasingly.

Care With Shemiras Einayim and Matters of Kedushah

Yosef HaTzaddik became the second-in-command in Egypt and the one responsible for supporting the entire known world during the famine, as it says, "He sold grain to all the populace" (*Bereishis* 42:6). Why was he given such a prestigious position? What was so special about him that he was the financial support of the world? The *Zohar* tells us that he was able to ward off the pressures of Potiphar's wife because he was careful in matters of *kedushah*. "One who shuts his eyes from seeing evil will dwell in heights, his bread will be granted, his water will be guaranteed" (*Yeshayah* 33:15–16). Rashi explains that "bread" is referring to *parnassah,* and one who is careful to guard his eyes will not need to seek it. Hashem will proactively provide for him. "Water" refers to his children and all their needs; those, too, will be provided by Hashem.

The *berachah* of guarding one's eyes is extraordinary! The *Kli Yakar* (*Ki Savo* 28:8) explains that Hashem has a treasure house that contains each person's fear of Heaven, as the verse says, "Fear of Hashem is his treasure" (*Yeshayah* 33:6). Hashem distributes *parnassah* to His children from this treasure house of *yiras Shamayim.*

Rav Yitzchok Blazer (*Shevivei Ohr,* p. 174) asks why, in *Bircas HaMazon*, we ask Hashem to support us "כִּי אִם לְיָדְךָ הַמְּלֵאָה הַפְּתוּחָה הַקְּדוֹשָׁה וְהָרְחָבָה — only from Your full, open, holy, wide hand." If Hashem's hand is open wide, why can't everyone come and take without delay or hardship? The answer is that Hashem's hand is described as holy. Therefore, only someone who acts with holiness, *kedushah*, can come and take from Hashem's hand, which is holy. When we act with *kedushah*, we can receive *parnassah* from the outstretched holy hand of Hashem. *Shem MiShmuel* (*Vayigash*) writes, "Nothing prevents a person from receiving Divine bounty like a deficiency in the *bris* [in matters of holiness]. And it is understood that the opposite is true: One who is protective of [his holiness] is a fit vessel to receive all kinds of abundance."

Hashem tells the Jewish Nation, וִהְיִיתֶם לִי סְגֻלָּה — be to Me a treasure. Rav Dovid Lelover homiletically explains that the word *segulah* can also hint to the Hebrew *nikud* (vowel) sign of *segol* — three dots in an upside-down triangle formation.

Hashem is telling us, the ultimate way to be His treasure is to guard your two eyes and mouth, which form the shape of a *segol*. Be a treasure to Me, guard your *segol*, guard what you see with your eyes and what you say with your mouth.

Rav Ephraim Wachsman told a beautiful story. There was a Yid who traveled from Monsey into the city each day. When traveling in general, and specifically into New York City, there are many challenges when it comes to guarding one's eyes. This Yid decided to incentivize himself to work on his shemiras einayim. Every time he looked away from something not tzanua, he added a dollar to a box. After a few months, he counted the money in his shemiras einayim container, which represented the number of times he had looked away, and was surprised that it was well over $2,000. That was two thousand times he had overcome his natural inclination to look! How extraordinary an accomplishment! But what was he going to buy with the money? As it was December and Chanukah was just around the corner, he decided to purchase a beautiful silver menorah. Rav Wachsman concluded, "In Shamayim, how beautiful, how bright, how holy are the lights of this Yid's menorah. A menorah that shines with purity, holiness, and moral strength."

May we all have the zechus to bring forth such light as well.

Honoring One's Parents

One of the many *berachos* of honoring one's parents is *parnassah* (*Tanna D'Vei Eliyahu Rabbah* 26). Dama ben Nesinah, a non-Jew, refused to wake his father despite the opportunity to earn a large profit, and was rewarded with vast wealth (*Kiddushin* 31a). If such is the reward for a non-Jew who is not commanded in this mitzvah, then certainly we, who are obligated in this mitzvah, will be rewarded greatly (Rav Chaim Palagi, *Tochachas Chaim, Toldos*).

Avoiding Lashon Hara

"It is the nature of people to seek *segulos* and *berachos* for success in *parnassah*," writes the Chofetz Chaim (*Shemiras HaLashon*). "But what will all the *segulos* and all the *berachos* help if he speaks *lashon hara* and *rechilus*? If they listened to me, I would tell them to be extra careful with their speech... as then certainly they will be blessed even more than they would be with any *segulah*!"

What distinguishes man from animal is our ability to speak. When we guard our mouths and speak in the way the Torah desires, then we elevate ourselves and make ourselves worthy of Hashem's *berachah*.

Igra D'Kallah writes that the *mahn's* holiness was such that through its consumption, one's speech was refined and pure and no words of nonsense or *lashon hara* were spoken.

Hafrashas Challah — Separating Challah

The Gemara (*Shabbos* 32b) writes that one receives blessing when separating *challah*. The Gemara quotes a verse in *Yechezkel* (44:30) as support for this: "Give the first of your dough to the Kohen to bring enduring blessing into your house.

Shlomo HaMelech requested of Hashem, הַטְרִיפֵנִי לֶחֶם חֻקִּי, ***H**atrifeini **l**echem **ch**uki* — provide for me my daily bread" (*Mishlei* 30:8). The first letters of these three words, rearranged, form the word חַלָּה, "*challah*," as one who is careful with the mitzvah of separating *challah* will merit having *parnassah* (see also *Megaleh Amukos, Parashas Shelach*).

Sandek

Serving as the *sandek* at a *bris* is a *segulah* for wealth. The baby rests on the legs of the *sandek* when the *bris milah* is performed. The *sandek's* legs are like the *Mizbei'ach* upon which the *ketores* was brought, and the *bris milah* is like the *ketores* offering. The *sandek* is rewarded with wealth just as the one who brought the *ketores* was rewarded with wealth (*Maharil, Milah* §1; *Rema* 265:11). However, the Vilna Gaon was of the opinion that the *sandek* does not receive a *berachah* for wealth.

> *Once Rav Eliezer Yehudah Finkel, the rosh yeshivah of Mir, and Rav Yitzchok Zev Soloveitchik, the Brisker Rav, attended a bris. There was a question as to which of these two great rabbanim should be the sandek. Rav Leizer Yudel said he would take the honor, as he needed the berachah of being a sandek to support his burgeoning yeshivah. The Brisker Rav pointed out that the Vilna Gaon held that being sandek is not a segulah for wealth. Rav Leizer Yudel said, "A check from the Rema is good enough for me!"*

> *Rav Avraham Genachowsky was asked to be sandek at a bris. At first he refused, saying that the honor should be given to someone else. But at the father's repeated insistence, Rav Avraham agreed. A short while later he received $55,000, clearly demonstrating that the berachah of wealth is showered upon the sandek.*
>
> *A few months later, Rav Avraham was again asked to be a sandek. While sitting with the baby on his lap, he resolved not to read any newspapers from that day on (even from chareidi sources). Reflecting on his two most recent opportunities to serve as sandek, Rav Avraham wrote in his journal, "And now I ask myself: Which sandeka'us brought me greater wealth?"*

Bircas Kohanim

Chazal tell us that when the Kohanim bless the congregation, Hashem stands over them and He Himself also blesses them, as it says (*Bamidbar* 6:23–27), "Speak to Aharon and his sons, saying, 'This is how you will bless Bnei

Yisrael, saying to them... and I shall bless them'" (*Bamidbar Rabbah* 11:2; *Shir HaShirim Rabbah* 2:9). There is nothing more powerful, more effective, or more precious than to receive a *berachah* directly from Hashem Himself. This is the very essence of *Bircas Kohanim*. It is no wonder that this mitzvah is called "a great and expansive gift" (*Avodas Kehunah*). The Kohanim are His agents, delivering Hashem's *berachah*.

Halachah states that a Kohen must recite *Bircas Kohanim* in an audible voice. This is suggested in the words "saying to them," on which Rashi comments, "so they can all hear." *Tur* (*Orach Chaim* 128) quotes the Yerushalmi, which adds further significance with the words: "With the voice of the Highest, Hashem; Hashem joins the voices of the Kohanim as they bless the people."

One should make every effort to hear *Bircas Kohanim*. In addition to its special *segulos*, it is a mitzvah for the Kohanim to bless the congregation and a mitzvah for the congregation to be blessed by the Kohanim (*Sefer Chareidim*). *Rabbeinu Bachya* (*Kad HaKemech, Berachah*) tells us that the world is sustained because of *Bircas Kohanim*! *Sifrei* writes that, when saying "*Yevarechecha Hashem,*" the Kohanim should think that Hashem should bless us with financial success and wealth. When saying "*v'yishmerecha,*" they should intend to bless us that Hashem guard the wealth with which He's blessed us, so that we don't lose it.

The *Zohar* (*Nasso* 147) explains that while the Kohanim bless the congregation, the congregation is to stand in fear and trepidation, aware that this moment is an *eis ratzon,* and *berachah* fills the entire world. The time of *Bircas Kohanim* is a time of extraordinary *rachamim* from Hashem. Therefore, it is a time when one who is experiencing a challenge can transform the *din*. Consequently, one who has a bad dream can annul it during *Bircas Kohanim*. The fifteen words of *Bircas Kohanim* contain all the *berachah* a person can ever require, in This World and the Next (*Akeidas Yitzchak; Yalkut Me'am Loez, Nasso*).

Rav Shimshon of Ostropoli (*Eretz HaChaim Shin*: 418) had a *kabbalah* that there are three times that are highly auspicious for *tefillos*: when the *aron kodesh* is opened (also when reciting the words "*Ant Hu zan l'chola um'farnes l'chola*" in *Berich Shemei*), during *hagbah* (lifting the sefer Torah after *Krias HaTorah*), and during *Bircas Kohanim*. Therefore, one who has a request should ask at this time and his *tefillah* will most certainly be accepted.

Rav Shimshon Pincus says: "The greatest *eis ratzon* in This World is the moments of *Bircas Kohanim*. This is the time that the gates of Heaven are open. What more can we want? *'Yevarechecha Hashem'* — Hashem will bless us with prosperity; *'v'yishmerecha'* — He will protect us from sin, He will shine His countenance upon us and grant us peace — the *berachah* that contains all *berachos*!

"A friend was suffering from ill health. I had him in mind during *Bircas Kohanim* and Hashem answered my *tefillos*. This fellow experienced a miraculous *refuah sheleimah*. Such is the power of *Bircas Kohanim*!" (*Nefesh Shimshon, Tehillim*, p. 135).

On Rosh Hashanah, the Brisker Rav had a minyan in his home. It was time for Bircas Kohanim, but the Kohen was late. The Brisker Rav waited quite some time for him to arrive.

After davening, a congregant asked the Rav why it was not considered an undue hassle for the tzibbur to wait so long for Bircas Kohanim. "People spend days or weeks traveling to receive a berachah from a rav," said the Brisker Rav. "During Bircas Kohanim, Hashem tells us, 'I will bless them.' This is a berachah directly from Hashem. There is no greater blessing than to be blessed directly by Hashem! Was the wait not worthwhile?" (Uvdos V'hanhagos L'Beis Brisk, Vol. 3, p. 170).

Reciting Tehillim

The *sefarim* write that a *segulah* for *parnassah,* as well as for many other things, is saying *Tehillim,* and saying the entire *sefer Tehillim* at one time, without interruption (Rav Pinchas of Koritz, *Imrei Pinchas, Seder HaYom* 123; Rav Menachem Mendel of Rimanov, *Be'eros HaMayim*).

Reciting Chapter 23 of Tehillim, Mizmor L'Dovid

This chapter of *Tehillim* is a *segulah* for *parnassah,* as Dovid HaMelech declares, "*Lo echsar* — I will not lack" (Rav Moshe Cordovero in his *Siddur Tefillah L'Moshe*).

Reciting the Thirteen Principles of Faith (Thirteen Ikkarim)

Rav Pinchas of Koritz instructed those struggling with *parnassah* to review the Thirteen Principles of Faith each day. The ultimate *segulah* is understanding that Hashem directs everything, and completely relying on Him. "The one who trusts in Hashem is surrounded by kindness" (*Tehillim* 32:10).

Iggeres HaRamban

The Ramban wrote a letter to his son and instructed him to read it every day. He promised that "on the days that you read it, the Heavens will respond to all your requests." One can read the letter aloud and ask Hashem for anything, including assistance with *parnassah* (*Taamei HaMinhagim,* p. 566).

Tefillah on Rosh Hashanah and Reciting Mizmor L'Dovid (Tehillim 24) on Rosh Hashanah and Yom Kippur at Night

Our *parnassah* for the entire year is determined on Rosh Hashanah, the day of Judgment. It behooves us to concentrate on our *tefillos* at this time. Rav Chaim Kanievsky commented, "My *hishtadlus*, the effort that I put into earning my livelihood, takes place twice a year — on the two days of Rosh Hashanah, when I daven to Hashem to provide for my family!"

Mateh Ephraim (582:23) writes that after Maariv the congregation should recite Chapter 24 of *Tehillim* with total concentration. Reciting this chapter is a *segulah* for *parnassah* for the entire year (*Arizal, Pri Eitz Chaim*). Perhaps the reason is that in this chapter we declare, "לַה׳ הָאָרֶץ וּמְלוֹאָהּ, To Hashem belongs the earth and all that fills it." These words strengthen our *emunah* that Hashem is the Master Controller of every aspect of creation, including our *parnassah*. The Ben Ish Chai writes that this chapter is *mesugal* for *parnassah* and that is why it is recited as the *shir shel yom* on Sunday, the first day of the new work week.

Concentrating on the Word "Ayei" in the Kedushah of Yamim Noraim

Rav Chaim Vital (*Shaar HaKavanos*) writes that it is a *segulah* to daven for *parnassah* while the chazzan says "אַיֵּה — *ayei*" in *Kedushah*. The chazzan stretches out the word "*ayei*" so the congregation will have time to daven the special *tefillah* printed in most *machzorim*. Rav Chaim Vital says that his rebbi, the Arizal, taught him that at that moment, one can daven that Hashem grant him either wealth, righteous and learned children, or *ruach hakodesh*.

Of the three, Rav Shimshon Pincus chose to daven that his children be righteous and successful in their learning. He then told his children, "Look how much I love you and care about you! I gave up the berachah of wealth so that my kinderlach should be righteous and learn Torah! Look how valuable you are to me!"

Purchasing a New Knife for Rosh Hashanah

Many have the custom to purchase a new knife for Rosh Hashanah, as it is a *segulah* for *parnassah*. The word חת״ך (*chasach*), which means "cut," is also the name of the angel that is connected to *parnassah;* his name is alluded to in the last letters of the words פּוֹתֵ**חַ** אֶ**ת** יָדֶ**ךָ** (*posei'a**ch** e**s** yade**cha***), open Your hands" (*Segulos Yisrael* quoting the Rebbe of Ziditchov; *Zichron Tov* of the Chozeh of Lublin). Using a sharp knife is also a *segulah* for *parnassah* (*Likkutei Maharich,* Vol. 2, p. 4).

Aliyah of Maftir Yonah on Yom Kippur at Minchah

In many shuls, the *aliyah* that is sold for the highest amount is the *aliyah* of *Maftir Yonah*. Rav Yosef Yitzchok Schneerson, the Rebbe Rayatz, said that buying this *aliyah* is a *segulah* for wealth (*Otzar Minhagei Chabad, Elul/Tishrei,* p. 234).

It is fascinating to note that *Sefer Sod Meisharim* writes that for the sixteen days that Yonah was in the fish's belly, he was sustained with *mahn*. This is suggested in the verse וַיְמַן ה׳ דָּג גָּדוֹל לִבְלֹעַ אֶת יוֹנָה (*Vayeman Hashem dag gadol livloa es Yonah*), Hashem appointed a huge fish to swallow Yonah (*Yonah* 2:1). The word "וַיְמַן" is composed of the words "וי," the *gematria* of which is sixteen, and "מן," implying that during the sixteen days that Yonah was in the fish's belly, he was sustained by *mahn*.

The *mekubal* Rav Seraya Deblitzky felt that there was no source for this *segulah*. He lightheartedly said that the *segulah* was for the *gabbai*, who could now pay the shul's bills with the money brought in by the sale. Additionally, Rav Chaim Kanievsky stated that there was no source for *Maftir Yonah* as a *segulah* for wealth (although there are other *segulos* associated with it; *B'Didi Havei Uvda,* p. 596; *Sefer Heichel Shlomo,* p. 156, quoting others as well).

Matzah on Pesach

Rav Tzadok HaKohen of Lublin explains that the matzah we eat on Pesach contains the taste of the *mahn* that fell in the Desert (*Kiddushin* 38). Pesach is the *yom hadin*, the day of judgment, when it is decided how that year's grain yield will perform (*Rosh Hashanah* 16a). Eating the matzah, which is permeated with the holiness and taste of the *mahn* and a demonstration of the time when Hashem miraculously provided our sustenance, is a *segulah* for *parnassah* for the whole year (see also *Tiferes Shlomo, Rimzei Pesach*).

The first three letters of the word אֲפִיקוֹמָן (*afikoman*) are an acronym of the words פּוֹתֵחַ אֶת יָדֶךָ (*posei'ach es yadecha*), open Your hand; for those who eat the *afikoman*, Hashem opens His hands with bountiful *berachah* (*Maor VaShemesh*). The *afikoman* is to be eaten while full, which further hints to the idea of Hashem providing us with bountiful satiety.

Shlissel Challah

There is a custom to bake *shlissel challos* the Shabbos immediately after Pesach. What is a *shlissel challah*? It is either a challah that is baked in the shape of a key or one that is baked with a key in it or with the imprint of a key in its dough.

What is the reason for this custom? The Apter Rebbe (*Ohev Yisrael*) explains that when the Jews came into Eretz Yisrael at this season, the *mahn* no longer descended and the Yidden needed to plant crops for food. So at this time of year, we ask

Hashem to unlock the gates of *parnassah*, to which only He holds the key (*Taanis* 2).

The numerical value of the word מַפְתֵּחַ, key, is 528 — the same numerical value of חַלָּה, מָן, פַּרְנָסָה — challah, *mahn*, and *parnassah*.

Sefer Ratz K'Zvi says something so beautiful regarding this custom. Matzah is called "*lechem oni,* the bread of the poor." We only resume eating the bread usually eaten by the middle-class and the wealthy after Pesach. The key in the challah reminds us, even when we are eating the bread of the affluent, that the key to *parnassah* is totally in Hashem's hands (*Taanis* 2a).

Additionally, during this time we count the Omer. Each day of the Omer represents a new *shaar* — a new gate of spiritual elevation. We ask Hashem to unlock these gates to allow us to bask in the spiritual treasures of each day of *sefiras ha'omer.*

Rav Pinchas of Koritz explains that the gates of Heaven are unlocked from the first night of Pesach until Pesach Sheini (the 14th of Iyar). The *shlissel challah* reminds us of this special time (*Imrei Pinchas Pesach*, 217).

Yad Ephraim explains that during Pesach, when chametz was forbidden, it was, so to speak, locked. The *shlissel challah* is a sign of its being unlocked.

The Belzer Rebbe says that the *shlissel challah* is a way of thanking Hashem for unlocking the doors to the "prison" that was Mitzrayim.

Rav Tzvi Hirsh Meisels explained the *shlissel challos* custom when he recounted the following story each year on the first Shabbos after Pesach:

> *Pesach night in Prague, after everyone left the shul, the gabbai locked the doors and made his way home, where he hung his large key ring on its hook. When he was about to make Kiddush, there was a loud clang; the keys had fallen to the floor. Assuming that he hadn't put it onto its hook carefully enough, he pushed it all the way onto the peg, so it would not fall again. But before he could begin Kiddush, the keys fell again.*

When they fell a third time, and yet a fourth time, the gabbai got spooked. He went to ask the Chief Rabbi, Rav Yehudah Leib Loew, the Maharal, what to do.

The Maharal suggested that the gabbai place each key on a separate peg, which would help them figure out what was going on. Lo and behold, this time only one key fell. It was the key to the aron kodesh!

The Maharal told him to run to the shul and open the aron kodesh to see if all was as it should be. To his shock, the gabbai found a bottle of red wine inside! On closer inspection, he saw that it was not wine; it was blood, planted there by the cardinal, who wanted to accuse the Jews of murdering a Christian child to use blood in baking their matzos.

The Maharal told the gabbai to carefully remove the bottle of blood, empty it, clean it well, fill it with wine, and return it to its place, without telling anyone. The gabbai did so and returned home to conduct his Seder.

The next morning, in the middle of davening, the police burst into the shul, followed by the cardinal and other church officials. They were screaming that a local Christian child had been murdered by the Jews, and that they were storing his blood in the aron kodesh. Opening the aron kodesh, the cardinal pointed to the bottle and shouted, "There it is, the child's blood! Those murderous Jews!"

The Maharal explained that it was a bottle of wine that they used for Kiddush and Havdalah. The police chief checked the bottle and confirmed that it was wine. The people of Prague were saved from the blood libel through the miraculous keys.

To recall the miracle that saved the Jews of Prague, the Maharal said that we should really have matzah with a key baked into it. Since that's not possible, we bake a key into a challah on the first Shabbos after Pesach (Otzroseihem shel Tzaddikim, Pesach, p. 678).

Torah Study

Sefarim are replete with indications that the *berachah* of *parnassah* is given to those who study Torah. The Gemara tells us that there are indications of this in the Torah, in *Neviim*, and in *Kesuvim* (*Avodah Zarah* 19b). When one toils in Torah, his wealth will increase! "One who accepts the yoke of Torah will have the yoke of financial pressure removed from him" (*Avos* 3:6). Hashem provides sustenance for one who steadfastly keeps mitzvos and studies Torah (*Machzor Vitri*). Hashem will prepare his sustenance for him!

The *Baal HaTurim* informs us that there are two verses in the Torah that contain all the letters of the Hebrew alphabet. One of them is the *pasuk* that tells us about the *mahn*: זֶה הַדָּבָר אֲשֶׁר צִוָּה ה׳ לִקְטוּ מִמֶּנּוּ אִישׁ לְפִי אָכְלוֹ עֹמֶר לַגֻּלְגֹּלֶת מִסְפַּר נַפְשֹׁתֵיכֶם אִישׁ לַאֲשֶׁר בְּאָהֳלוֹ תִּקָּחוּ, "This is the thing that Hashem has commanded: 'Gather from it, for every man according to his consumption — an *omer* per person — according to the number of your people, everyone according to whoever is in his tent shall you take.'"

This teaches us that Hashem will provide *parnassah* without toil for whoever fulfills the Torah, which contains all the letters of the *alef-beis*, just as He did in the Wilderness.

Rav Naftali Tzvi Yehudah Berlin (*Ha'amek Davar, Toldos* 26:5) writes that those who study Torah are counted as soldiers in the army of Hashem and their needs are provided for by Hashem. Women who take the role of breadwinner to support their husbands learning are valiant soldiers in this holy army as well.

"If you keep the Torah and mitzvos, I will provide rain (*parnassah*) in its correct time," Hashem promises (*Vayikra* 26:3–4). Rashi explains this to mean that if you delve into the Torah, you will be given rain at the appropriate time.

The Lubavitcher Rebbe explained that learning Torah and keeping mitzvos is the wedding contract we made with Hashem; like a husband, He is obligated to provide for our sustenance and needs when we fulfill our side of the deal.

The *Chasam Sofer* (*Derashos*, p. 279) writes that a *segulah* for *parnassah* is to refrain from eating in the morning until one has learned Torah. He learns this from the verse, "You shall not eat bread or [flour made from] parched grain or fresh grain... until you bring the offering of your God. [This is] an eternal law, for your generations, in all your dwelling places" (*Vayikra* 23:14). One should not eat until he brings a *korban;* one should not eat until he sanctifies the day, which in our times, in lieu of *korbanos,* is accomplished by studying Torah. Once he has done that, he can eat — Hashem will see to it that he will have food. It is "an eternal law, for your generations, in all your dwelling places."

Rising Above Nature

Rav Yechiel Michel of Zlotchov imparted a most wonderful *segulah.* There are times when a person is seeking something elusive — perhaps it is *parnassah*, or children, or health — but it seems that it is not within *teva*, the world's natural order, for him to find what he is seeking. He should perform a mitzvah that is above *his* nature. He should perform a mitzvah that he struggles with. When one rises above his nature, Hashem will reciprocate and rise above nature to provide the sought-out blessing (*Igra D'Pirka* §24).

Thank You, Hashem!

Hakadosh Baruch Hu says, "When I see people who have no Torah learning and no good deeds, neither them nor their forefathers, yet they thank Me, praise Me, and daven to Me, I pay heed to them and *double their sustenance*" (*Tanna D'Vei Eliyahu*). Such is the awesome power of thanking and praising Hashem!

The Shelah writes that praising Hashem for all the *chesed* He has done for him creates a stream of additional *berachah* and prosperity. He sees an indication of this in the verse that begins by speaking of a singular *chesed* and then mentions a multitude of *chasadim*: "They will thank Hashem for His kindness [singular: one kindness], and for His wonders to the children of men" (*Tehillim* 107:8). Showing appreciation to Hashem for one kindness spurs Hashem to do myriad kindnesses.

The Ksav Sofer says that Hashem provided *mahn* on a daily basis, and didn't provide a large quantity at one time, so that we would thank Him on a regular basis. If Bnei Yisrael received a month's worth of support all at once, they might not remember to thank Him all the time. Because they depended on it every day, and there was no guarantee that it would fall on the morrow, the recipients thanked Hashem continuously for His miraculous *chesed.*

Seder HaYom tells us something so powerful about the potency of thanking Hashem. In the *Shemoneh Esrei*, we have two *berachos* thanking Hashem for miraculously providing for us on a moment-by-moment basis: *Modim* and *V'chol HaChaim.* The moment in which we thank Hashem is an *eis ratzon*, a propitious time, to daven and plead for our needs. The pipeline of plentitude is opened by gratitude. So immediately following the two blessings of thanksgiving comes the *berachah* of *Sim Shalom,* in which we ask Hashem to grant us peace, blessing, goodness, favor, *chesed*, mercy, and more.

Promoting Unity and Avoiding Mockery

The Shelah (*Yoma* §197) writes, "One disagreement nullifies one hundred sources of *parnassah.*" *Shalom* and harmony invite the Presence of Hashem, which is a conduit for *parnassah*. There is no greater receptacle for *berachah* than peace (*Uktzin* 1:12). *Machlokes*, on the other hand, diminishes *parnassah,* as the Torah indicates when telling us what Yaakov said when Yosef disappeared: "*Vayeitzei ha'echad* — The one went away"; the "one," the unity, was gone, and as a result, "*tarof toraf* — he has surely been torn to pieces" (*Bereishis* 44:28; see *Chasam Sofer* there).

Shevet Mussar (Ch. 37) writes that *machlokes,* feuding, is so harmful and so despised by Hashem that when Bnei Yisrael committed the sin of serving the Golden Calf, the *mahn* still fell, because the nation was united. Yet, on the day that Korach and the 250 elders disagreed with Moshe and created a *machlokes,* the *mahn* did not fall. One should take every measure to avoid disagreement; there is no blessing in *machlokes.* Giving in to a client, a partner, or an employee to avoid disagreement is a wise business decision.

The Gemara (*Avodah Zarah* 18b) tells us that the *parnassah* of a *leitz,* a mocking person, will be diminished. The Chofetz Chaim (*Michtavim* §2) urges people to avoid reading newspapers and magazines that are filled with mockery and disparage the Torah, and that spread lies and *lashon hara*, as this itself prevents one from enjoying financial success.

To apply that today, one must also take care to avoid websites that are replete with contempt for Torah values and that spread *lashon hara.*

Living Within Your Means!

One of the most practical and greatest *segulos* for *parnassah* is living within your means. Societal pressures are often overwhelming and cause us to make unwise financial decisions, creating stress, discord, and pain. The Chofetz Chaim (*Biur Halachah* 529:1; Rav Pinchas of Koritz, *Shaar Toras Ha'adam* 144) urges people to spend wisely and not cave in to the pressures of spending more than they can afford. The key is to be strong and resolute to ensure you are making wise choices and not just to impress a neighbor. This is a monumental struggle in our close-knit communities. Each of us, even if we have the means, needs to be cognizant that our purchases, our *simchahs*, and our spending habits influence our children, neighbors, and overall community.

Rav Yechezkel Abramsky (*Chazon Yechezkel, Tanach,* p. 382) said that everyone cries when they say, in the Yamim

Noraim davening, "*Adam yesodo mei'afar v'sofo le'afar* — Man began as dust and will end as dust." Why do we cry? It is the way of the world that people are born and then pass away. We should cry when we say "*B'nafsho yavi lachmo* — With his life his bread will come," as we sacrifice our souls and eternal world in the pursuit of money. Of course, we need to go to work to pay the mortgage, taxes, tuition, clothing, food, and the like, and an Orthodox Jewish lifestyle is not cheap. But to what standards are we aspiring? In Western culture, success is almost always defined by the amount of money you make, the size of your home, the type of car you drive, the watch you wear, and the brand of clothing you dress in. There is no escaping that. The Jewish world has adopted much of this lifestyle, as well. But as Torah-true Yidden we need to understand the value of living within our means. When we live beyond them, we sacrifice our souls and our lives in the pursuit of a status symbol that can never bring everlasting or sincere happiness.

How many years have gone by, how many relationships have been ruined, how much spiritual advancement has stalled in the persistent pursuit of ever-rising standards? Let us distinguish between what is truly needed, and what we think we need because that is what everyone around us has. A woman who tells her husband, "I would rather you come home earlier from work so you could learn at night, or spend time with the children," is a hero. She understands that happiness comes from within. She has *emunah* that what she and her family have is what Hashem wants them to have.

When Avraham went to Egypt, he was not wealthy, and he must certainly have lodged at inexpensive inns. Yet, when he left Egypt a wealthy man, he lodged at the very same places he had been to before, although he was now a wealthy man, laden with livestock, silver, and gold. His newfound wealth did not change his lifestyle. He still patronized the same inexpensive lodgings he used when he was poor. He was in control of his life, not allowing money or society to dictate his lifestyle or his priorities. Avraham understood that money has been deposited by Hashem to be invested in *eternal* gains and not in frivolities or unnecessary luxuries (Rav Pam, *Atarah LaMelech,* p. 18).

With an ounce of forethought, a pound of restraint, and a focus on our priorities, we can ensure that we are not sacrificing our souls just to keep up with the Joneses and the Friedmans.

Shlomo HaMelech tells us, "*U'mosar ha'adam min habeheimah ayin* — The superiority of man over beast is naught" (*Koheles* 3:19). The verse may also be read as "The superiority of man over beast is *ayin* — his ability to say 'no.'"

After World War II, a relative of ours who had thus far been a refugee found out that she was the heir of a large estate. She was only twenty-two. At that moment she davened, "Hashem, please ensure that I can control the money and the money does not control me." Like Avraham, she lived a life of control, and invested wisely in mitzvos, *tzedakah*, and *chesed,* all of which are part of her eternal legacy and something that her family strives to emulate.

Listen to the words of Morgan Housel in his best-selling book, *The Psychology of Money*:

Everyone needs the basics. Once they're covered there's another level of comfortable basics, and past that there's basics that are both comfortable, entertaining, and enlightening. But spending beyond a pretty low level of materialism is mostly a reflection of ego, a way to spend money to show people that you have money.

Think of it like this, one of the most powerful ways to increase your savings is not to raise your income. It's to raise your humility.

When you define savings as the gap between your ego and your income you realize why many people with decent income save so little. It is a daily struggle against instinct to extend your peacock feathers to their outermost limits and keep up with others doing the same.

Savings can be created by spending less. You can spend less if you desire less. ***And you will desire less if you care less about what others think of you. Money relies more on psychology than finance.***

Using Your Money Well

Rav Yosef Chaim of Baghdad, the Ben Ish Chai, writes that the word for someone who is wealthy is עָשִׁיר, *ashir*, which is composed of two words, יֵשׁ, *yesh*, and רָע, *ra* (*Od Yosef Chai, Korach*). A person who uses his financial means to give *tzedakah*, learn and support Torah, and acquire mitzvos and the like will find that his money is "*yesh*," it is always with him and it will escort him into the Next World. As the Mishnah says, in the Next World Hashem will give each *tzaddik* 310 worlds of *berachah* and abundance; the *gematria* of יֵשׁ (*yesh*) is 310. On the other hand, one who uses the *berachah* of wealth for indulgences and transient pleasure is using the money for רָע (*ra*). A truly wealthy person ensures there is no "רָע" by breaking up the word, placing the "יֵשׁ" in the middle of the "רָע." The Noam Elimelech says that that is why, when Hashem showed Moshe Rabbeinu what a shekel coin should look like, He showed him a coin of fire. Fire can be constructive or destructive. It can warm and illuminate, and it can destroy and burn. The same is true with money; one can use it to warm the hearts of others and illuminate their lives, or one can use it to destroy.

May Hashem give each of us the Heavenly assistance to use the money He gives us for mitzvos and good things.

Being Happy With What You Have

Focusing on your *berachah* is a *segulah* for wealth. It will not necessarily increase the number of dollars in your bank account, but it will increase your appreciation for what you have.

In a famous study, volunteers watched a video of a basketball game. They were told to count the number of times the white team passed the ball. About twenty-five seconds into the video, a mascot in a full gorilla suit walked straight through the action, traveling across the screen for a full five seconds as the team continued to pass the ball.

After the video, the viewers were asked how many times the players passed the ball, as well as some additional questions, such as: Did you see anyone in the video besides for the basketball players? Did you see a gorilla?

Unbelievably, nearly *half* of the two hundred volunteers (46%) did not notice the gorilla! When they saw the tape again, they saw the gorilla, and were shocked and surprised that they had missed seeing it the first time.

How could such a large percentage have not seen a large hairy creature passing right in front of the camera? Psychologists explained it is because they were laser-focused on something else (counting the number of passes). This caused their neural filters to simply dump the gorilla sighting into their mental spam folder. This is called inattentional blindness, the inability to see what is right in front of us if we are not directly focused on it.

We are busy. So busy. Family, work, shul, community, Shabbos, Yom Tov, and more. When we are focused on other aspects of life, we are likely to suffer from inattentional blindness to much of the good that is showered on us. When we are on the move, in the car, at work, at shul, with friends, traveling, or shopping, it is difficult to take a step back and appreciate what we have. The nice carpet, the view, the fact that we have space for the kids to play, toys, plenty of food, running water, showers, heating, closets, clothing, the ability to learn and daven, and, of course, each other.

The Chazon Ish often said, "If things are good, who said they need to be better?" This is a refrain that one should repeat often. A *chassan* complained to the Chazon Ish that his future father-in-law had gifted him a Shas Warsaw, which included only a limited number of *meforshim*. To learn well, he said, he needed a Shas Vilna, with all the *meforshim*. "You need to accept everything Hashem gives you," the Chazon Ish responded. "I know a *talmid chacham* who blossomed with only a Shas Warsaw." Perhaps the Chazon Ish was referring to himself, as he learned from a Shas Warsaw his whole life! (*Maaseh Ish*, Vol. 1, p. 40).

Many situations can be seen as either a cup that is half-full or half-empty. The optimist looks at the half-cup of milk and appreciates what he has. The pessimist looks at the half-empty part and feels bad about what is not there. Rav Yaakov Galinsky explains that the word חָכָם — a wise person — forms the acronym חֲצִי כּוֹס מְלֵאָה — the half cup is full. He works towards always having an attitude of gratitude and appreciates the good that Hashem has bestowed upon him in life.

Rabbi Jonathan Sacks writes: "A consumer society... encourages us to spend money we don't have, on products we don't need, for a happiness that won't last. The reason such happiness does not last lies in the fundamental difference between hedonic happiness, a momentary feeling of pleasurable sensation, and eudaemonic happiness, which is the lasting feeling brought by having lived a good, meaningful, and worthy life. Hedonic happiness requires constant stimulation. Hence the idea of the 'hedonic treadmill': Getting what we want only temporarily satisfies desire. We almost immediately find new things to desire, so that though we may be better off materially, we do not become happier psychologically" (*Morality*, p. 106).

◆§ *Wealth Is Appreciating What We Have*

During the first Shabbos in isolation when Covid-19 began, I told the children about Rav Yehoshua Neuwirth, author of *Shemiras Shabbos K'Hilchasah*. In the introduction to the *sefer*, there is a short biography in which the author recounts that as a young child, running from the Nazis, Rav Neuwirth and his family hid in a concealed room for three years. During this time, he did not go outside once! He could not even look out the window! Can you imagine three years isolated from the world and not seeing sunlight? We then went around the table and had the children recount the good they have, despite the quarantine. Food, Shabbos yogurts, the ability to go outside and play, games, books, each other, and so much more. Covid-19 gave us the time to introspect, to gain appreciation, and *see,* perhaps for the first time, how much *berachah* Hashem showers on each of us.

The Maharal's brother, Rav Chaim, writes that the word "עָשִׁיר" is formed from the first letters of the words עֵינַיִם, שִׁנַּיִם, יָדַיִם, רַגְלַיִם (*einayim, **sh**inayim, **y**adayim, **r**aglayim)* — eyes, teeth, hands, legs. If you are blessed with eyes that see, teeth that chew and enhance your smile, and hands and feet to move with, then you are wealthy! (*Iggeres HaTiyul*).

"Greater is the one who benefits from his hands than one who fears Heaven," says the Gemara (*Berachos* 8a). The Maharal explains that the Gemara is telling us that great is the one who enjoys his work, who is happy and satisfied with his lot (*Nesivos Olam, Nesiv HaOsher* 1). Such a person is praiseworthy in This World and will be happy and calm in the Next World as well, because he does not spend his days pursuing the fleeting dream that more and newer will bring him joy. The Vilna Gaon (*Even Shlomo*, Ch. 3) writes that the sign of a kosher animal is that it chews its cud. It is happy with the food it has and rechews it again and again. The non-kosher animal swallows its food and just wants more and more.

Rav Shlomo Kluger (*Imrei Shefer*) writes that a person who is dissatisfied with his lot prevents his wealth from increasing. On the other hand, when one is happy and content with what he has, Hashem says, "Look, he is happy with what I have given him. If I give him more, he will not just want more after that."

Being happy with your lot is a *segulah* for wealth. This is alluded to in Yaakov's *berachah* for Naftali (*Devarim* 33:23), "Naftali is satiated with his lot," and therefore he is "filled with Hashem's blessings."

A Yid walking along the side of the street was struck by a car. Miraculously, he was okay and did not even suffer a broken bone. He brought cake and schnapps to shul to thank Hashem for the unbelievable miracle he had experienced.

The next day, another congregant set up cake and schnapps after Shacharis for a miracle that occurred to him. Amazed at two congregants experiencing open miracles on successive days, everyone gathered around to hear the man's account of supernatural Divine intervention. The man said, "I was walking outside, and baruch Hashem I was ***not*** *hit by a car" (Otzros HaTorah, Mizmor L'Sodah, p. 62).*

תפילות לפרנסה

Tefillos for Parnassah

פרשת המן

The commentators cite Yerushalmi that one who recites this chapter every day is assured that his food will not be lacking. *Levush* explains that this chapter teaches that God provides each day's sustenance — just as He provided the *mahn* each day in the Wilderness.

Many recite the following paragraph before the פָּרָשַׁת הַמָּן.
[It is omitted on Shabbos and Yom Tov.]

יְהִי רָצוֹן מִלְּפָנֶיךָ, יהוה אֱלֹהֵינוּ וֵאלֹהֵי אֲבוֹתֵינוּ, שֶׁתַּזְמִין פַּרְנָסָה לְכָל עַמְּךָ בֵּית יִשְׂרָאֵל, וּפַרְנָסָתִי וּפַרְנָסַת אַנְשֵׁי בֵיתִי בִּכְלָלָם, בְּנַחַת וְלֹא בְצַעַר, בְּכָבוֹד וְלֹא בְבִזּוּי, בְּהֶתֵּר וְלֹא בְאִסּוּר — כְּדֵי שֶׁנּוּכַל לַעֲבֹד עֲבוֹדָתֶךָ וְלִלְמוֹד תּוֹרָתֶךָ — כְּמוֹ שֶׁזַּנְתָּ לַאֲבוֹתֵינוּ מָן בַּמִּדְבָּר, בְּאֶרֶץ צִיָּה וַעֲרָבָה.

שמות טז:ד-לו

וַיֹּאמֶר יהוה אֶל מֹשֶׁה, הִנְנִי מַמְטִיר לָכֶם לֶחֶם מִן הַשָּׁמָיִם, וְיָצָא הָעָם וְלָקְטוּ דְּבַר יוֹם בְּיוֹמוֹ, לְמַעַן אֲנַסֶּנּוּ הֲיֵלֵךְ בְּתוֹרָתִי אִם לֹא. וְהָיָה בַּיּוֹם הַשִּׁשִּׁי, וְהֵכִינוּ אֵת אֲשֶׁר יָבִיאוּ, וְהָיָה מִשְׁנֶה עַל אֲשֶׁר יִלְקְטוּ יוֹם יוֹם. וַיֹּאמֶר מֹשֶׁה וְאַהֲרֹן אֶל כָּל בְּנֵי יִשְׂרָאֵל, עֶרֶב וִידַעְתֶּם כִּי יהוה הוֹצִיא אֶתְכֶם מֵאֶרֶץ מִצְרָיִם. וּבֹקֶר וּרְאִיתֶם אֶת כְּבוֹד יהוה, בְּשָׁמְעוֹ אֶת תְּלֻנֹּתֵיכֶם עַל יהוה, וְנַחְנוּ מָה, כִּי תַלִּינוּ עָלֵינוּ. וַיֹּאמֶר מֹשֶׁה, בְּתֵת יהוה לָכֶם בָּעֶרֶב בָּשָׂר לֶאֱכֹל וְלֶחֶם בַּבֹּקֶר לִשְׂבֹּעַ, בִּשְׁמֹעַ יהוה אֶת תְּלֻנֹּתֵיכֶם אֲשֶׁר אַתֶּם מַלִּינִם עָלָיו, וְנַחְנוּ מָה, לֹא עָלֵינוּ תְלֻנֹּתֵיכֶם, כִּי עַל יהוה. וַיֹּאמֶר מֹשֶׁה אֶל אַהֲרֹן, אֱמֹר אֶל כָּל עֲדַת בְּנֵי יִשְׂרָאֵל, קִרְבוּ לִפְנֵי יהוה, כִּי שָׁמַע אֵת תְּלֻנֹּתֵיכֶם. וַיְהִי כְּדַבֵּר אַהֲרֹן אֶל כָּל עֲדַת בְּנֵי יִשְׂרָאֵל, וַיִּפְנוּ אֶל הַמִּדְבָּר, וְהִנֵּה כְּבוֹד יהוה נִרְאָה בֶּעָנָן.

❧ THE CHAPTER OF MAHN ☙

The commentators cite Yerushalmi that one who recites this chapter every day is assured that his food will not be lacking. *Levush* explains that this chapter teaches that God provides each day's sustenance — just as He provided the *mahn* each day in the Wilderness.

Many recite the following paragraph before the פָּרָשַׁת הַמָּן.
[It is omitted on Shabbos and Yom Tov.]

May it be Your will, HASHEM, *our God and the God of our forefathers, that you prepare a livelihood for Your entire people, the House of Yisrael — and my livelihood and the livelihood of the members of my household among them — with ease and not with pain, with honor and not with disgrace, in a permissible and not in a forbidden manner, so that we will be able to perform Your service and study Your Torah, as You nourished our forefathers in the Wilderness, in a desolate and arid land.*

Shemos 16:4–36

HASHEM *said to Moshe, "Behold I will cause bread to rain down on you from heaven; and the people will go out and gather each day's portion in its day, so that I can test whether they will walk according to My teaching or not. And it will be on the sixth day that they will prepare what they will bring; for there will be double what they will gather day by day." Moshe and Aharon said to all the Children of Yisrael: "This evening you will know that* HASHEM *removed you from the land of Egypt. And in the morning you will see the glory of* HASHEM *when He hears your complaints against* HASHEM*; for what are we, that you complain against us?" Then Moshe said, "[This will occur] when* HASHEM *gives you meat to eat in the evening and bread in the morning to satisfaction, when* HASHEM *will have heard your complaints that you charge against Him; for what are we? — not against us are your complaints, but against* HASHEM*!" Moshe said to Aharon, "Say to the entire congregation of the Children of Yisrael, 'Draw near before* HASHEM*, for He has heard your complaints.'" And it happened that when Aharon spoke to the entire congregation of the Children of Yisrael, they turned toward the Wilderness and behold! — the glory of* HASHEM *was seen in a cloud.*

וַיְדַבֵּר יהוה אֶל מֹשֶׁה לֵּאמֹר. שָׁמַעְתִּי אֶת תְּלוּנֹּת בְּנֵי יִשְׂרָאֵל, דַּבֵּר אֲלֵהֶם לֵאמֹר, בֵּין הָעַרְבַּיִם תֹּאכְלוּ בָשָׂר, וּבַבֹּקֶר תִּשְׂבְּעוּ לָחֶם, וִידַעְתֶּם כִּי אֲנִי יהוה אֱלֹהֵיכֶם. וַיְהִי בָעֶרֶב, וַתַּעַל הַשְּׂלָו וַתְּכַס אֶת הַמַּחֲנֶה, וּבַבֹּקֶר הָיְתָה שִׁכְבַת הַטַּל סָבִיב לַמַּחֲנֶה. וַתַּעַל שִׁכְבַת הַטָּל, וְהִנֵּה עַל פְּנֵי הַמִּדְבָּר דַּק מְחֻסְפָּס, דַּק כַּכְּפֹר עַל הָאָרֶץ. וַיִּרְאוּ בְנֵי יִשְׂרָאֵל, וַיֹּאמְרוּ אִישׁ אֶל אָחִיו, מָן הוּא, כִּי לֹא יָדְעוּ מַה הוּא, וַיֹּאמֶר מֹשֶׁה אֲלֵהֶם, הוּא הַלֶּחֶם אֲשֶׁר נָתַן יהוה לָכֶם לְאָכְלָה. זֶה הַדָּבָר אֲשֶׁר צִוָּה יהוה, לִקְטוּ מִמֶּנּוּ אִישׁ לְפִי אָכְלוֹ, עֹמֶר לַגֻּלְגֹּלֶת, מִסְפַּר נַפְשֹׁתֵיכֶם, אִישׁ לַאֲשֶׁר בְּאָהֳלוֹ תִּקָּחוּ. וַיַּעֲשׂוּ כֵן בְּנֵי יִשְׂרָאֵל, וַיִּלְקְטוּ הַמַּרְבֶּה וְהַמַּמְעִיט. וַיָּמֹדּוּ בָעֹמֶר, וְלֹא הֶעְדִּיף הַמַּרְבֶּה, וְהַמַּמְעִיט לֹא הֶחְסִיר, אִישׁ לְפִי אָכְלוֹ לָקָטוּ. וַיֹּאמֶר מֹשֶׁה אֲלֵהֶם, אִישׁ אַל יוֹתֵר מִמֶּנּוּ עַד בֹּקֶר. וְלֹא שָׁמְעוּ אֶל מֹשֶׁה, וַיּוֹתִרוּ אֲנָשִׁים מִמֶּנּוּ עַד בֹּקֶר וַיָּרֻם תּוֹלָעִים וַיִּבְאַשׁ, וַיִּקְצֹף עֲלֵהֶם מֹשֶׁה. וַיִּלְקְטוּ אֹתוֹ בַּבֹּקֶר בַּבֹּקֶר, אִישׁ כְּפִי אָכְלוֹ, וְחַם הַשֶּׁמֶשׁ וְנָמָס. וַיְהִי בַּיּוֹם הַשִּׁשִּׁי, לָקְטוּ לֶחֶם מִשְׁנֶה, שְׁנֵי הָעֹמֶר לָאֶחָד, וַיָּבֹאוּ כָּל נְשִׂיאֵי הָעֵדָה, וַיַּגִּידוּ לְמֹשֶׁה. וַיֹּאמֶר אֲלֵהֶם, הוּא אֲשֶׁר דִּבֶּר יהוה, שַׁבָּתוֹן שַׁבַּת קֹדֶשׁ לַיהוה מָחָר, אֵת אֲשֶׁר תֹּאפוּ אֵפוּ, וְאֵת אֲשֶׁר תְּבַשְּׁלוּ בַּשֵּׁלוּ, וְאֵת כָּל הָעֹדֵף הַנִּיחוּ לָכֶם לְמִשְׁמֶרֶת עַד הַבֹּקֶר. וַיַּנִּיחוּ אֹתוֹ עַד הַבֹּקֶר כַּאֲשֶׁר צִוָּה מֹשֶׁה, וְלֹא הִבְאִישׁ,

HASHEM spoke to Moshe, saying, "I have heard the complaints of the Children of Yisrael; speak to them, saying: In the afternoon you will eat meat and in the morning you will be sated with bread; and you shall realize that I am HASHEM, your God." And it happened in the evening that the quail came up and covered the camp, and in the morning there was a layer of dew surrounding the camp. The layer of dew evaporated and behold! — upon the surface of the Wilderness was revealed something thin, as thin as frost upon the ground. The Children of Yisrael saw and said to each other, "What is this?" — for they did not know what it was; then Moshe said to them: "This is the food that HASHEM has given you to eat. This is the thing that HASHEM has commanded, 'Gather from it, for each man according to his consumption — an omer per person — according to the number of your people, everyone according to whoever is in his tent shall you take.'" The Children of Yisrael did so; they gathered, he who took much and he who took little. Then they measured in an omer, and whoever took more did not have extra and whoever took less was not lacking; each one gathered according to his consumption. Then Moshe said to them, "Let no one leave over from it until morning." But they did not heed Moshe, and some men left part of it over until morning and it bred worms and became putrid, and Moshe became angry at them. They would gather it every morning, everyone according to his consumption, and when the sunlight grew hot it would melt. It happened on the sixth day that they gathered a double measure of food, two omers for each one; and all the leaders of the congregation came and told Moshe. He said to them: "This is what HASHEM spoke of; tomorrow is a day of rest, a holy Shabbos to HASHEM; what you wish to bake, bake; and what you wish to cook, cook; and whatever is left over, put away for yourselves in safekeeping until the morning." They put it away until the morning, as Moshe commanded; and it did not become putrid

וְרִמָּה לֹא הָיְתָה בּוֹ. וַיֹּאמֶר מֹשֶׁה, אִכְלֻהוּ הַיּוֹם, כִּי שַׁבָּת הַיּוֹם לַיהוה, הַיּוֹם לֹא תִמְצָאֻהוּ בַּשָּׂדֶה. שֵׁשֶׁת יָמִים תִּלְקְטֻהוּ, וּבַיּוֹם הַשְּׁבִיעִי שַׁבָּת, לֹא יִהְיֶה בּוֹ. וַיְהִי בַּיּוֹם הַשְּׁבִיעִי, יָצְאוּ מִן הָעָם לִלְקֹט, וְלֹא מָצָאוּ.

וַיֹּאמֶר יהוה אֶל מֹשֶׁה, עַד אָנָה מֵאַנְתֶּם לִשְׁמֹר מִצְוֹתַי וְתוֹרֹתָי. רְאוּ כִּי יהוה נָתַן לָכֶם הַשַּׁבָּת, עַל כֵּן הוּא נֹתֵן לָכֶם בַּיּוֹם הַשִּׁשִּׁי לֶחֶם יוֹמָיִם, שְׁבוּ אִישׁ תַּחְתָּיו, אַל יֵצֵא אִישׁ מִמְּקֹמוֹ בַּיּוֹם הַשְּׁבִיעִי. וַיִּשְׁבְּתוּ הָעָם בַּיּוֹם הַשְּׁבִעִי. וַיִּקְרְאוּ בֵית יִשְׂרָאֵל אֶת שְׁמוֹ מָן, וְהוּא כְּזֶרַע גַּד לָבָן, וְטַעְמוֹ כְּצַפִּיחִת בִּדְבָשׁ. וַיֹּאמֶר מֹשֶׁה, זֶה הַדָּבָר אֲשֶׁר צִוָּה יהוה, מְלֹא הָעֹמֶר מִמֶּנּוּ לְמִשְׁמֶרֶת לְדֹרֹתֵיכֶם, לְמַעַן יִרְאוּ אֶת הַלֶּחֶם אֲשֶׁר הֶאֱכַלְתִּי אֶתְכֶם בַּמִּדְבָּר בְּהוֹצִיאִי אֶתְכֶם מֵאֶרֶץ מִצְרָיִם. וַיֹּאמֶר מֹשֶׁה אֶל אַהֲרֹן, קַח צִנְצֶנֶת אַחַת וְתֶן שָׁמָּה מְלֹא הָעֹמֶר מָן, וְהַנַּח אֹתוֹ לִפְנֵי יהוה, לְמִשְׁמֶרֶת לְדֹרֹתֵיכֶם. כַּאֲשֶׁר צִוָּה יהוה אֶל מֹשֶׁה, וַיַּנִּיחֵהוּ אַהֲרֹן לִפְנֵי הָעֵדֻת לְמִשְׁמָרֶת. וּבְנֵי יִשְׂרָאֵל אָכְלוּ אֶת הַמָּן אַרְבָּעִים שָׁנָה, עַד בֹּאָם אֶל אֶרֶץ נוֹשָׁבֶת, אֶת הַמָּן אָכְלוּ עַד בֹּאָם אֶל קְצֵה אֶרֶץ כְּנָעַן. וְהָעֹמֶר עֲשִׂרִית הָאֵיפָה הוּא.

and there were no worms in it. Then Moshe said, "Eat it today for today is a Shabbos to HASHEM; today you will not find it in the field. You are to gather it for six days; but the seventh day is Shabbos, on it there will be none." But it happened on the seventh day that some of the people went out to gather, and they did not find.

HASHEM said to Moshe: "How long will you refuse to observe My commandments and My teachings? See — because HASHEM has given you the Shabbos, therefore He provides you on the sixth day with food for two days; let every man remain in his place; let no one leave his domain on the seventh day." So the people rested on the seventh day. The House of Yisrael called it mahn. It was like coriander seed, it was white, and it tasted like dough kneaded with honey. Moshe said: "This is the matter that HASHEM commanded: An omerful of it is to be a keepsake for your generations, so that they can see the food that I fed you in the Wilderness when I took you out of the land of Egypt." Moshe said to Aharon, "Take a single earthenware jar and place in it an omerful of mahn, and set it down before HASHEM as a keepsake for your generations." Just as HASHEM commanded Moshe, so Aharon set it down before the Aron of Testimony as a keepsake. The Children of Yisrael ate the mahn for forty years until they arrived at a populated land; they ate the mahn until they arrived at the edge of the land of Canaan. The omer is one-tenth of an eifah.

תפלה על הפרנסה

This prayer is recited after פָּרָשַׁת הַמָּן.
[It is omitted on Shabbos and Yom Tov.]

אַתָּה הוּא יהוה לְבַדֶּךָ, אַתָּה עָשִׂיתָ אֶת הַשָּׁמַיִם וּשְׁמֵי הַשָּׁמַיִם, הָאָרֶץ וְכָל אֲשֶׁר עָלֶיהָ, הַיַּמִּים וְכָל אֲשֶׁר בָּהֶם, וְאַתָּה מְחַיֶּה אֶת כֻּלָּם. וְאַתָּה הוּא שֶׁעָשִׂיתָ נִסִּים וְנִפְלָאוֹת גְּדוֹלוֹת תָּמִיד עִם אֲבוֹתֵינוּ. גַּם בַּמִּדְבָּר הִמְטַרְתָּ לָהֶם לֶחֶם מִן הַשָּׁמַיִם, וּמִצּוּר הַחַלָּמִישׁ, הוֹצֵאתָ לָהֶם מַיִם, וְגַם נָתַתָּ לָהֶם כָּל צָרְכֵיהֶם, וְשִׂמְלָתָם לֹא בָלְתָה מֵעֲלֵיהֶם. כֵּן בְּרַחֲמֶיךָ הָרַבִּים וּבַחֲסָדֶיךָ הָעֲצוּמִים, תְּזוּנֵנוּ וּתְפַרְנְסֵנוּ וּתְכַלְכְּלֵנוּ וְתַסְפִּיק כָּל צָרְכֵנוּ, וְצָרְכֵי עַמְּךָ בֵּית יִשְׂרָאֵל הַמְּרֻבִּים, בִּמְלוּי וּבְרֶוַח, בְּלִי טֹרַח וְעָמָל גָּדוֹל, מִתַּחַת יָדְךָ הַנְּקִיָּה, וְלֹא מִתַּחַת יְדֵי בָשָׂר וָדָם.

יְהִי רָצוֹן מִלְּפָנֶיךָ, יהוה אֱלֹהַי וֵאלֹהֵי אֲבוֹתַי, שֶׁתָּכִין לִי וּלְאַנְשֵׁי בֵיתִי כָּל מַחְסוֹרֵנוּ, וְתַזְמִין לָנוּ כָּל צָרְכֵנוּ. לְכָל יוֹם וָיוֹם מֵחַיֵּינוּ דֵּי מַחְסוֹרֵנוּ, וּלְכָל שָׁעָה וְשָׁעָה מִשְּׁעוֹתֵינוּ דֵּי סִפּוּקֵנוּ, וּלְכָל עֶצֶם מֵעֲצָמֵינוּ דֵּי מִחְיָתֵנוּ, כְּיָדְךָ הַטּוֹבָה וְהָרְחָבָה, וְלֹא כְּמִעוּט מִפְעָלֵינוּ, וְקֹצֶר חֲסָדֵינוּ, וּמִזְעֵיר גְּמוּלוֹתֵינוּ. וְיִהְיוּ מְזוֹנוֹתַי, וּמְזוֹנוֹת אַנְשֵׁי בֵיתִי וְזַרְעִי וְזֶרַע זַרְעִי, מְסוּרִים בְּיָדְךָ, וְלֹא בְּיַד בָּשָׂר וָדָם.

PRAYER FOR LIVELIHOOD

This prayer is recited after פָּרָשַׁת הַמָּן.
[It is omitted on Shabbos and Yom Tov.]

It is You alone, HASHEM, You have made the heaven, the most exalted heaven, the earth and everything upon it, the seas and everything in them, and You give them all life. It is You Who always performed miracles and great wonders with our forefathers. Also in the Wilderness You rained down for them food from heaven, and from the flinty rock You withdrew water for them, and You also provided them all their needs, and their clothing did not wear out upon them. So in Your abundant mercy and powerful kindness, may You nourish us, sustain us, and support us, and supply all our needs and the abundant needs of Your people the House of Yisrael, with fullness and relief, without travail or great effort, from beneath Your pure hand and not from beneath mortal hands.

May it be Your will, HASHEM, my God and the God of my forefathers, that You prepare for me and for the members of my household all our deficiencies and make ready all our needs, every single day of our days according to our needs — every single hour of our hours our adequate supply; and for every bone of our bones sufficient nourishment, in accordance with Your good and generous hand, and not according to the paucity of our accomplishment, the shortness of our kindness, and the diminution of our generosity. May my nourishment and the nourishment of the members of my household, my offspring and the children of my offspring be committed to Your hand and not to the hand of flesh and blood.

תפלה לפרנסה מהשל"ה

של"ה נר מצוה מס' תמיד קלד

אַתָּה הוּא הָאֱלֹהִים הַזָּן מִקַּרְנֵי רְאֵמִים וְעַד בֵּיצֵי כִנִּים, וְאַתָּה הוּא הַמֵּכִין כָּל צָרְכֵיהֶן, וְנוֹסָף עַל הַצְּרָכִים הַהֶכְרֵחִיִּים אַתָּה הוּא הַנּוֹתֵן בְּמִלּוּי וְרֶוַח וְעֹשֶׁר וְכָבוֹד, כָּל זֶה עוֹשֶׂה בְּנִדְבַת לִבְּךָ הַטּוֹב. כִּי אַתָּה הוּא נָדִיב בֶּאֱמֶת, לֹא כְּמוֹ שֶׁקּוֹרִין לִפְעָמִים לְאָדָם אֶחָד נָדִיב, כִּי נְדִיבוּתוֹ אֵינָהּ אֲמִתִּית רַק לְתַשְׁלוּם גְּמוּל אוֹ בִּשְׁבִיל טוֹבָה שֶׁקִּדְּמוּהוּ וַהֲרֵי הוּא כְּסוֹחֵר, אָכֵן מִי הִקְדִּימְךָ וְשִׁלַּמְתָּ, וּבְנִדְבַת לִבְּךָ הַטּוֹב טוֹב וּמֵטִיב אַתָּה לַכֹּל.

וְלִי אֲנִי עַבְדְּךָ הֵטַבְתָּ עַל כֹּל, וְנָתַתָּ לִי עֹשֶׁר וְכָבוֹד מִיָּדְךָ הַכֹּל, בֵּרַכְתַּנִי מִכֹּל בַּכֹּל כֹּל. נָתַתָּ לִי סְפָרִים הַרְבֵּה, וְכֶסֶף וְזָהָב לָרֹב, וּמַלְבּוּשֵׁי כָבוֹד וְדִירָה בְּכָבוֹד, קָטֹנְתִּי מִכָּל הַחֲסָדִים אֲשֶׁר עָשִׂיתָ אֶת עַבְדֶּךָ, וְיָרֵא אָנֹכִי מְאֹד לְנַפְשִׁי שֶׁלֹּא יִהְיֶה חָס וְשָׁלוֹם עֹשֶׁר שָׁמוּר לִי לְרָעָה לְהַאֲכִילֵנִי הַמְעַט מִזְּכֻיּוֹתַי שֶׁבְּיָדִי, וּבְאִם הוּא כֵן, קַח נָא אֶת בִּרְכָתִי וְאַל אֶרְאֶה בְּרָעָתִי לָעוֹלָם הַבָּא עוֹלָם הַנִּצְחִי. וּבְאִם רְצוֹנְךָ הַטּוֹב לְמֵיהַב וְלֹא לְמִשְׁקַל, תֵּן בְּלִבִּי וּבְלֵב כָּל הַנִּלְוִים אֵלַי שֶׁלֹּא לְהִשְׁתַּמֵּשׁ בְּמַתְּנוֹתֶיךָ לְתַעֲנוּגִים גּוּפָנִיִּים, וְיִתְפַּרְנְסוּ מִמֶּנּוּ בַּעֲלֵי תוֹרָה אֲנָשִׁים כְּשֵׁרִים אֲנָשִׁים הֲגוּנִים, עֲשׂוֹת צְדָקָה הַרְבֵּה וּגְמִילוּת חֲסָדִים לַקְּרוֹבִים וְלָרְחוֹקִים, וּדְבַר יהוה יָקוּם, יִהְיוּ לְרָצוֹן אִמְרֵי פִי, וְהֶגְיוֹן לִבִּי לְפָנֶיךָ יהוה צוּרִי וְגֹאֲלִי.

❧ TEFILLAH FROM THE SHELAH ☙ FOR SUCCESS IN PARNASSAH

Sefer HaShelah

It is You, the God Who nourishes from the horns of re'eimim to the eggs of lice, and it is You Who prepare all their needs, and in addition to their necessities, it is You Who give in fullness and generously, wealth and honor. All this is done from the generosity of Your good heart, for it is You Who are truly generous. This is unlike a person who is sometimes called "generous," for his generosity is not genuine, but rather as a repayment or for a favor that preceded it, and such a person is like a merchant. But You, who preceded You, for You to pay? From the generosity of Your good heart, You are good to all and benefit all.

And to me, Your servant, you have benefited over all; You have given me wealth and honor, and You have blessed me from everything, in everything, with everything. You have given me many books, silver and gold in large quantities, clothing of honor, and an honorable dwelling. I have been diminished by all the kindness that You have done Your servant, and I fear greatly for my soul that it not be, Heaven forbid, "Riches preserved for their owner to his misfortune," to have me consume the minimum of my merits that are in my hand. And if so, please take away my blessing, so that I may not see my misfortune in the eternal World to Come. If it is Your good will to give and not to take, place in my heart and in the hearts of all accompanying me not to use Your gifts for physical pleasures, but that masters of Torah, proper people, and good people be sustained by it; [May we] do much charity and to grant kindness to those near and far, and may the word of HASHEM stand. May the expressions of my mouth and the thoughts of my heart find favor before You, HASHEM, my Rock and my Redeemer.

תפלה כשהולך לעשות עסק מבעל השל"ה

של"ה שער האותיות

One who goes out to engage in business makes the following statement:

אֲנִי הוֹלֵךְ לַעֲשׂוֹת זֶה
בִּרְשׁוּת הַשֵּׁם יִתְבָּרֵךְ וּלְמַעַן שְׁמוֹ.

He continues with the following short prayer:

רִבּוֹנוֹ שֶׁל עוֹלָם! בְּדִבְרֵי קָדְשְׁךָ כָּתוּב לֵאמֹר: "וְהַבּוֹטֵחַ בַּיהוה חֶסֶד יְסוֹבְבֶנּוּ", וּכְתִיב "וְאַתָּה מְחַיֶּה אֶת כֻּלָּם". חֲלוֹק לִי מֵחַסְדְּךָ לִתֵּן בְּרָכָה בְּמַעֲשֵׂה יָדַי בִּפְעֻלָּה זוֹ.

תפלה להצלחת הפרנסה מהחתם סופר

Set aside money for *tzedakah l'ilui nishmas* R' Meir Baal HaNess, and recite:

הֲרֵינִי מִתְנַדֵּב מָעוֹת זֶה לִצְדָקָה לְעִלּוּי נִשְׁמָתוֹ שֶׁל רַבִּי מֵאִיר בַּעַל הַנֵּס, כְּדֵי שֶׁהַקָּדוֹשׁ בָּרוּךְ הוּא, בִּזְכוּת רַבִּי מֵאִיר בַּעַל הַנֵּס, יַצְלִיחֵנִי בְּמִסְחָר זֶה שֶׁאֲנִי עוֹשֶׂה וְכָל אֲשֶׁר אֶעֱשֶׂה אַרְוִיחַ, וְיָרוּם קַרְנִי וְיִגְבַּהּ מַזָּלִי לִהְיוֹת דְּבָרַי נִשְׁמָעִים בִּפְנֵי כָּל שׁוֹמְעָם, וְאֶהְיֶה לְחֵן וּלְחֶסֶד וּמְכֻבָּד בְּעֵינֵי כָּל רוֹאַי מֵעַתָּה וְעַד עוֹלָם. אֱלָהָא דְמֵאִיר עֲנֵנִי. אֱלָהָא דְמֵאִיר עֲנֵנִי. אֱלָהָא דְמֵאִיר עֲנֵנִי.

אֶקְרָא לֵאלֹהִים עֶלְיוֹן לָאֵל גֹּמֵר עָלָי. חָנֵּנִי אֲדֹנָי, כִּי אֵלֶיךָ אֶקְרָא כָּל הַיּוֹם. עָזְרֵנוּ אֱלֹהֵי יִשְׁעֵנוּ עַל דְּבַר כְּבוֹד שְׁמֶךָ, וְהַצִּילֵנוּ וְכַפֵּר עַל חַטֹּאתֵינוּ לְמַעַן שְׁמֶךָ. עֲשֵׂה לְמַעַן יְמִינֶךָ, עֲשֵׂה לְמַעַן תּוֹרָתֶךָ, עֲשֵׂה לְמַעַן קְדֻשָּׁתֶךָ. יִהְיוּ לְרָצוֹן אִמְרֵי פִי וְהֶגְיוֹן לִבִּי לְפָנֶיךָ, יהוה צוּרִי וְגוֹאֲלִי. אָמֵן וְכֵן יְהִי רָצוֹן.

⚜ TEFILLAH FROM THE SHELAH TO BE RECITED ⚜ UPON STARTING WORK

One who goes out to engage in business makes the following statement:

I go to do this with the permission of HASHEM, may He be blessed, and for His sake.

He continues with the following short prayer:

Master of the Universe! In Your holy Writings the following is written: "He who trusts in HASHEM, may kindness surround him." It is also written, "You give them all life." Grant me a portion of Your kindness to give blessing to my handiwork in this action.

⚜ TEFILLAH FROM THE CHASAM SOFER ⚜ FOR SUCCESS IN BUSINESS

Set aside money for *tzedakah l'ilui nishmas* R' Meir Baal HaNess, and recite:

I hereby donate this money to charity for the ascension of the soul of R' Meir Baal HaNess, so that the Holy One, Blessed is He, in the merit of R' Meir Baal HaNess, grant me success in this business that I am doing; may I be successful wherever I turn and may I profit in all that I do. May He exalt my pride and may my star rise so that my words are listened to by all who hear them. May I be for grace and for kindness and honored in the eyes of all who see me from now and forever. God of Meir answer me. God of Meir answer me. God of Meir answer me.

I will call upon God, Most High, to the God Who fulfills for me. Show me favor, O God, for to You do I call the whole day. Assist us, O God of our salvation, for the sake of Your Name's glory, rescue us, and atone for our sins for Your Name's sake. Act for Your right hand's sake, act for Your Torah's sake, act for Your sanctity's sake. May the expressions of my mouth and the thoughts of my heart find favor before You, HASHEM, my Rock and my Redeemer. Amen, and so may it be Your will.

תפלה לפרנסה מר׳ שלמה אלקבץ

ספר ראשית חכמה שער אהבה

אַתָּה הָאֵל הַזָּן מִקַּרְנֵי רְאֵמִים עַד בֵּיצֵי כִנִּים, וְאֵין בְּיַד שׁוּם מַלְאָךְ וְשַׂר לָזוּן, וּלְפַרְנֵס, וּלְכַלְכֵּל כַּלְכָּלָתְךָ. כַּכָּתוּב עַל יְדֵי דָוִד עַבְדֶּךָ: עֵינֵי כֹל אֵלֶיךָ יְשַׂבֵּרוּ, וְאַתָּה נוֹתֵן לָהֶם אֶת אָכְלָם בְּעִתּוֹ. פּוֹתֵחַ אֶת יָדֶךָ, וּמַשְׂבִּיעַ לְכָל חַי רָצוֹן. וּכְתִיב: נֹתֵן לֶחֶם לְכָל בָּשָׂר, כִּי לְעוֹלָם חַסְדּוֹ. וּמַפְתֵּחַ זֶה הוּא בְּיָדְךָ לְצָרֵף וּלְלַבֵּן בְּנֵי אָדָם לְשֶׁיִּבְטְחוּ בְךָ וְיֵדְעוּ כִּי מוֹשִׁיעַ אֵין בִּלְתֶּךָ.

תפלה להצלחת הפרנסה מבעל פלא יועץ

פלא יועץ ערך הפרנסה

הֲרֵינִי הוֹלֵךְ לְהִתְעַסֵּק בְּמַשָּׂא וּמַתָּן, וּבְטוּחֲנִי בַּיהוה שֶׁהוּא יִתֵּן לִי כֹּחַ לַעֲשׂוֹת חָיִל, לְהִתְפַּרְנֵס אֲנִי וּבְנֵי בֵיתִי בְּדֶרֶךְ כָּבוֹד, וְלַעֲשׂוֹת צְדָקָה וּגְמִילוּת חֲסָדִים, וּכְדֵי שֶׁאוּכַל לְקַיֵּם כָּל מִצְוֹת בּוֹרְאִי כְּתִקּוּנָן. עָזְרֵנוּ אֱלֹהֵי יִשְׁעֵנוּ עַל דְּבַר כְּבוֹד שְׁמֶךָ. אַל תֵּפֶן לְרִשְׁעֵנוּ. עֲשֵׂה עִמָּנוּ צְדָקָה וָחֶסֶד לְמַעַן שִׁמְךָ הַגָּדוֹל. יִהְיוּ לְרָצוֹן אִמְרֵי פִי וְהֶגְיוֹן לִבִּי לְפָנֶיךָ יהוה צוּרִי וְגֹאֲלִי.

৩ TEFILLAH FROM RAV SHLOMO ALKABETZ ৯ FOR PARNASSAH

You are the God Who nourishes from the horns of re'eimim to the eggs of lice, and no angel or minister has the ability to nourish, sustain or support Your support. As is written by Dovid, Your servant: "The eyes of all look to You with hope and You give them their food in its proper time. You open Your hand and satisfy the desire of every living thing." It is also written: "He gives nourishment to all flesh, for His kindness endures forever." This key is in Your hand to smelt and purify people, when they trust in You and know that there is no other savior.

৩ TEFILLAH FROM THE PELE YOETZ ৯ BEFORE STARTING WORK

I am about to go to engage in business and I have confidence that HASHEM *will give me the ability to be successful, to earn a livelihood for myself and my household with dignity, and to give charity and extend kindness, and so I that will be able to correctly fulfill all the commandments of my Creator. Assist us, O God of our salvation, for the sake of the glory of Your Name. Do not turn to our wrongdoing. Treat us with charity and kindness for the sake of Your great Name.*

May the expressions of my mouth and the thoughts of my heart find favor before You, HASHEM, *my Rock and my Redeemer.*

תפלה קדם מסחר מהחיי אדם

בית אברהם — צוואת החיי אדם

הֲרֵינִי הוֹלֵךְ לַעֲסוֹק בְּמַשָּׂא וּמַתָּן בֶּאֱמוּנָה כְּדֵי לְפַרְנֵס אוֹתִי וְאֶת בְּנֵי בֵיתִי, וִיהִי רָצוֹן שֶׁתִּשְׁלַח בְּרָכָה בְּמַעֲשֵׂה יָדַי וּבְכָל אֲשֶׁר אֶפְנֶה, אֲנִי וְכָל הָעוֹסְקִים בִּשְׁבִילִי, נַצְלִיחַ וְנַשְׂכִּיל, כִּי עָלֶיךָ הִשְׁלַכְתִּי יְהָבִי וְאַל אֵבוֹשָׁה כִּי בָטַחְתִּי בָךְ. וּתְצַוֶּה לַמַּלְאָכִים הַמְמֻנִּים עַל הַפַּרְנָסָה שֶׁיּוֹלִיכוּ הַקּוֹנִים אֶצְלִי, וְתִמְצָא סְחוֹרָתִי חֵן בְּעֵינֵיהֶם, וְהַצִּילֵנִי מִכָּל נִדְנוּד וְחִלּוּל הַשֵּׁם, וְאַל תְּבִיאֵנִי לִידֵי נִסָּיוֹן, וְיִתְקַדֵּשׁ שִׁמְךָ עַל יָדִי.

תפלה מבעל האור לשמים

It is in this *tefillah* that we declare our total reliance on Hashem and understand that we are in His hands and under His control. *Bitachon* in Hashem is the very key to access *parnassah* and *berachah*.

רִבּוֹן הָעוֹלָמִים יָדַעְתִּי כִּי הִנְנִי בְּיָדְךָ לְבַד, כַּחֹמֶר בְּיַד הַיּוֹצֵר, וְאִם גַּם אֶתְאַמֵּץ בְּעֵצוֹת וְתַחְבּוּלוֹת וְכָל יוֹשְׁבֵי תֵבֵל יַעַמְדוּ לִימִינִי לְהוֹשִׁיעֵנִי וְלִתְמֹךְ נַפְשִׁי מִבַּלְעֲדֵי עֻזְּךָ וְעֶזְרָתֶךָ אֵין עֶזְרָה וִישׁוּעָה, וְאִם חָלִילָה יַחְפְּצוּ כֻּלָּם לְהָרַע אָז אַתָּה בְּחֶמְלָתְךָ תָּשִׂים עֵינֶיךָ עָלַי וְתַשְׁקוֹף עָלַי לְטוֹבָה מִמְּעוֹן קָדְשֶׁךָ, הִנֵּה חֲבָלִים נָפְלוּ לִי בַּנְּעִמִים וִישׁוּעָתִי בָּאָה וְעֶזְרָתִי תִּגָּלֶה, לָכֵן עָזְרֵנִי רִבּוֹן הָעוֹלָמִים לִהְיוֹת עֵינַי פְּתוּחוֹת לִרְאוֹת תָּמִיד אֲמִתּוּת הַדָּבָר הַזֶּה, וִיהִי תָּקוּעַ וְקָבוּעַ אֱמוּנָתְךָ בְּלִבִּי בְּכָל עֵת לְבַל אָסוּר לֹא בְּדִבּוּר וְלֹא בְּמַעֲשֶׂה וְלֹא

༄ TEFILLAH FROM THE CHAYEI ADAM ༄ FOR PARNASSAH

Beis Avraham (R' Avraham Danzig)

Behold! I am going to engage in business with faith in order to support myself and my household. May it be Your will that You send blessing to my activity, and wherever I turn — I and those working for me — may we succeed and act wisely, for I have cast my burden on You, and may I not be ashamed, for I have placed my trust in You. Command the angels who are charged over sustenance to bring customers to me, and may my merchandise find favor in their eyes. Save me from the slightest hint [of sin] or desecration of the Name. Do not bring me into the power of challenge, and may Your Name be sanctified by me.

༄ TEFILLAH FROM THE OHR LASHAMAYIM ༄ FOR PARNASSAH

It is in this *tefillah* that we declare our total reliance on Hashem and understand that we are in His hands and under His control. *Bitachon* in Hashem is the very key to access *parnassah* and *berachah.*

Master of the World, I know that I am in Your hands alone, like clay in the hands of a craftsman. Even if I mightily attempt with ideas and plans and all of the planet's inhabitants stand by my right side to support me, without Your power and assistance there is no aid nor salvation. Even if, God forbid, everyone will desire to harm me, You, with Your compassion, please pay attention to me and positively gaze down upon me from Your Holy Abode. Behold, portions have fallen to me in pleasant places, my salvation is coming, and my aid will be revealed. Therefore, Master of the World, enable me to keep my eyes open to constantly recognize the truth of this matter. [My] faith in You should always be firm and enduring within my heart and for every instant, and nothing to the contrary should ever enter my mind, my words, actions, or

בְּמַחֲשָׁבָה לַעֲבֹד זוּלָתְךָ חָלִילָה כִּי אִם תִּרְדֹּף נַפְשִׁי רְצוֹנְךָ הַטּוֹב בֶּאֱמֶת, גַּם עָזְרֵנִי לְבַל יָמוּשׁ מֵרַעְיוֹנַי וּמִלְּבִּי גְּדֻלָּתְךָ וּגְבוּרוֹתֶיךָ וְהוֹפָעַת חַיּוּתְךָ בְּכָל רֶגַע, וְקֹטֶן עֶרְכִּי בֵּין מַעֲשֶׂיךָ וּמָה נֶּחְשָׁב אֲנִי בֵּין יְצוּרֶיךָ וּכְאַיִן אֲנִי נֶגֶד בְּרוּאֶיךָ, אִם גַּם הָיִיתִי נָקִי מִכָּל חֵטְא וּמַה גַּם כִּי עֲוֹנוֹתַי רָבוּ לְמַעְלָה רֹאשׁ נְקַלּוֹתִי מִכָּל בְּרוּאֶיךָ, כִּי הֵם עוֹשִׂים רְצוֹנְךָ אֲשֶׁר לְכָךְ נוֹצְרוּ וַאֲנִי בְּגֹבַהּ לִבִּי מְתֹעָב בְּעֵינֶיךָ, וְעָזְרֵנִי לִהְיוֹת מִדַּת הַכְּנָעָה וּשְׁפְלוּת רוּחַ דָּבוּק בְּלִבִּי וּבְרַעְיוֹנַי בְּכָל עֵת וּבְכָל רֶגַע, וְתִהְיֶה יִרְאָתְךָ עַל פָּנַי לְבִלְתִּי אֶחֱטָא, וְיִשְׂמַח לִבִּי תָּמִיד בְּךָ אֲשֶׁר בְּרָאתַנִי לִכְבוֹדֶךָ, וְאַהֲבָתְךָ תִּבְעַר בְּקִרְבִּי בְּכָל עֵת, וּמֵחָכְמָתְךָ תַּאֲצִיל עָלַי לִהְיוֹת נֶגֶד עֵינַי גְּדֻלָּתְךָ וּגְבוּרוֹתֶיךָ וּמִעוּט עֶרְכִּי וְחֶסְרוֹן בִּינָתִי, וְלֹא יִגְבַּהּ לִבִּי וְלֹא אֶרְדֹּף אַחַר הַכָּבוֹד וּגְדֻלָּה וָעֹשֶׁר, כִּי אִם תִּכְסֹף נַפְשִׁי לַעֲשׂוֹת רְצוֹנְךָ הַיָּשָׁר בְּעֵינֶיךָ, וְאֶהְיֶה מוּכָן בְּכָל רֶגַע לִמְסֹר נַפְשִׁי רוּחִי וְנַפְשִׁי וְגוּפִי וּמְאֹדִי עַל קְדֻשַּׁת שְׁמֶךָ, וְהָסֵר כָּל הַמָּסַכִים הַמַּבְדִּילִים בֵּינִי לְבֵינֶךָ, וְהַחֲזִירֵנִי בִּתְשׁוּבָה שְׁלֵמָה לְפָנֶיךָ, וְיִנְעַם לִי כָּל אֲשֶׁר תַּעֲשֶׂה עִמָּדִי, וְלֹא יְבַלְבְּלֵנִי שׁוּם עִנְיָן מֵעֲבוֹדָתְךָ הָאֲמִתּוּת, וְלֹא תַעֲלֶה קִנְאַת אָדָם עָלַי וְלֹא קִנְאָתִי עַל אֲחֵרִים, וְלֹא אֶתְאַוֶּה לְשׁוּם דָּבָר זוּלַת רְצוֹנֶךָ, וְהוֹרֵנוּ דֶּרֶךְ חֻקֶּיךָ לְעָבְדְּךָ בְּלֵב נָבָר וָזָךְ וּבְשִׂמְחָה וְרוּחַ נְמוּכָה וּבְאַהֲבַת עַמְּךָ יִשְׂרָאֵל,

thoughts to serve anything besides for You, God forbid. My true desire should only be to do what You — in your goodness — desire.

Please assist me as well that my thoughts and feelings should never forget Your greatness, power, and emanation of life into every moment, and the smallness of my value amongst all that You have made. And what am I considered amongst all Your handiwork, and I am nothing in comparison to all that You have created. Even if I were free from all sin — and all the more so that my sins have overwhelmed me — I am still less valuable than all Your creations. For they perform the desired task that they were created for, while I with my haughtiness have made myself abhorrent before You.

Please assist me that the attribute of self-effacement and humility should cleave to my heart and thoughts all the time. Awe of You should always be upon me, so that I shall not sin. I should always rejoice in the fact that You created me for Your glory. Love for You should always flare up within me. Please grant me from Your wisdom so that Your greatness and power and my miniscule value and lack of understanding should always be on my mind,

[Please Hashem assist me] that I should not become arrogant, nor pursue honor, prestige, and wealth. Rather I should only desire to fulfill Your will — that which is upright in Your eyes. I should be prepared, at any moment, to sacrifice myself, my soul, my body, and my possessions for the sanctification of Your name. [Please] remove all the barriers that separate myself from You and return me — with complete repentance — to You. I should recognize the pleasantness of all that You do for me. Nothing should distract me from serving You properly. I should not be jealous of anyone, nor should anyone be jealous of me. Nor should I desire anything besides for Your will.

[Hashem,] teach me the way of your statutes, so that I can serve You with a simple and pure heart, with joy, with a humble spirit, and with love of Your nation, Yisrael.

וְיִתְקַדֵּשׁ שִׁמְךָ עַל יָדַי וְעַל יְדֵי זַרְעִי וְזֶרַע זַרְעִי עַד סוֹף כָּל הַדּוֹרוֹת, וְלֹא יִמָּצֵא פְּסוּל בָּנוּ חָלִילָה, וְנִנָּצֵל מֵחִלּוּל הַשֵּׁם, וְנִזְכֶּה לַעֲסֹק בְּתוֹרָתְךָ לִשְׁמָהּ בִּתְמִידוּת מִתּוֹךְ הַרְחָבָה, בִּתְשׁוּבָה וּבְדַעַת וּבְשִׂמְחָה וְלֵב טָהוֹר, וְנִשָּׁמֵר מִכָּל חֵטְא וּמִכָּל עָוֹן, וְנִשְׂמַח בְּדִבְרֵי תוֹרָתֶךָ וּבְמִצְוֹתֶיךָ לְעוֹלָם וָעֶד, וְנִזְכֶּה לְתַקֵּן אֶת אֲשֶׁר הֶעֱוִינוּ וְלֹא נֵבוֹשׁ בָּעוֹלָם הַזֶּה וְלֹא נִכָּלֵם לָעוֹלָם הַבָּא אָמֵן כֵּן יְהִי רָצוֹן.

Your Name should be sanctified through me, my children, and my descendants throughout all the generations. No imperfection should be found in us, God forbid, nor should we commit any desecration of Your Holy Name. We should merit to toil in Your Torah, constantly, for its sake, in a state of calm, repentance, understanding, joy, and a pure heart. We should be protected from any sin or iniquity, and we should rejoice in Your Torah and mitzvos forever. We should merit to rectify all that we have done wrong, and we should not be embarrassed in This World or ashamed in the World to Come! Amen! So may it be Your will!

This volume is part of
THE ARTSCROLL® SERIES
an ongoing project of
translations, commentaries and expositions on
Scripture, Mishnah, Talmud, Midrash, Halachah,
liturgy, history, the classic Rabbinic writings,
biographies and thought.

For a brochure of current publications
visit your local Hebrew bookseller
or contact the publisher:

Mesorah Publications, ltd

313 Regina Avenue
Rahway, New Jersey 07065
(718) 921-9000
www.artscroll.com